"McNulty reestablishes Marcuse's credentials as a first-rate philosopher, while at the same time affirming Marcuse's political commitments to critical Marxism and democratic socialism. With writing that is philosophically sophisticated, accessible and engaging, McNulty elaborates Marcuse's theoretical positions on questions of epistemology, metaphysics, the philosophy of science, aesthetics and philosophical anthropology. Ranging confidently over the entire body of Marcuse's work, McNulty has given us an excellent introduction to Marcuse's critical philosophy."
—**John Abromeit**, *State University of New York at Buffalo, USA*

"In this lucid and imaginative study, McNulty painstakingly reconstructs the key elements of Marcuse's philosophy and demonstrates its enduring relevance. As the need for exploring new directions in thought and action becomes more pressing than ever, being guided so brilliantly into the heart of Marcuse's engaged thinking could hardly be more valuable."
—**Espen Hammer,** *Temple University, USA*

Marcuse

Herbert Marcuse (1898–1979) is known to many as a leading figure of 1960s counterculture, and a "Guru of the New Left." However, the deeper philosophical background to Marcuse's thought is often forgotten, especially his significant engagement with German idealism, ancient philosophy, and a broad spectrum of problems and issues from the philosophical tradition.

This much-needed book introduces and assesses Marcuse's philosophy and is ideal for those coming to his work for the first time. Jacob McNulty covers the following topics:

- Marcuse's life and the background to his thought, including his formative period as a student of Husserl and Heidegger and as a philosopher in Horkheimer's Institute
- Marcuse's recasting of metaphysics in light of Marxian and Freudian thought
- Marcuse and German idealism, especially the role of Kant and Hegel
- Marcuse's philosophy of human nature, his use of the late Freud's ideas of Eros and Thanatos
- Marcuse as a critic of state and monopoly capitalism
- Meaning, propaganda, and ideology: the political implications of language and also the centrality of free speech
- Marcuse's aesthetics
- Marcuse's legacy and his relationship to contemporary analytical philosophy (especially "analytic critical theory").

An outstanding and engaging introduction to a central figure in twentieth-century radical thought, *Marcuse* is essential reading for those in philosophy and related disciplines including political theory, sociology, and media and communication studies.

Jacob McNulty is an Assistant Professor of Philosophy at Yale University, USA. He is the author of *Hegel's Logic and Metaphysics* (2023). His work on Rousseau, Fichte, and others has appeared in the *European Journal of Philosophy*, *Journal of the History of Philosophy*, and *British Journal for the History of Philosophy*.

The Routledge Philosophers

Edited by Brian Leiter

University of Chicago, USA

The Routledge Philosophers is a major series of introductions to the great Western philosophers. Each book places a major philosopher or thinker in historical context, explains and assesses their key arguments, and considers their legacy. Additional features include a chronology of major dates and events, chapter summaries, annotated suggestions for further reading, and a glossary of technical terms.

An ideal starting point for those new to philosophy, they are also essential reading for those interested in the subject at any level.

Also available:

Freud, second edition
Jonathan Lear

Habermas
Kenneth Baynes

Peirce
Albert Atkin

Plato
Constance Meinwald

Plotinus
Eyjólfur Emilsson

Einstein
Thomas Ryckman

Merleau-Ponty, second edition
Taylor Carman

Leibniz, second edition
Nicholas Jolley

Bergson
Mark Sinclair

Arendt
Dana Villa

Cassirer
Samantha Matherne

Adam Smith
Samuel Fleischacker

Descartes
David Cunning

Marx
Jaime Edwards and Brian Leiter

Marcuse
Jacob McNulty

For more information about this series, please visit: https://www.routledge.com/The-Routledge-Philosophers/book-series/ROUTPHIL

Jacob McNulty

Marcuse

Routledge
Taylor & Francis Group

LONDON AND NEW YORK

First published 2025
by Routledge
4 Park Square, Milton Park, Abingdon, Oxon OX14 4RN

and by Routledge
605 Third Avenue, New York, NY 10158

Routledge is an imprint of the Taylor & Francis Group, an informa business

© 2025 Jacob McNulty

British Library Cataloguing-in-Publication Data
A catalogue record for this book is available from the British Library

Library of Congress Cataloging-in-Publication Data
Names: McNulty, Jacob, 1989- author.
Title: Marcuse / Jacob McNulty.
Description: Abingdon, Oxon : Routledge, 2025. |
Includes bibliographical references and index.
Identifiers: LCCN 2024026951 (print) | LCCN 2024026952 (ebook) |
ISBN 9781032308746 (hardback) | ISBN 9781032308722 (paperback) |
ISBN 9781003307075 (ebook)
Subjects: LCSH: Marcuse, Herbert, 1898-1979.
Classification: LCC B945.M2984 M37 2025 (print) |
LCC B945.M2984 (ebook)
| DDC 191—dc23/eng/20240804
LC record available at https://lccn.loc.gov/2024026951
LC ebook record available at https://lccn.loc.gov/2024026952

ISBN: 978-1-032-30874-6 (hbk)
ISBN: 978-1-032-30872-2 (pbk)
ISBN: 978-1-003-30707-5 (ebk)

DOI: 10.4324/9781003307075

Typeset in Joanna
by codeMantra

For My Parents

Contents

Preface and acknowledgments

Herbert Marcuse was perhaps the most visible and widely discussed philosopher of the 1960s. His best-selling work *One-Dimensional Man* offered a statement of the philosophy behind the social upheavals of the era. A mentor to Angela Davis and Abbie Hoffman, he could often be seen addressing student activists, not only in the US but in Europe and South America as well. Yet like other philosophers who achieve popular acclaim, Marcuse's academic reputation has suffered. Though it endeared him to his students and colleagues, Marcuse's approachability, good humor, and charm may have worked against him in this regard. Another obstacle to his reception is his association with social movements widely seen to have failed, at least in their most radical aims. Indeed, Marcuse shares with the student movement a reputation for naïveté and utopianism. Even among the minority of academic philosophers interested in Marx and in the Frankfurt School of critical theory, with which he was affiliated, Marcuse is neglected. He is frequently passed over in favor of thinkers viewed as either more rigorous, profound, or timely; for example, Adorno, Horkheimer, Benjamin, and Habermas, all of whom are subjects of ongoing discussion and debate.

I belong to a small but growing group of readers who believe Marcuse's neglect is totally unjustified. Marcuse's clarity, plain-spokenness, and approachability as an author do not signal a lack of sophistication. They are, rather, expressions of his singular gift, which was to have integrated the most abstruse doctrines from philosophy and its history and the concrete concerns of radical politics. In his writing, political fervor, historical experience, and deep philosophical learning coalesce. Though consistently scholarly and intellectually serious, this was a synthesis mercifully free from the pretentious characteristic of so much left-aligned academic writing. I will attempt to present the synthesis as clearly as possible, and to begin (or continue) a conversation about whether and to what extent it succeeds.

This book, as a contribution to the *Routledge Philosophers Series*, provides an introduction to Marcuse's thought, suitable for advanced undergraduates and graduate students but also useful for researchers in the field. But although its primary aim is to inform, it has an agenda—one it partly shares with some other recent authors. My aim is to present Marcuse as a serious philosopher in his own right, chiefly by exploring the continuities between his thought and the philosophical tradition. Any reader of continental philosophy and social thought in the twentieth century knows that an author's claim to be a Marxist can mean almost anything, and should not be taken at face value. Yet Marcuse, whatever his faults, was clear and consistent in defending Marx's critique of capitalism and the need for a socialist alternative. As a Marxist, Marcuse is part of a movement whose relationship to traditional philosophy is often one of extreme skepticism or even hostility. To grasp the difficulty, one need only think of Marx's own invective against Hegel, a thinker Marcuse insists is indispensable to critical theory. Yet in each of the following chapters, I will offer a sympathetic account of Marcuse's efforts to reconcile Marxist views and traditional philosophical doctrines: for example, Hegel's idealism; Plato's realism about universals; and Kant's aesthetic formalism. In the background of this book is my suspicion that Marcuse's Frankfurt School colleagues are less trustworthy than he is in this connection; in particular, the compromises they have brokered between bourgeois or non-Marxist thinkers and Marx seem lopsided in favor of the former.

Though Marcuse never himself characterized his project in this way, I will approach it as a response to a dilemma that I believe has plagued Marxist philosophical thought in the twentieth century. Down one path are the broadly anti-philosophical forms of Marxism—or, at least, those opposing *traditional* philosophy. I mean those which insist that Marxism is, or is at least continuous with, empirical science (natural, social, or otherwise). Though appealingly naturalistic, these forms of Marxism are often hostage to fortune. They risk scorn at the hands of the mainstream of current, non-Marxist empirical research. Down the second path are those forms of Marxist social thought which define themselves as philosophical, in a more traditional sense, chiefly by attempting to fuse Marxism with non-Marxist doctrines from the tradition: for example, Kantian ethics, Hegelian idealism, or moral realism. Yet in their effort to avoid the pitfalls of vulgar or "mechanistic" Marxism, these movements risk a break with anything distinctively Marxist at all. The dilemma is between being dissolved in non-Marxist (social) science or non-Marxist philosophy. I suggest that Marcuse's thought is a satisfying *via media* between these options.

The first chapter provides an overview of Marcuse's life and thought, looking at his philosophical formation as a student of literature, romanticism and, later, existential phenomenology; his activism and military service, particularly in World War I but also in the Office for Strategic Services during World War II; and, finally, his role in the student movement. The second chapter describes his epistemology, defining it as a form of Hegelian idealism adapted to a historical materialist framework. The third analyzes Marcuse's debt to Plato, and a form of essentialist metaphysics Marxists often avoid. The fourth concerns Marcuse's philosophy of science, abstracting somewhat from his better-known theory of technology. Its aim is to explore Marcuse's anti-realist and instrumentalist view of science, which prepares the way for his well-known thesis that science and technology are inseparable (both from one another and from what Marxists call "the forces of production"). The fifth chapter concerns Marcuse's aesthetics, and his effort to defend doctrines like those from classical German aesthetics, but this time in the context of a critical theory of society. The sixth examines Marcuse's debt to Freud and psychoanalysis, focusing on his effort to fuse the late Freud's vision of human life as a contest between Eros and Thanatos with the Marxist theory of history. The seventh concerns Marcuse's view of the politics of his time. It discusses his view that the main competitors in twentieth-century geopolitics—fascism, communism, and liberalism—share an underlying basis in monopoly or state capitalism (though this is obviously something of a misnomer in the case of Soviet communism).

The three main works on which I rely are *Reason and Revolution*, *Eros and Civilization*, and *One-Dimensional Man*. However, I also refer intermittently to other books, unpublished writings, the classic philosophical essays of the 1930s, interviews, and other lectures. I am greatly indebted to Douglas Kellner for his *Collected Papers of Herbert Marcuse* Project, an absolutely invaluable resource without which books like this one would be impossible.

I am not the first to pursue a recovery of Marcuse's legacy, and I want to be sure to acknowledge the pioneering work of Andrew Feenberg, Marcuse's last student. For decades now, Feenberg has been a vocal advocate of Marcuse's thought, insisting it be given a hearing as serious philosophy, in particular as a sophisticated Marxist response to the legacy of Heideggerian phenomenology, and as an original and compelling critique of technology. I am here following a line of thought initiated by Feenberg, and I refer to Feenberg's writings throughout this volume, and have benefited from them greatly. While I have endeavored to record my debts to these writings, I wish to offer a blanket acknowledgment of them here in the preface. As the reader will see, they are the works of secondary literature I recommend most frequently in the pages to follow.

I have also benefited greatly from Douglas Kellner's *Herbert Marcuse and the Crisis of Marxism*, especially its discussion of Marcuse's analyses of fascism, liberal capitalism, and Soviet communism. (Of course, this is not to diminish the value of Kellner's perspective on Marcuse's philosophical ideas but only to register the way he manages to relate them compellingly to the historical and sociological doctrines Marcuse developed).

In the course of producing this manuscript, I accumulated many debts. My first and most important is to the editor of this series, Brian Leiter, and to Tony Bruce at Routledge.

I was extremely fortunate to have several colleagues read and comment upon the entire manuscript: Arash Abazari, John Abromeit, Fred Rush, Tom Whyman, and Ulrika Carlsson. Individual sections, at different times and in different stages of readiness, were read and commented on by Andrew Feenberg, Toni Koch, Brian O'Connor, Kenneth Walden, Steven Klein, Johnny Thakkar, Vid Simonti, and Paul Redding. Ulrika later assisted with the preparation of the manuscript.

I also benefited from the five referee reports commissioned by Routledge. I apologize to any colleagues or friends who helped with the manuscript and I may have inadvertently omitted.

As stated, my primary aim is introductory, and it is my hope that students with little prior knowledge of Marcuse or the sources on which he drew can profit from this book. However, I also hope that what I have to say will constitute a modest intervention on behalf of a thinker I have come to feel is unfairly neglected.

Abbreviations

I cite works by Marcuse using the following abbreviations. Full citation information is given in the Bibliography.

AD   *The Aesthetic Dimension*
CPHM *Collected Papers of Herbert Marcuse*, 5 vols. (N.B. I always state the name of the paper in question, since noting the volume is generally not sufficient to specify the source.)
CPT   *A Critique of Pure Toleration* (N.B. All page references are to Marcuse's essay "Repressive Tolerance," and do not refer to either of the other two essays by Moore and Wolf.)
CR   *Counterrevolution and Revolt*
EC   *Eros and Civilization: A Philosophical Inquiry into Freud*
EL   *An Essay on Liberation*
FL   *Five Lectures: Psychoanalysis, Politics and Utopia*
HO   *Hegel's Ontology and Theory of Historicity*
N   *Negations*
ODM   *One-Dimensional Man: A Study in the Ideology of Advanced Industrial Society*
RR   *Reason and Revolution: Hegel and the Rise of Social Theory*
SA   *A Study on Authority*
SM   *Soviet Marxism*

Chronology

1898	Herbert Marcuse is born in Berlin to an upper-middle-class Jewish family.
1911	Studies in Gymnasium.
1916	Drafted into the German army.
1922	Completes PhD thesis at Freiburg on the German Künstlerroman.
1924	Marries mathematician Sophie Wertheim.
1928	Returns to Freiburg to study philosophy, this time under Husserl and Heidegger. First child, Peter, born.
1932	Completes second thesis ("Habilitationschrift"), *Hegels Ontologie und die Grundlegung einer Theorie der Geschichtlichkeit.* Breaks with his supervisor, Heidegger, who has by this time joined the Nazi Party. The second thesis is never formally accepted.
1933	Hired by Horkheimer's Institute for Social Research, which is temporarily headquartered in Holland. Then flees Germany for Switzerland where the Institute has relocated.
1934	Emigrates to United States to work for the Institute at Columbia University.
1936	Contributes to the Frankfurt School's massive *Studie über Autorität und Familie*. Publishes "The Concept of Essence" in the Zeitschrift für Sozialforschung.
1941	*Reason and Revolution: Hegel and the Rise of Social Theory*.

1942–50	Works for the U.S. Government, first at the Office for Strategic Services (alongside Franz Neumann) and then as head of the Central European section of the State Department.
1951	Sophie Wertheim dies of cancer.
1954–65	Teaches at Brandeis, and encounters student-activists Abbie Hoffman and Angela Davis.
1955	Eros and Civilization: An Inquiry into Freud.
1956	Marries the widow of his friend Franz Neumann, Inga Neumann.
1958	Soviet Marxism: A Critical Analysis.
1964	One-Dimensional Man: Studies in the Ideology of Advanced Industrial Society.
1965–70	Relocates to University of California, San Diego. "Repressive Tolerance" published.
1969	An Essay on Liberation.
1973	Inga Neumann dies.
1976	Marries Erica Sherover, student and activist.
1978	The Aesthetic Dimension: Toward a Critique of Marxist Aesthetics. Translation of German work published a year before.
1979	Dies of a stroke shortly after his 81st birthday during a trip to Germany where he was invited by Habermas to visit the Max Planck Institute in Starnberg.

One
Life and thought

1. From Berlin to San Diego

Herbert Marcuse was born on July 18, 1898, in Berlin, Germany.[12] His family was Jewish, though assimilated: moderately observant, they attended synagogue on high holidays, but did not keep kosher. Carl, Marcuse's father, was a businessman, and the family was comfortably middle-class.

Marcuse's early years were spent studying in a *Gymnasium*. At 17, however, Marcuse was drafted into the army and was forced to leave school. Like so many of his generation, he was to serve in World War I, though he was never directly in harm's way. For the duration of the war he remained in Germany, because of poor eyesight.[3] Still, Marcuse's military career, which only lasted two years, represents an important phase of his development. As he would tell an interviewer decades later, his interest in radical politics dates from this time (CPHM 5: 190).

At the end of the war, in what was to be a pivotal event in his political education, Marcuse joined a soldiers' council in Berlin. These councils were the precursors of the soviets, which were meant to be the building blocks of a future socialist society. Yet Marcuse soon became disenchanted when the soldiers voted to reinstate their former officers (CPHM 6: 428). Like many of his generation, Marcuse was severely disillusioned by the complicity of the oppressed with their oppressors. This early disappointment was a harbinger of things to come. The socialist revolution in Germany would be defeated, its leaders Rosa Luxemburg and Karl Liebknecht betrayed

DOI: 10.4324/9781003307075-1

and murdered. This defeat led Marcuse to withdraw from political action and commence a course of study at university.

Marcuse developed a scholarly interest in Marxism at this time. He wanted to know why the socialist revolutions in central Europe failed. Though the young Marcuse viewed the rise of the Soviet Union with enthusiasm, his optimism was to be short-lived. Lenin was replaced by Stalin, who soon "revealed himself for what he was: a liquidator" (CPHM 6: 429).

Here, then, we see the ingredients that formed Marcuse's life-long political outlook: a fervent commitment to socialism, ready to manifest itself in political engagement and in theoretical research; disillusionment with the Soviet Union; and a clear-headed appreciation of the limitations of mass and working-class movements in post-industrial Western societies. This last tendency in Marcuse's thought may be less familiar to those used to thinking of him as a utopian or optimistic thinker.

When he entered university, first at Berlin and then at Freiburg, Marcuse did not first turn to philosophy or politics, but to German literature. This was to be an interest his whole life long, and Marcuse would later describe his book The Aesthetic Dimension as him having come full circle. Marcuse wrote a dissertation on the German romantic novel and its themes. During these years, he met the woman who was to be his first wife, Sophie Wertheim, a mathematician. They were married in 1924, and soon began to establish a life for themselves in Germany.

In the late 1920s Marcuse returned to Freiburg to undertake a Habilitation: the second dissertation required in German academia of those hoping to become academic philosophers. At Freiburg, Marcuse studied under Husserl, the founder of phenomenology, and later with Heidegger, Husserl's renegade pupil. The fruit of this apprenticeship was a work on Hegel, later published and translated under the title Hegel's Ontology and Theory of Historicity. The work is marked by Heidegger's concern with "the question of being": the question, repressed since philosophy's beginnings, of what it means for anything to be.[4] Yet it also evinces preoccupations of Marcuse's later work: it is intensely preoccupied with the organic, with the dialectic, and with history. As Habermas remarks, Marcuse's writings of this period are surprisingly scholarly given his later trajectory

(CPHM 2: 234). In addition to participating in the Hegel renaissance then taking place in Germany, Marcuse published in leading academic journals.

Given their obvious political differences, the relationship between Marcuse's mature thought and Heidegger's project in *Being and Time* has aroused considerable scholarly controversy.[5] Later, Marcuse would break with Heidegger, experiencing his embrace of National Socialism as a profound betrayal. Yet the young Marcuse was gripped by *Being and Time*, and did not see signs of Heidegger's reactionary attitudes.[6] Indeed, the young Marcuse regarded Heidegger's thought as promising from a Marxist perspective, and as marking a profound break with traditional philosophy.[7]

Heidegger pursued his alternative form of phenomenology against an unusual backdrop. He employed the framework of ontology, and "the question of Being." What is it for anything—a number, a tool, a person—to be or exist at all? In a move reminiscent of Kant's Copernican turn, Heidegger sought an answer to this question from the human standpoint, and not from an impersonal one. The question of Being could only be pursued by human beings, because we are those beings who raise this question of ourselves. "Dasein," Heidegger's term for us, represents "that being whose being is at issue for it." Heidegger's account of human life was unprecedented in its insistence that the human being, unlike the Cartesian subject or Husserlian ego, proves inseparable from its world: in particular, a world of artifacts, social roles and shared meanings.

Without delving into the considerable literature that has arisen on the subject, one brief remark on the affinity Marcuse saw between Heidegger and Marx is in order. We can begin to clarify this puzzling idea by recalling Heidegger's opposition to traditional philosophy's attempts to separate the self, the subject, or the I from its world. So long as the Cartesian subject, Husserlian ego, or Kantian "I" was able to hold itself apart from its world, philosophy seemed to have shored up a central plank of bourgeois ideology: specifically, its embrace of different cults of inwardness and consequent disparagement of efforts to radically transform society.[8] Once the human being was recognized as "thrown into a world" of social roles, artifacts, and tasks, the escape route offered by traditional (bourgeois) philosophy was blocked, and the need for social transformation had to be squarely faced. One could no longer embrace the traditional Christian, Stoic, or Kantian options of avoiding contaminating one-self with political activity and focusing instead on the attainment of inner goods like salvation, wisdom, or moral righteousness. Needless to say, Heidegger had not himself gone nearly this far and Marcuse never labored under the misapprehension that Heidegger was himself a progressive. Indeed, Marcuse was keenly aware of incompatibilities between Heidegger's thought and Marxism. He was to complain later that his teacher's notion of "historicity" was far too abstract, and that the apparent concreteness of existential phenomenology was "phony" and "false."[9] Heideggerian histori-cism did not incorporate the concrete realities of history featuring in Marx's theory: class relationships, forces of production, and so on. Indeed, the biological underpinnings of Dasein, e.g., sex differences, do not enter into Marcuse's analysis (CPHM 3: 167). And so on. Still, the young Marcuse saw a modest affinity between Heidegger and Marx. He would certainly not be the last to see in Being and Time other possibilities than the ones its author intended.

However, the rise of the Nazis put an end to Marcuse's hopes of an academic career in Germany, and, later, threatened his life. No doubt, relations soured between Marcuse and Heidegger because of Heidegger's involvement with the Nazis, and Heidegger never approved Marcuse's Habilitationschrift on Hegel. Long a critic of modern society, technology, and the Enlightenment, Heidegger had now become an enthusiastic supporter of the Nazis. He would later join the party, even going so far as to become the Nazi rector of the University of Freiburg. This was felt as a betrayal by Heidegger's former students, many of whom, like Marcuse, were Jewish. Not only Marcuse's career prospects, but his very life was imperiled by the rise of the Nazis. In interviews later in life, Marcuse would remark that, had he stayed in Germany, he would have almost cer-tainly been deported to a concentration camp ("Bill Moyers: A Con-versation with Herbert Marcuse" CPHM 3: 61).

It was at this time that Marcuse was to become associated with the group of intellectuals with whom his life and thought would become forever linked: Max Horkheimer's Institute for Social Research, which had temporarily become headquartered in Switz-erland. With a letter of recommendation from Husserl, Marcuse was able to join the Institute and emigrate from Germany. The Institute had begun in Frankfurt the previous decade, funded by a bequest from the wealthy, left-wing student Felix Weill. Its members shared Marcuse's interest in understanding the reasons socialist revolutions in Europe had failed. Like Marcuse, most were Jewish and from upper-middle-class German families. The members of the Institute shared an interest in Marx, and believed that a new interdisciplinary form of social science was required for understanding the realities of the modern world: fascism; monopoly capitalism; mass culture; secularization; antisemitism; and world war. Yet most were also steeped in classical German philosophy from Kant to Hegel and interested in drawing on the heritage of traditional philosophy to avoid "mechanistic" or reductive forms of Marxism. Many were also interested in Freud and his new method of psychoanalysis which they felt could help uncover the dark, irrational forces at work in modern culture. Still, the interdisciplinary cast of Frankfurt School critical theory meant that its members included musicologists, political scientists, literary critics, and others. Together, they would create landmark works of social theory that are indispensable to the history of Marxism and of the progressive left.

In light of Marcuse's subsequent reputation as an activist and public figure rather than a scholar, it is worth noting that this was not the case in the first incarnation of the Frankfurt School. As Habermas writes, in a remembrance of Marcuse on the occasion of his hundredth birthday: "Not Adorno, but Marcuse assumed the role of the philosopher in the division of labor Horkheimer established at the New York Institute. He was the one who wrote the commentary to the programmatic essay 'Traditional and Critical Theory'" (CPHM 2: 234). Here, Habermas alludes to a foundational text of critical theory, Horkheimer's essay "Traditional and Critical Theory" (1972). The essay calls for a break with the mode of intellectual inquiry that had dominated Western philosophy and science, one in which the knowing subject and the object known are considered radically distinct. A physicist does not consider himself part of the elementary particles he studies, but a social scientist is in many ways part of the object of his study (society). Instead of a traditional theory, a critical theory would acknowledge the embeddedness of the knowing subject in his object of study. This embeddedness received further support from Marxism, which understood scholarly activity and the university ("knowledge production") as part of economic production more generally. The upshot: a change in the way society was known and understood would change society itself, since such knowing and understanding is internal to social life. Social life is not simply patterns of behavior among human beings, but a shared set of understandings of what one does when one participates. Hence, theoretical work assumes a practical significance by virtue of its ability to alter the self-understandings that constitute social practices.

In his companion essay to Horkheimer's piece, Marcuse describes an agenda that should guide this study's focus. This agenda will attempt to avoid two extremes: the naiveté of traditional philosophy, so often oblivious to the role of social and historical conditions in the formation of philosophical systems; and the crass reductionism of a "sociology of knowledge," which considers the embeddedness of ideas in their economic surroundings to be totally discrediting. As Marcuse writes:

> it is certainly true that many philosophical concepts are mere "foggy ideas" arising out of the domination of existence by an uncontrolled economy and, accordingly, are to be explained precisely by the material conditions of life. But in its historical forms philosophy also contains insights into human and objective conditions whose truth points beyond previous society and thus cannot be completely reduced to it. Here belong not only the contents dealt with under such concepts as reason, mind, freedom, morality, universality, and essence, but also important achievements of epistemology, psychology, and logic.
> (N 109)

Virtually every one of the concepts Marcuse lists will be part of our investigation, and in each case we will want to be mindful of the dilemma he describes. It is a dilemma between, on one hand, a traditional ideal of philosophical truth as transcending history and, on the other, an attempt to dissolve the heritage of philosophy in history, sociology, and economics. Just how can traditional philosophical ideas retain their claim to truth when their thoroughgoing interconnections with social life are exposed? This is the tightrope that Marcuse thinks critical theory will have to walk in its attempt to carry traditional philosophy forward in a nontraditional way.

The Frankfurt School was a movement in almost perpetual exile. Soon, when Switzerland seemed threatened with invasion, the Institute would relocate to the United States, where it would first be housed at Columbia University in Morningside Heights, and later in California. Marcuse followed this migration, and his association with the Institute was both formative and long-lasting. Not all of the School's members would escape persecution. Walter Benjamin, though never officially a member of the Institute, counts as one of its guiding intellectual lights. Frankfurt School authors followed Benjamin in their conviction that the micro-analysis of cultural forms (architecture, literature, mass-culture) could be a part of Marxist social science. Yet Benjamin would die by his own hand when his attempt to escape Europe seemed doomed. His death would be traumatic for all the School's members.

World War II marks another of the most important phases of Marcuse's career as a politically engaged intellectual. When he emigrated to the US, Marcuse contributed to the global struggle against fascism by joining the Office for Strategic Services (OSS), a precursor to the CIA. He served on the European desk of the OSS, preparing reports on the German enemy. There, he was joined by other émigrés from the German academic community, including Franz Neumann, another member of the Frankfurt School. Carl Schorske, who would later become a famed historian of fin-de-siècle Vienna, was also on the desk. He remembers the atmosphere on the Europe desk in a piece entitled "Encountering Marcuse" (Cobb and Abromeit 2004: 253–60). As Schorske explains, Neumann was the natural leader, issuing orders and divvying up tasks; Marcuse, though serious in his work, brought a geniality and good humor that helped lighten the mood. Discussions ranged widely, moving from topics immediately related to the war effort to others in German history, literature, and culture; this made the OSS a kind of second graduate school for its younger and less experienced members.

After the war, Marcuse moved from the OSS to the State department. He became active in denazification, the effort by the US and its allies to purge German society of Nazis. He was also part of the emerging Cold War against Russia, and contributed to the OSS's reports on the Soviet Union. Those interested in a clearer picture of the activities of Marcuse and Neumann in the OSS can now consult a collected edition of their writings, most of which (but not all) concern National Socialism (Neumann, Marcuse, and Kirchheimer 2013). Marcuse later recalled the OSS's growing interest in "Indochina" during this period (CPHM 6: 430). It was a harbinger of the war in Vietnam, during which Marcuse would become synonymous with the student protest movement.

Remarkably, Marcuse managed during the early years of the war to produce a comprehensive study of Hegel's thought that has since become a classic: *Reason and Revolution: Hegel and the Rise of Social Theory*. Its opening remarks clarify the real-world political stakes of this scholarly work: "In our time, the rise of Fascism calls for a reinterpretation of Hegel's philosophy" (RR vii). The study is not only one of the finest overviews of Hegel's thought and of subsequent nineteenth-century philosophy available, it is also a welcome corrective to a better-known piece of anti-Hegelian polemic from the same period: Popper's *The Open Society and Its Enemies* (1945). Popper's study locates the philosophical origins of totalitarianism in Hegel and Marx (though also considerably earlier, in Plato). These thinkers stand accused of an outlook that is fundamentally hostile to scientific and rational inquiry, as well as the "open" societies in which these enterprises thrive: specifically, societies in which there is a free and fair competition between diverse viewpoints, and in which the ones best able to withstand counterargument prevail. With their claim to a superior, dialectical mode of knowledge, Hegel and Marx appear in Popper's retelling as dogmatists, unwilling to submit their beliefs to rational scrutiny. As with the religious dogmatism of the Middle Ages, the only way to promote such beliefs is with force and violence. This was a method the bloodthirsty followers of Hegel and Marx in Nazi Germany and the Soviet Union had employed with relish.

Marcuse's *Reason and Revolution* provides a counterweight to Popper's influential text, finding in Hegel and Marx a "negative" philosophy opposed to "positivism" in all its forms. In Marcuse's retelling, Hegel and Marx appear as radically critical thinkers, and it is their dogmatic opponents—both in the contemporary context and during their own time—who have paved the way for fascism. The disagreement between the two camps, "positive" and "negative" philosophies, turns on whether some "positive" fact is treated as foundational for philosophy, or whether instead it is the human being's ability to criticize, or "negate," that is emphasized instead. Crucially, this dogmatism is not limited to metaphysicians, moralists, and religious believers, but includes naturalists, empiricists, and scientific figures as well. One implication of Marcuse's argument is that positivists are unwitting abettors of political regression. We will turn to a fuller examination of Marcuse's thesis in Chapter 2, though his interpretation of Hegel will be important throughout. We will attempt to see if Marcuse makes good on his claim that the thinking of Hegel and Marx is indispensable for the progressive left and incompatible with the far right.

During the 1950s, Marcuse pursued a conventional academic career as a professor, mostly at Brandeis University in Boston. Since his thought is so firmly associated with the counterculture of the 1960s, it is worth remembering that many of his most important ideas and relationships are products of the previous decade. It was during this time that Marcuse met Abbie Hoffman, then a student at Brandeis but later an important figure in the student movement (born in 1936, Hoffman is one of many counterexamples to the still widespread but misleading idea that the student revolutionaries were baby-boomers and products of postwar privilege). Hoffman was the subject of a famous trial surrounding his activities during the protests at the 1968 Democratic convention and would later go underground. Marcuse also owes his relationship with the Harvard sociologist Barrington Moore, Jr. to this period. Along with the Harvard philosopher Robert Paul Wolff, they would collaborate on the later work *Critique of Pure Toleration*, the source of one of Marcuse's most notorious ideas: "repressive tolerance." The *Critique* is discussed in Chapter 6, where we consider Marcuse's views on free speech and the liberal ideal of a tolerant society.

It was also during the 1950s that Marcuse authored one of his two most famous books, *Eros and Civilization*. A fascinating and original synthesis of Marx and Freud, *Eros and Civilization* argues that a non-repressive society can only be achieved through the overthrow of capitalism. The book has a reputation for unrealistic utopianism and is still associated with the hippies and their experiments in free love. Yet it appeared in 1955, and as we will see when we discuss it in greater detail, its ideas on human sexuality are anything but simplistic or naïve. A key idea in my reconstruction will be that Eros is not identical with sex; that the identification of the two is more characteristic of the repressive society we currently inhabit than of the future one Marcuse envisioned; and, perhaps most surprisingly of all, that it is the present repressive society which is perverted, and not its successor, since repression and perversion are two sides of the same coin. Regarding its association with the 1960s, it is worth noting that the 1955 book's origins lie earlier, in lectures given at the University of Washington in 1950–51 (EC xxviii). Interestingly, Marcuse seems not to have ever undergone analysis himself, nor to have been formally trained in the practice of it.[10] His interest in psychoanalysis, though deep and enduring, remained an intellectual interest rather than a personal practice.

The 1950s were productive and fulfilling years for Marcuse, but they were not without personal tragedies and complications. Marcuse's first wife died of cancer in 1951. In 1954, he wedded Inga Neumann, the widow of his friend and Frankfurt School colleague Franz Neumann. In 1958, *Soviet Marxism* appeared, a study of the communist system in the USSR. The book grew out of work done by Marcuse and others on the OSS, and was published by Columbia University Press. Like other members of the Frankfurt School, Marcuse was deeply critical of Soviet communism, which he viewed as totalitarian. Yet Marcuse was no cold warrior, and it is clear that he viewed liberal capitalism as sharing the totalitarian tendencies of the Eastern bloc. As we will see in a subsequent chapter, the disturbing parallels between liberal capitalism and Soviet communism are shared by fascist regimes as well. These commonalities arise from a shared reliance on a highly centralized, industrial mode of production. Firms are monopolistic rather than competitive. Their goals are inseparable from those of the state, military, and police. This thesis, reminiscent of Adorno and Horkheimer, may seem totalizing and pessimistic to some. We will need to critically examine Marcuse's contention that state and monopoly capitalism (or its communist equivalent) poses the threat of totalitarianism, even in officially democratic societies. Marcuse drew on this analysis to criticize Soviet communism, but in one important sense his critique is indebted to orthodox historical

materialism: it draws on the idea that societies, whatever their official ideological orientation, remain controlled by their underlying
mode of economic production. Marcuse's critical analysis of Soviet
communism will be crucial to Chapter 6, where it is considered
alongside his diagnoses of liberalism and fascism.

Once again, however, Marcuse's life as a scholar was upended by
the political tumult of the era. In the 1960s, when he was over 70
years old, Marcuse achieved unexpected renown as a public figure.
He was initially drawn into politics by the civil rights movement,
and later by the war in Vietnam. During these years, Marcuse became
known as "the father of the student left," or even its "guru." Yet he
resented these labels and was always modest about his own role in
the movement. Marcuse was also clear that the student movement
could not replace the working class, even if the latter had given up
its interest in overthrowing capitalism (CPHM 3: 156). Rather, the
student left would, in Marcuse's view, serve a preparatory role in
bringing about a larger upheaval. Marcuse addressed student groups
not only in the United States but across the world, especially in
Latin America and Europe. Indeed, Marcuse was in Paris during
the '68 rebellions, where his thought seemed to many to represent
a welcome alternative to the doctrinaire Marxism of the French
Communist Party. Marcuse was revered in part for his lack of preten-
tiousness or condescension to student activists. Members of my generation may recognize these qualities in Bernie Sanders or Jeremy
Corbyn, two other figures whose advanced years and plain-spoken
style belie their adoration by youth in revolt. This period also saw
Marcuse move to the University of San Diego. (An endearing detail:
Marcuse was pleased to be in close proximity to the San Diego Zoo,
then one of the largest in the world.)[11]

As is well known, Marcuse was an important mentor to the
scholar-activist Angela Davis, who had herself studied Hegel and
Marx in Berlin. Later, he would defend Davis when she was dismissed
from her position at UCLA for being a member of the Communist
Party. Marcuse is remembered as a beloved presence on campus, and
groups of students took to escorting him between buildings. In an
era when so many leaders of the left had been murdered, it is not
difficult to see why Marcuse's friends and admirers would have been
concerned about his security. He often received death threats and

other alarming letters (CPHM 6: 207). During this period, Marcuse met his last wife, Erica ("Ricky") Sherover, a scholar-activist. The two were wed in 1976 after Marcuse's second wife, Inga, died of cancer.

Whether on campus or not, Marcuse remained active as a philosophical author, and in the 1960s wrote his best-known book. *One-Dimensional Man* addressed new impediments to the overthrow of capitalism, those presented by the rising standard of living, the cooption or disappearance of the traditional working class, mass media, modern science and technology, and, most famously, repressive desublimation. One of Marcuse's best-known concepts, "repressive desublimation" concerns the aggressive and sexual energies which lie behind most subversive activity. These energies used to be "sublimated," in that they were redirected into cultural and scientific activity, and in this way prevented from finding an antisocial outlet. In modern society, however, these energies attain a more direct outlet. Late capitalism is powerful enough to permit its members a little light rebellion, and they become grateful to the social order for the opportunities it affords them to indulge. Yet this permissiveness is repressive because it serves to reconcile people to a false social order. Formerly, the scientific and cultural production made possible through repression led to the formation of autonomous, self-disciplined individuals: specifically, individuals with the psyches described by Freud, in which higher cultural ideals, found in the super-ego, are employed by the ego to hold aggression and sexuality from the id in check. Yet late capitalist society, though more permissive, presides over a mass of heteronymous individuals: those without higher ideals, and unable to gain the upper hand over their desires. Such individuals, though freer in a superficial sense, prove easier to govern and are more thoroughly enslaved than their predecessors.

Though it was admired by student activists, *One-Dimensional Man* is also a substantial, scholarly work. For a widely read, or at least best-selling, book, it is unusually engaged with philosophy and its history. Its treatment of science and technology is informed by Heidegger's idea of technology as a mode of world-disclosure, less a set of tools and techniques than an outlook which affects the way the world shows up to its inhabitants.[12] Its critique of the one-dimensional society draws on a contrast with the two-dimensional one that Plato and Aristotle inhabited. In their outlook, the presence of a second ideal world of forms—or, in Aristotle's case, of potentialities present in the things of this world—provided resources for social critique. The forms, otherworldly or substantial, made possible a comparison between how things and human beings were, and how they might be. With the rise of modern science and instrumental reason, the possibility of social critique is now limited.

Marcuse also sharply criticizes the "analytic" philosophy that predominated in the Anglophone academy of his time. He does so for what he sees as its complicity in the one-dimensional society, and its defense of a one-dimensional, or conformist, mode of thought. Marcuse's critical discussions of analytic philosophy may not be rigorous by scholarly standards, and he does have a perhaps unfortunate tendency to group disparate figures and movements together: the early and later Wittgenstein; the logical positivists; the ordinary-language philosophy of Austin, Ryle and behaviorism; Quine's naturalism; and so on. Yet Marcuse discerns in these disparate movements a common tendency to discredit modes of thought and experience that challenge the status quo. In the name of the verifiable, the scientific, or ordinary usage, these movements, one and all, discredit any appeals to a second dimension. While it may be that Anglophone philosophy has, in the meantime, become more ecumenical—indeed, more friendly to social critique—Marcuse's observation is warranted at least to this extent. Ethics, politics, and other areas of thought that had been central to the history of philosophy were marginalized in the analytic tradition prior to the post-war period. *One-Dimensional Man* will be an important source in the chapters on science and technology, metaphysics, and epistemology below. It is the primary source most frequently referred to in this study.

Then as now, leftist intellectuals faced political pressure over their outspoken stances. In 1968, Ronald Reagan (then governor of California) and other conservatives, objected to Marcuse's reappointment at UCSD (Feenberg 2023: 17; "Mr. Harold Keen: Interview with Herbert Marcuse," CPHM 1: 128–37; Katsiaficas, "Afterword: Marcuse as Activist," CPHM 3: 192–93).[13] Under political pressure, Marcuse retired from university teaching in 1970.

Marcuse's final published book, *The Aesthetic Dimension*, written just a year before his death, brings his thought full circle. It constitutes a return to the themes of his earliest work on German literature. In it, he defends the idea that it is a work of art's form, rather than its content, which makes it revolutionary. For this reason, politically didactic works may be self-defeating. Similarly, works with no overt political content, but which are aesthetically innovative at the level of their form, may have unacknowledged revolutionary potential. Though he was not uncritical of American mass culture, Marcuse saw in rock-and-roll and the culture of the new left examples of how art can effect change by projecting the image of a non-repressive world. He rejected the vulgar Marxist idea that art, as part of the ideological superstructure, could only ever be epiphenomenal and therefore causally impotent. Marcuse's aesthetics will be our focus in Chapter 5.[14]

Marcuse remained an active speaker and lecturer to the end. In 1979, while on a trip to Germany where he had been invited to give a lecture by Habermas, Marcuse suffered a serious stroke and died. Habermas would later pay tribute to Marcuse in a piece entitled "The Different Rhythms of Philosophy and Politics: For Herbert Marcuse on his 100th Birthday." There, Habermas noted that Marcuse's public persona had eclipsed his scholarly work. This was so even as other figures from the Frankfurt School had seen their reputations improve among scholars and academics. Habermas's observation is a common one among Marcuse's admirers and students (Davis 2004: 43). Often, the observation seems to be accompanied by a sense of indignation (in my view, entirely justified). It seems unfair that Marcuse's writings should suffer such conspicuous neglect. No doubt the rise of postmodernism, with its mistrust of "metanarratives' like Marxism and psychoanalysis, made Marcuse less congenial to North American academics than other Frankfurt School authors.

Leftist thinkers cannot inspire revolutions single-handedly by means of their writings. Typically, they will merely provide counsel to social movements already well underway. We live in extremely tumultuous times, not dissimilar to those in which Marcuse found himself repeatedly caught up. The 2008 financial crisis was the worst global economic catastrophe since the Great Depression. It brought an end to the triumphal mood in capitalist countries that followed the fall of the Soviet Union. The "end of history," it seemed, had not come. With the war on terror, Americans once again had to confront the reality of the military–industrial complex and the perverse incentives that so often stimulate the premature rush to war. In the wake of the financial crisis, new forms of far-right, nationalist, and xenophobic politics are resurgent, often exploiting forms of misogyny and racism in the population that have become impossible to ignore. These developments have galvanized segments of the left not heard from in recent decades. In countries like the United States and Great Britain, a socialist alternative to unfettered, free-market capitalism seems increasingly attractive, even to the electorate (or at least its younger members). The environmental movement is resurgent, as the alarming effects of climate change become increasingly difficult to ignore. The #MeToo movement has brought attention to pervasive sexual harassment in the entertainment industry and society in general. The protests against police brutality that erupted in the wake of the murder of George Floyd are by some counts the largest in recent history.

It is philosophy, not contemporary politics, which forms the focus of this volume. Still, it seems to me that Marcuse's thought is incredibly timely. Though he rejected Soviet communism, Marcuse never wavered in his belief in socialism. He saw the continuities between capitalism and far-right politics and knew that fascism, vanquished abroad, might triumph at home in unforeseen ways. He understood the roots of far-right movements in the contradictions of late capitalism, on one hand, and in the vicissitudes of the id, on the other. He was prescient about the women's liberation and environmental movements, showing tremendous faith in them in their infancy. Marcuse was no class reductionist who viewed the fight for economic justice as excluding others focused on the rights of marginalized groups. Yet he was also no proponent of neo-liberal identity politics, the depressingly familiar program of compensating for an increasingly brutal and unequal economic system by ensuring that the ruling class administering it is diverse. In short, Marcuse sought a united left opposition, while remaining true to the socialist heritage.

Given his reputation as an optimist, even a utopian, it is also worth noting that Marcuse could often be quite clear-eyed about the dim prospects for the left in America. After the high-tide of 1960s activism passed, Marcuse often noted that the United States was not in a pre-revolutionary situation, and acknowledged the value of supporting liberal moderates in elections. Still, it would seem that, of all the figures in the Frankfurt School, Marcuse is one whose politics exhibit the clearest parallels with the left of today. Even the type of generational politics he represented—an alliance between the very old and the very young—remains familiar (we might think of Bernie Sanders and Greta Thunberg). It is legitimate to question Marcuse's legacy, and that of the student movement which seems to have failed in so many of its aims. Yet we should also be aware that this mistrust may be a product of an equally questionable legacy: the total eclipse of socialist and labor politics in all areas of public life in the West during the neoliberal era.

Given the timeliness and urgency of Marcuse's political message, a reader could be forgiven for being disappointed that the study to follow focuses on arcane philosophical topics. In a way, this reaction would be appropriate, because a question that will recur in what follows is that of what, if anything, radical politics and traditional philosophy might contribute to one another. Marcuse's life and thought suggest optimism on this score. Even as he maintained his engagement in political life, Marcuse kept faith in traditional philosophy: Plato and Aristotle; Kant and Hegel; Marx, Nietzsche, and Freud (whom he insisted on reading philosophically); Husserl and Heidegger. This book is written with the conviction that political engagement in the present and intellectual engagement with philosophy's past are not competing but complementary. It attempts to show how an admirably engaged intellectual never ceased to find, in the most unlikely areas of traditional philosophy, inspiration for left-wing political aims. It suggests caution to those who would see Marcuse's life and thought as inconsistent. These detractors would include vulgar Marxists for whom the point of philosophy is not to interpret the world but to change it. If this remark is read as calling for an end to philosophy, then Marcuse is not an adherent of it. They might also include proponents of logical positivism, behaviorism, naturalism, ordinary-language philosophy, Wittgensteinianism, and other schools of twentieth-century analytical philosophy. These figures will need to contend with Marcuse's insistence that it is the philosophical tradition, and not its scientific cutting edge, which contains the most vital resource for critical theory in the present.

Before concluding, it is worth attempting to give a sense of the personal qualities that so endeared Marcuse to his students and colleagues. These are captured well by Richard Bernstein:

> But he never gave up hope; he never submitted to the despair of thinking that the power of negativity could not assert itself. He searched—in what sometimes seems like a desperate manner—for the signs of those social movements and tendencies that were progressive and liberating. He was open to new possibilities and enthusiastically supported them in speech and deed. He never accepted the lament over the death of the New Left, and he claimed that the women's movement may yet turn out to be the most radical movement of our times. To the end he personified the demand for happiness and liberation. In all his activities he was "life affirming." Those who knew him even slightly were deeply affected by his charm, his humor, his playfulness, his sheer zest and delight in living, his own capacity for the pleasure of being alive. It is this quality that evoked such profound resonances among those who were inspired by him. I have been primarily focusing on Marcuse as a negative thinker, as one of the most persistent radical critics of our time, but what was so beautiful about Marcuse (and I am using "beautiful" in a way in which he would have used it) is that there was a deep harmony between Marcuse as a thinker and Marcuse as a man, and so much hostility and resentment among those who envied him.
>
> (1986: 188)

Marcuse told an interviewer that he had found "joy in living" (CPHM 3: 163). One can hardly imagine this being said by Adorno, or, indeed, many other members of the Institute. The contrast in temperament is reflected in an anecdote related by Marcuse's son Peter (CPHM 1: x–xi), who recalled the preparations for family visits to the homes of Adorno and of Horkheimer (the latter of whom employed servants). Beforehand, the children were cautioned to be on their best behavior. Both Horkheimer and Adorno were known to be formal, strict, and unforgiving.

Clearly, Marcuse the elder did not fit the mold of the dour, unapproachable German professor (those who visited his office would be greeted by a photo of hippopotami, Marcuse's favorite animal). As Peter Marcuse observes, it may be these temperamental differences which made Herbert more comfortable than the others living and working in the U.S. Marcuse remained in America, while Adorno and Horkheimer returned to Germany immediately after the war. There, they assumed positions of authority in the academy. Both would be sharply critical of the student movement and clash with their rebellious students during the 1960s. Horkheimer even went so far as to support the Vietnam War, and Adorno is infamous for calling the police to quell student upheavals on the campus of the University of Frankfurt. Marcuse's trajectory in this era was, obviously, very different.

2. Thematic overview: Marxism and philosophy

On the one hand, it is a truism that the thinkers of the Frankfurt School, Marcuse included, were Marxists. On the other hand, it can often be difficult to explain the nature and extent of their commitment to Marx's teachings. Indeed, this problem is not limited to studies of the Frankfurt School. The label "Marxist" has meant so many things to so many people that it is almost vacuous. This is especially so in traditions and periods when almost everybody is eager to lay claim to Marx's legacy (for example, French philosophy of the 1960s). Why, then, begin with what might seem to be an unpromising angle of approach?

The reason is that it is the unique character of Marcuse's Marxism that is his greatest distinction. Marcuse is a Marxist author who succeeds in defending Marx's legacy without either betraying it in favor of some alternative philosophical creed or allowing it to ossify into a rigid dogma. In my view, this is a rare achievement, and it is not clear that Marcuse's peers in the Western Marxist tradition and the Frankfurt School managed to square the circle of achieving an authentic but non-dogmatic Marxism (their other achievements notwithstanding). As I hope to show, Marcuse represents what is perhaps the high-water mark of a distinctly *philosophical* form of Marxism. By this, I mean one in which Marxism appears as a culminating development in the history of philosophy, rather than as the repudiation of the latter. Less abstractly, I locate in Marcuse's thought motifs from the history of philosophy that Marxists have often regarded with suspicion. Though not all of them will be discussed in this study, they include the following: philosophical, and not just political, idealism, i.e., anti-realism; utopianism; rationalism; a belief in universal and necessary truths, moral and scientific; rejection of reductionist forms of empiricisms, physicalism, and naturalism; an interest in the essences or "Ideas" of things; and so on. Most Marxists have repudiated some, or even all, of these ideas as little more than ideological mystifications that shield society from critique. Thus the challenge facing us will be that of showing how Marcuse reconciles Marxism and (at least some of) these motifs from the philosophical tradition—ones Marxists have dismissed as being on a par with theology and religion.

I have alluded to a dilemma between fidelity to Marx and dogmatism, and I want to expand upon it here. Marxist thinkers in the twentieth century faced a dilemma between orthodox Marxism and its various revisionary forms.[15] Orthodoxy risked complicity with the totalitarian regimes of the USSR, and, correspondingly, with a form of Marxism that seemed equally rigid, dogmatic, and ill-adapted to the realities of twentieth-century history and politics (often, these forms of Marxism are derided as "economistic," "mechanistic," "deterministic," or "vulgar"). Though Engels did not live to see the rise of the USSR, his Marxism, as set forth in the *Dialectics of Nature* and *Socialism: Utopian and Scientific*, seems (and has seemed to its critics) to contain the germ of the form of Marxism that would prevail in the Soviet Union. This was less because of Engels' substantive views than because of the methodological precept that Marxist social science should be seen as continuous with the natural sciences. Once it assumed its mature form, this scientific socialism seemed to carry with it the threat of a physicalist, determinist, and reductionist account of human beings, which seems uncomfortably close to the dehumanizing outlook of so many Marxist regimes—and which may have facilitated their grave human-rights abuses. Clearer examples of orthodox Marxism than that of Engels himself come from the period of the Second International: the Erfurt Program (criticized by Engels) and the writings from that period of figures like Kautsky and Plekhanov. Lenin's *Materialism and Empiriocriticism*, with its reflection on the theory of knowledge, also helped shape this movement.[16]

Engels' *Dialectics of Nature* and the writings of his epigones would often be the critical target of Western Marxists, so-called because none of them lived and worked behind the Iron Curtain. These figures sought to transcend orthodox Marxism by integrating insights from Hegel and classical German philosophy. To be fair, they often claimed their project was no betrayal of Marx himself, but merely an attempt to reach back to an earlier phase of his career: the young Marx, who was steeped in Hegel's metaphysics, especially the idea of Spirit (*Geist*) whose telos is reconciliation with its world (whereas a failure to realize this telos is alienation, a category Marx would adapt to his critique of capitalism). The young Marx's writings were never published, and were only discovered in 1932. They were quickly seized upon by Hegelian Marxists as a sanction for their approach, and decried by proponents of orthodoxy who dismissed these writings as mere juvenilia. Lukács is a more interesting case, having written a landmark work of Hegelian Marxism (*History and Class Consciousness*) a full decade before the young Marx's writings had been discovered. Had the young Marx not existed, Western Marxists would have invented him.

In any case, Western thinkers looked to Hegelian Marxism to address the deficits of the orthodox variety, and, in particular, its insistence that culture, philosophy, and art could only ever be "epiphenomenal," i.e., causally impotent in comparison to all-powerful economic forces. Here, I refer to the orthodox Marxist doctrine of historical materialism, or, more accurately, the idea of the "primacy of the productive forces." Western Marxists looked to this new form of Marxism to explain the failures of socialist revolution in central Europe, and believed that attention to consciousness was required for this. Wilhelm Reich's Freudian analysis of why rebelling workers were so easily pacified (in his view, because of the conservative tendency of the super-ego, at work even in those who are outwardly rebellious) counts as an instance of this new form of non-orthodox, psychologically oriented Marxism. These Western Marxists, among them Lukács and the Frankfurt School, avoid the risks of orthodoxy through innovation. Yet the latter carries risks of its own. Innovation risks betraying Marxism in the name of programs that were, at best, non-Marxist and, at worst, incompatible: for example, liberalism. One innovator who ran the latter risk is Habermas, whose revival of Kant's Enlightenment rationalism on the basis of the philosophy of language has often seemed to contradict main tenets of Marxism, such as its insistence on the priority of concrete material interests over abstract thought.

When evaluated as a response to the dilemma between orthodoxy and innovation, Marcuse's project seems to me to be among the most successful ever devised. In particular, Marcuse succeeded in innovating within the Marxist paradigm without betraying it for another. A prime example is the project of *Eros and Civilization*. This work undertakes a rapprochement between Marx and Freud, and undoubtedly reflects the Western Marxist belief that Marx's own account of human psychology was inadequate. Yet this synthesis of Freud and Marx preserves a core doctrine of Marx, and one even his most devoted supporters have been reluctant to accept: the theory of exploitation, arguably the main teaching of *Capital* insofar as it was devoted to showing that the capitalist's profit, the very life-blood flowing through the veins of the capitalist system, represents a kind of theft from labor, a usurpation of unpaid labor.

The main thesis of *Eros and Civilization* is that members of modern societies suffer from "surplus repression," and therefore from avoidable neurosis. Essentially, they must repress their erotic and aggressive instincts more than is necessary. Not every society in every period of history would demand this surplus repression of them. Why, then, must we suffer it? The answer is given by Marx. Workers are, in Marx's terms, exploited. Capitalism demands limitless growth and profit without end. Hence workers are forced to produce "surplus value," i.e., more value for their employers than is necessary to meet real human needs. No doubt this summary of Marcuse's thesis is inadequate and we will need to fill in the details. Yet it does serve to illustrate the way in which Marcuse's innovations preserve core Marxist doctrines. Elsewhere, Marxists have been quick to abandon Marx's own theory of exploitation. They have felt it depends on his labor theory of value: in particular, his idea that the determinant of value is the average socially necessary labor time required for its production. They have also held that the doctrine of exploitation is ill-suited to a world in which the dichotomy between labor and capital is not as stark as it once was. As we will see, this last point is well understood by Marcuse, who was interested in the way much of the industrialized proletariat had become white-collar workers and therefore more conservative. The upshot of all of this is that the Marxian doctrine of exploitation, the central teaching of the *Capital* project, survives largely intact in the pages of Marcuse's most important works.

As further confirmation of Marcuse's fidelity to Marx's project, it is worth comparing his modest departures from orthodoxy with the more dramatic ones of two other Frankfurt School authors: Adorno and Horkheimer. In their masterwork, *Dialectic of Enlightenment*, they part company with an idea that would seem to be a sine qua non of any Marxist analysis of modern society: the orthodox Marxist idea of capitalism itself.[17] Marxists typically regard capitalism as a unique epoch in the history of production, succeeding feudalism and slavery, and defined by private ownership of the means of production, the dichotomy between capitalist and laboring classes, and the imperative of ever-expanding profits; and the primary means by which this is achieved is "generalized commodity production" (when most of production is devoted to producing articles for purchase and sale). Yet while they remain critical of capitalism, Adorno and Horkheimer treat it as a symptom of something larger: "enlightenment." Contrary to what the latter term might suggest, this outlook is transhistorical, present throughout the entirety of the history of civilization and even at its very inception. Whatever name we use for it, the outlook that interests Adorno and Horkheimer is driven by fear of the alien and unpredictable. It manifests itself in "identity thinking," an all-consuming desire to assimilate what is novel to more of the same. Capitalism is an expression of enlightenment insofar as it treats every qualitatively distinct object as a quantity of exchange value. Yet so too are other, broader tendencies in modern society. One is the process of secularization Weber called "disenchantment." Another, also Weberian, is the associated displacement of value-laden and tradition-based modes of reasoning by the instrumental variety. Yet Adorno and Horkheimer even go so far as to locate identity-thinking in the use of concepts, and therefore to implicate science and reason themselves. In Adorno and Horkheimer, then, Marxism has become subsumed by a broader theory, inspired by Weber, Nietzsche, and others. History is no longer primarily the history of class struggles, but of the dialectic of myth and enlightenment.

Not only in his critique of capitalism, but also in his vision of a socialist alternative, Marcuse is more straightforwardly Marxist than his peers in the Western Marxist tradition. Adorno and Benjamin were both deeply reticent about the form a future socialist society would take. Both were inspired by the Old Testament idea of a prohibition on graven images, roughly the idea that one should not depict God lest one profane what is sacred. This may seem like an unwelcome intrusion of mysticism into what is otherwise meant to be a secular, scientific project, but it had a clear rationale in the failures experienced by socialism in the twentieth century. Adorno and Benjamin seem to follow those who thought the failures of Soviet communism could be traced to orthodox Marxism itself and its status as implicitly bourgeois. Consider for example the orthodox idea that it is the base rather than the superstructure that is primarily efficacious in history. This inspired regimes which viewed the expansion of productive power as their world-historical mission, often at terrible human cost. In light of this disillusioning experience, many were led to question the ideal of maximizing productive power itself. Was it not tacitly complicit with the bourgeois ideology that views nature and other human beings as so much raw material to be manipulated for the sake of power and profit? Marx himself had rejected utopian socialism, and warned against attempts to envision a socialist future that did not treat it as already tacitly present in the womb of the capitalist present. Adorno and Benjamin radicalize this position, refusing to describe a socialist alternative to capitalism for fear that they will simply reproduce the pathologies of the latter.

While Marcuse acknowledged that he could not provide a detailed blueprint for a future socialist society, he was not willing to forgo any speculation on this score either. When one examines Marcuse's account of this society, it is surprisingly faithful to Marx's own views. Once again, *Eros and Civilization* provides an example. Marx declares in *Capital* III that a socialist society will be one in which freedom is achieved through the shortening of the working day, and this seems to follow straightforwardly from Marcuse's analysis as well. Surplus repression is eliminated only through the elimination of surplus labor, which means a shorter working day. Admittedly, this remark from *Capital* III is only one half of an ambivalent teaching. Elsewhere, Marx suggests that it is not less work per se but, rather, fulfilling work that will allow us to be free. This time, freedom is meant in a more Kantian sense, not so much as the ability to do what one pleases but the ability to act from reason alone, to develop one's talents, and participate in the moral community. This Marxist teaching also finds a parallel in Marcuse. Marcuse held that the antithesis of duty and desire was an artifact of capitalist civilization, and that work would become play in a non-repressive society. Doubtless, this may seem utopian or exaggerated. Yet it was Marcuse's conviction that human beings are naturally social, and can enjoy cooperation for shared ends set by their nature. This is also a Marxist teaching. Of course, Marx derived it from Aristotle, whereas Marcuse derived it from Freud. Yet this disparity is encouraging. The presence of Aristotelian essentialist ideas in Marx's writings, early and late, sometimes seem to commentators to be a holdover from his youthful, Hegelian phase. They seem to represent a failure on his part to embrace a properly scientific point of view, in which human nature is a function of the mode of production and not an ontological, unchanging fact. In light of these concerns, it is note-worthy that Marcuse was using the most advanced social science of his day, Freudian psychology, in order to lend support to a classical image of human beings as naturally social. Encouragement on this score comes not from Aristotle's idea that the human being is a *zoon politikon*, but rather from Freud's observation that so much of human behavior and development can be explained by a force he calls "eros"—a constructive "anabolic" force that seeks ever-greater unities. Though most of *Eros and Civilization* is about Freud, there is little doubt that Marcuse is there attempting to show that the latest psychology has borne out Marx's views: both his critique of capitalism and his case for a socialist alternative.

Admittedly, Marcuse makes other more significant departures from Marx which are not so easily explained away. Like other Western Marxists and members of the Frankfurt School, he rejects the "vulgar Marxist" idea that art, culture, religion, and philosophy are "epiphenomenal," or causally impotent. This rejection is important to Marcuse's aesthetics and his conviction that art can have a progressive role. Yet here as ever, Marcuse's rejection of dogmatic Marxism is compatible with loyalty to the basic Marxist teaching. Marcuse concedes that art and culture are never by themselves sufficient to bring about revolutionary transformation of society. If historical conditions are not ripe, then no revolution will occur. The class structure must be incompatible with the available means of production. Yet it does not follow from this that art and culture are impotent. They have an impact, even if they cannot be the decisive factor. Marcuse saw this effect at work in the influence of hippie culture and rock-and-roll on the American population. Its influence was not limited to the superstructure but, as we will later see, constituted an "ingression into the base." That is to say, it disrupted the military–industrial complex, not once and for all but in isolated instances. In any case, Marcuse's insistence that culture may have some role is a much more modest departure from Marx's teaching than it might at first seem. It is certainly more modest than a familiar Hegelian-Marxist idea, occasionally entertained by Lukács and later adopted by Adorno. This is the idea that capitalism, like Hegel's Geist, constitutes a totality unified by a single principle: the law of exchange, which demands equivalents for equivalents. Whatever its merits, this idea is revisionary. It collapses the ideological and legal superstructure into the economic base so that there remains only the undifferentiated medium Adorno calls "society."

A final item worth noting when one appraises Marcuse's Marxism is his role as a voice in the anti-war movement. Marcuse retained a version of the Leninist idea that imperialism is the highest phase of capitalism, and applied it to America's military–industrial complex and its interventions in foreign countries. It is a common objection to capitalism that its obsession with profit and limitless growth leads to overproduction. Marcuse adds that it will also lead to destruction, insofar as the latter is also profitable. This profitable form of destruction can be found in war, still the source of a significant portion of the American gross domestic product. Marcuse, like others, flags the danger inherent in a world in which war is a means of stimulating a stagnant economy. Unlike the many leftists who make this observation, however, Marcuse offers a deeper analysis of the phenomenon with his Freudian–Marxist theory of the instincts.

Though faithful to Marx's critique of capitalism and case for a socialist alternative, Marcuse does depart from Marx and Engels in more radical ways: specifically when it comes to the philosophical foundations of their position. This will become clear when we consider his philosophical outlook in subsequent chapters, but I will indicate a few of the main ways here.

First, Marcuse, like others in the Frankfurt School, embraces a version of idealism deriving from Kant and Hegel. As we will see, there are numerous moments in Marcuse's writings when he is deeply critical of the realist idea that our senses put us in touch with reality as it is in itself. He often descries this as "positivism." In its place, Marcuse advocates the idea that the facts are "mediated" by society. This view resembles those of Kant and Hegel, though they would have insisted that it is the transcendental subject or Spirit which constitutes the facts. Yet Marxism is often thought to require a realist perspective, which treats nature as existing and having the character it does independent of human practices and interests. One could make the case for an idealist Marx, and certain Western Marxists have attempted to do so. There is some evidence for this in the young Marx. In "Theses on Feuerbach," Marx declares that reality is a product of "human sensuous activity" and criticizes previous naturalists, empiricists, and materialists for neglecting this fact which was emphasized by German idealism (though in an inadequate way, focused predominantly on reason and not on our material interests and the labor activities aimed to satisfy them).

Second, Marcuse differs from other Marxists in embracing a metaphysics reminiscent of Plato and Aristotle in which things have essences or natures. Whereas for Plato, these essences are forms, unchanging archetypes transcending the sensible world, for Aristotle they are instead substantial forms, present in things as their principles of motion and rest. Yet both are essentialists, and Marcuse appears to follow them in emphasizing the hidden potentials things have by virtue of their natures. For Marcuse, this is especially true of human beings who live stunted lives in a repressive society. Yet it is also true of nature, which appears in such a society as so much raw material to be exploited for the sake of profit.

Indeed, it is because of its essentialism that classical philosophy qualifies as "two-dimensional." It is an outlook that preserves the possibility of critique by maintaining a distinction between how things could and should be, and how they in fact are. By contrast, positivism, in abandoning metaphysics, ethics, and aesthetics in favor of what is empirically verifiable, is one-dimensional. Any statements concerning the way things could or should be, as opposed to how they are, cannot qualify as knowledge, i.e., they are non-cognitive. Such statements merely express personal preferences.

Clearly, this combination of classical philosophy and Marxism is peculiar, and might even seem self-contradictory. When we turn to a more detailed examination of Marcuse's views in this area, we will need to ask how he reconciles this metaphysics with the modern scientific worldview, and with historical materialism. Does this synthesis of Plato and Marx not risk complicity with reactionary critics of modernity, like Thomists, Heideggerians, and others who want to "re-enchant the world"? Marcuse appears to think there is no incompatibility.

In my view, it is appropriate that Marcuse accepts Marx's diagnosis of capitalism's ills and socialist prescription, on the one hand, while rejecting some of the underlying philosophical commitments of Marxism, on the other. The latter are fairly ill-defined, and often not defended in any systematic way. Marx's materialism is not physicalism, the thesis that the universe is composed only of the entities and forces recognized in the physical sciences. It is a view about the relationship between the economic base and the legal and political superstructure, together with the domain of ideology. Of course, it is extremely doubtful that Marx believed in an immaterial soul. Yet where on the spectrum of positions between physicalism and dualism Marx's views might lie is a question his writings do not answer. It is hard not to sympathize with those authors who argue that Marx was an anti-philosopher, or that he viewed many traditional philosophical questions as pointless, unanswerable, or confused. For our purposes, however, the point is that Marx's statements on the great questions of philosophy often rule out (or in) very little. Indeed, they are far more numerous in his early writings, something which further complicates the task of inferring anything from them about his position. To the extent that Marcuse contradicts Marx, it is better when it concerns abstract philosophical questions than the concrete details of his critique of capitalism and case for a socialist alternative.

Summary

Herbert Marcuse's formative years were spent in Berlin, where he had a political awakening in response to World War I and the socialist movement. After initially studying literature, and writing a thesis on Romanticism, he turned to the study of philosophy and began doctoral work at Freiburg. Like many others of his generation, he was fascinated by the phenomenological movement, and its promise to unite abstract philosophical concerns with concrete existential problems of human life. Yet the rise of the Nazis, and their embrace by his supervisor Martin Heidegger, made the prospect of an academic career doubtful for the young Marcuse. Marcuse soon emigrated from Germany, and became affiliated with Horkheimer's Institute for Social Research: a group of eclectic Marxist intellectuals who believed intellectual work should serve the end of human liberation. Marcuse would soon find himself in the USA, working for the Institute and also contributing to the war effort as a member of the OSS. The 1950s saw Marcuse deepen his interest in psychoanalysis, and publish one of his great masterworks, *Eros and Civilization*. Personally, they were marked by tragedy, and the death of Marcuse's first wife Sophie Wertheim. Marcuse would marry twice more, first wedding the widow of his friend Franz Neumann (Inga) and later the activist and philosopher Erica "Ricky" Sherover. During the 1960s, Marcuse would relocate to San Diego and become an inspiration to the student movement, as well as a mentor to scholar-activist Angela Davis and Abbie Hoffman. Though it brought visibility, this was a development that would somewhat tarnish his academic reputation. Henceforth Marcuse would often be viewed as a merely popular philosopher, though in fact his fidelity to the founding mission of critical theory is unmatched among his contemporaries. Marcuse's *One-Dimensional Man* was among the most discussed philosophical works of the '60s. Marcuse would die en route to a conference in Germany, but not before completing his final work, a study in aesthetics.

Substantively, the main contribution this book will assess is Marcuse's attempt to reconcile the concerns of traditional philosophy, e.g., the nature and possibility of knowledge, with a Marxist outlook. Marxism, even when anti-philosophical, often seeks intellectual nourishment from traditional philosophy, but thereby risks compromising its political radicalism and concreteness. Traditional philosophy, for its part, often finds in Marxism an anti-philosophical and reductive program that would dissolve the great questions of philosophy into the class struggle. Whether Marcuse successfully overcame this dilemma is the central question of this book.

Notes

1 In this biographical overview, I have mostly drawn on the account of Marcuse's life given by Kellner (1984: Ch. 1 "Origins: Politics, Art and Philosophy in the Young Marcuse") as well as Andrew Feenberg's piece "Remembering Herbert Marcuse" (2023: Ch. 1).

2 Axel Honneth (2003: 496–504) has suggested that some of Marcuse's independence as a thinker can be explained by the fact that he was an "outsider." Marcuse, unlike the other core members of the Institute, came from Berlin and not Frankfurt.

3 In the Lebenslauf (Curriculum Vitae) from his dissertation, Marcuse reports that this was due to his poor eyesight. See https://www.marcuse.org/herbert/pubs/22diss/HerbDissLLtrans.html.

4 Excellent discussions of Marcuse's earliest work on Hegel can be found in Feenberg (2005) (2023). In the chapters to follow, I will focus instead on the Hegelianism of *Reason and Revolution*. Of course, the two approaches are not necessarily in tension. However, it seems to me that the earlier Hegelianism, with its rather ontological cast—its focus on being, life, and the *Science of Logic*—bears less directly on critical social theory. *Reason and Revolution* is presented as a contribution to the struggle against fascism, as having continuities with Marx and Marxism, and as a "negative philosophy" in opposition to positivism.

5 See Feenberg (2005) and Abromeit (2010).

6 Extremely helpful here is Olafson's interview with Marcuse about his teacher Heidegger (Marcuse and Olafson 1977; also in CPHM 3: 165–76). See also Marcuse's early writings on Marxism (2005), many of which combine Marxism with existentialist phenomenology.

7 "I first, like all the others, believed there could be some combination between existentialism and Marxism, precisely because of their insistence on concrete analysis of actual human existence, human beings, and their world" (CPHM 3: 166).

8 As Arash Abazari points out to me, Husserl and Kant's transcendental egos have little to do with *psychological* inwardness. Both thinkers are anti-psychologistic. Still, both are offering theories of self-consciousness, which implicates them in the error Heidegger saw as pervasive in the tradition. Even if one rejects the traditional Cartesian idea of the mind as "inner theatre," appeals to self-consciousness in later figures would remain objectionable in holding the subject apart from its world.

9 "But I soon realized that Heidegger's concreteness was to a great extent a phony, a false concreteness, and that in fact his philosophy was just as abstract and just as removed from reality, even avoiding reality, as the philosophies which at that time had dominated German universities, namely a rather dry brand of neo-Kantianism, neo-Hegelianism, neo-Idealism, but also positivism" (CPHM 3: 166)

10 "I have never been analyzed. I apparently didn't need it. Psychologically, I hope, I am not interesting at all. I am fairly normal" ("Conversation with Marcuse in *Psychology Today*," CPHM 5: 189).

11 In an article for the *San Diego Reader*, Fokos (2007) discusses Marcuse's love of the zoo and of hippopotami. She quotes Kellner on the subject: "He thought the hippopotamus was a metaphor for all sorts of things. He saw it as the wonder in nature, that nature could produce something so extravagant."

12 The most thorough and philosophically sophisticated study of Heidegger's influence on Marcuse's thinking about technology is and remains Feenberg's *Marcuse and Heidegger: The Catastrophe and Redemption of History* (2005); but see also his more recent treatment of these topics (2023: Chs. 5–6). For an alternative perspective, see Abromeit and Cobb (2004: 131–52) which questions the extent of Marcuse's debt to Heidegger. The Marcuse–Heidegger relationship is not a prominent topic of the present study. This is not because I take sides in this controversy, but because I have little of substance to add to what has already been said by the main participants.

13 As I write these words, in August 2023, one of the most popular new nonfiction books—a *New York Times* bestseller—treats Marcuse as a forerunner of the (alleged) takeover of American higher education by critical race theory: *America's Cultural Revolution* by Christopher Rufo.

14 Sometimes ideology is distinguished from the superstructure. Whereas the latter is a set of legal and political institutions that stabilize the base, the former is the set of ideas that do so. See Cohen (2000: 216).

15 The distinction I draw here between orthodox Marxism and revisionary versions should not be equated with another: the distinction between the writings of Marx and Engels themselves, and those of their followers—in the Western Marxist tradition and the Soviet Union. "Orthodox Marxism," in the sense in which I will use it in this study, refers to a family of views that claim inspiration from Marx and Engels, but which appear later. When arguing that Marcuse and others criticize orthodox Marxism as reductive, I should not be taken to claim that Marcuse (or these others) criticize Marx and Engels themselves. Hence when I claim, e.g., that many orthodox Marxists regarded the ideological superstructure as "epiphenomenal," this is not inconsistent with, e.g., Engels' famous statement in the 1890 letter to Borgius that he and Marx never wanted to deny that the ideological superstructure has some weak causal role:

> According to the materialist conception of history, the ultimately determining element in history is the production and reproduction of real life. More than this neither Marx nor I have ever asserted. Hence if somebody twists this into saying that the economic element is the only determining one, he transforms that proposition into a meaningless, abstract, senseless phrase.
>
> (Marx, K. and Engels, F. 1978: 760)

Thanks to Arash Abazari for discussion of this issue, and for the reference to Engels' letter.

16 I owe my understanding of "mechanistic" forms of Marxism descending from the later Engels to Avineri (1968: 65–66).

17 As Arash Abazari reminds me, there is an important caveat to this claim: an earlier version of Dialectic of Enlightenment—the 1944 Philosophische Fragmente—contained Marxist language, e.g., concerning class, that was expunged from the 1947 version. Hence it is worth considering the possibility that Adorno and Horkheimer's approach is consistent with Marxism, but was amended. It is sometimes speculated that this was Horkheimer's doing, and that his motivation was to avoid political persecution in Cold War America. There is also the suspicion that Horkheimer himself had begun to drift rightward, a trend that culminated in his later support for the Vietnam War. For further discussion, see van Reijen and Bransen (2002).

Further reading

Feenberg, A. (2023) Towards a Ruthless Critique of Everything Existing, London: Verso. [Ch. 1 offers a vivid portrait of Marcuse, in San Diego, Paris and elsewhere, from his last student, the philosopher of technology and scholar of modern European thought Andrew Feenberg.]

Jay, M. (1973) The Dialectical Imagination: A History of the Frankfurt School and the Institute of Social Research, 1923–1950, Boston/Toronto: Little, Brown & Company.

Kellner, D. (1984) Herbert Marcuse and the Crisis of Marxism, London: Macmillan. [One of the first and best comprehensive overviews of Marcuse's life and thought. The biographical chapter is an important source for the present discussion.]

Katz, B. (1982) Herbert Marcuse and the Art of Liberation: An Intellectual Biography, London: Verso.

Marcuse, H., Neumann, F., and Kirchheimer, O. (2013) Secret Reports on Nazi Germany: The Frankfurt School Contribution to the War Effort, ed. R. Loudani with a foreword by R. Geuss, Princeton: Princeton University Press.

Two
Epistemology

This chapter concerns Marcuse's epistemology, or theory of knowledge. It may seem questionable to attempt to ascribe *any* epistemological views to Marcuse. After all, he does not explicitly address the topic of epistemology—at least not in the way most contemporary or traditional philosophers do. We will not find in his writings responses to skepticism about the external world (or other minds); arguments for foundationalism or coherentism; attempts to identify necessary and sufficient conditions on knowledge as opposed to justified true belief; and so on. Certainly, no such epistemological projects are present on the *surface* of his writings, and it would therefore be somewhat misleading to present epistemology as a central concern of this particular philosopher and critical theorist. Nevertheless, the present study is written with the conviction that Marcuse's critical theory of society is best understood against the backdrop of his deep immersion in the philosophical tradition and his preoccupation with enduring questions—even if his answers were anything but traditional. If we examine Marcuse's writings more closely, we will, I think, find a recurrent preoccupation with (at least) one perennial epistemological topic.

While Marcuse does not share all of contemporary or classical philosophy's concerns in the theory of knowledge, he does, I think, address one recurrent topic from the history of epistemology. Admittedly, this is a broader topic than the term "epistemology" might imply, since it concerns not only the possibility of knowledge but the more general issue of the interface between mind and the world which knowledge presupposes (a more accurate title for this chapter might refer to the area of philosophy where epistemology

DOI: 10.4324/9781003307075-2

and philosophy of mind intersect). The specific topic I have in mind is the controversy between realists and anti-realists—or, though the two controversies are not exactly equivalent, realists and idealists. Provisionally, we can characterize this debate in very broad terms as one between those who insist the human mind can come to know a mind-independent reality, existing and having the character it does independently of us, and those who maintain, on the contrary, that the reality we know is in some sense mind-dependent (either for its existence or its character). What is more, I will argue that Marcuse takes sides in this debate, and is an idealist—albeit of a very heterodox sort. Marcuse's idealism is unconventional, given his Marxist commitments. We can anticipate why when we recall that Marx defined himself as a historical materialist, a self-designation often presented as the very inverse of idealism.

Marxists have often expressed their anti-idealism along the following lines. Idealism, in its over-emphasis on thinking or the mind, envisions human beings upside down, walking on their heads with their feet in the air (Marx 1976: 102). The latter is a position whose absurdity is meant to be self-evident in this analogy. Materialism inverts this allegedly absurd picture, placing the human being right-side up with her feet planted firmly on the ground once more. Henceforth, it is social consciousness that derives from social being, and not the reverse; ideas that derive from reality, and not reality that derives from ideas; thought that is the predicate and human beings its subject, rather than the reverse (Marx and Engels 1978: 4, 18). Rhetoric aside, the substance of the point is clear: Marxism is the opposite of classical idealism, and in that sense irreconcilable with it. Are there any prospects for a Marcusean critical theory of society that is idealist, even if only in some non-traditional sense?

My argument will be that Marcuse's position is best characterized in terms that will at first seem a contradiction in terms: as idealist materialism. Following German idealism, it acknowledges that the world we know depends on us. Yet following Marx, Marcuse will add that it is society and the mode of production that determine the way the world "shows up" to knowers. To some, the former tenet will seem a profound betrayal of Marxism, especially if the latter is understood as a realist doctrine. On this interpretation, Marxism holds that nature, the body, society, and the world more generally are real, and were so well before they became objects of consciousness or knowledge. Idealism, by contrast, appears to require that reality is dependent on the human being, and even if one emphasizes human interests and practices as opposed to the human mind, this position can still seem to put the cart before the horse. Just how such a position, at once Hegelian and Marxist, could be even so much as coherent will be difficult to show. Yet my aim is to show that Marcuse does in fact hold such a position, and that it is not incoherent.[1]

As if all this were not complex enough, there is an additional dimension to Marcuse's epistemological project: his critique of positivism. It is well known that the Frankfurt School arrived at its program for a critical theory of society by contrasting its own rather politicized conception of knowledge-production with the more austerely scientific one of the Vienna circle. Yet when Marcuse speaks of positivism he does not just have in mind the *logical* positivism of the Vienna circle, but a tendency he sees as pervasive in modern philosophy. As we will see, Marcuse includes Comte, Schelling, and others in this tradition. Indeed, he goes so far as to suggest in one place that the whole of (modern?) philosophy constitutes a dispute between idealism and positivism. As he writes in an unpublished piece, "Idealism and Positivism": "I have chosen idealism and positivism as the two types of philosophical thinking which have dominated the entire history of Western thought" (CPHM 5: 92). For Marcuse, the crux of this longstanding debate between idealism and positivism is the idealism–realism issue. Marcuse's Hegelian-Marxist idea that reality is constituted by society is meant to be an alternative to the positivist one. What, then, is positivism for Marcuse?

We will delve more deeply into this issue in this chapter, but for now the following should be sufficient. Positivism, in Marcuse's sense, consists in the realist view that "the facts" are out there waiting to be apprehended by us. Of course, positivism is also closely associated with empiricism, the effort to make philosophy scientific, and finally, with a radical critique of metaphysics. Yet the realist dimension is central in Marcuse's presentation, and forms the target of his attack. Contra positivism, Marcuse will argue that "the facts" are constituted by society, understood in a Hegelian-Marxist way. An important issue to consider is whether this position is subjectivist in the pejorative sense. Is it a position that leaves us out of touch with the world in the way that perhaps Berkeleyan idealism or skepticism about the external world threaten to do? I argue that it is not, and that it is the role of Marx in Marcuse's idealism that blocks any move to such a "subjective idealism." However, I will leave for later the question of whether Marcuse's idealist position implies a conception of science in which the possibility of objectivity or truth is fatally undermined. This topic will be deferred to the chapter on Marcuse's philosophy of science.[2]

1. "Going behind" the facts

Our point of departure is an extremely rich though obscure passage in *One-Dimensional Man*, where Marcuse appears to defend an idealist conception of knowledge. I hope to arrive at a preliminary statement of Marcuse's idealist position by unpacking this passage, which I believe contains all of the doctrine's key components. Marcuse begins with the paradoxical statement that, under present social conditions, truly grasping the facts may require "going behind" them:

> Under the repressive conditions in which men think and live, thought—any mode of thinking which is not confined to pragmatic orientation within the status quo—can recognize the facts and respond to the facts only by "going behind" them. Experience takes place before a curtain which conceals and, if the world is the appearance of something behind the curtain of immediate experience, then, in Hegel's terms, it is we ourselves who are behind the curtain. We ourselves not as the subjects of common sense, as in linguistic analysis, nor as the "purified" subjects of scientific measurement, but as the subjects and objects of the historical struggle of man with nature and with society. Facts are what they are as occurrences in this struggle. Their factuality is historical, even where it is still that of brute, unconquered nature.
>
> (ODM 189)

Several things are worth noting about the position articulated in this paragraph.

The first is a point of background: the longstanding debate in philosophy between realists and idealists is here approached in more contemporary terms—specifically, in terms of "facts." Are the facts simply out there waiting to be apprehended by us? Or are they, instead, constructed by us? At issue here are facts, rather than things, a distinction famously drawn by Wittgenstein in the *Tractatus* (2001: 5). As a preliminary, a fact is the kind of thing that can be preceded by a "that" clause. The cat is not a fact, but *that* the cat is black is one. Facts, then, have structure, something Marcuse actually emphasizes.[3] The same elements, structured differently, might not constitute a fact (that "black is a cat"). It is also sometimes said that facts are abstract in a way that their subject-matter is not. The cat may be black, but the *fact* that the cat is black does not—cannot—have any color. For all this, however, a fact is not identical to a proposition, the linguistic or intentional entity through which a fact is represented. Whereas propositions can be false, facts typically cannot.

It might seem that very little turns on this, but it is at least a preliminary indication that Marcuse's opponent will be a positivist inspired by the early Wittgenstein, perhaps a member of the Vienna circle.

Substantively, it could be that the relevant debate about whether the world is mind-independent or not is adjudicated differently, depending on whether it is facts or things that concern us. Anticipating slightly, it may be that idealism is less rebarbative when it concerns the mind-dependence of facts, rather than of things. An element of realism could be retained—at least for the constituents of facts, if not for the facts themselves. This would make Marcuse's idealism qualified rather than absolute. Later, I will return to the issue of how this framing in terms of facts affects the dispute.

A second important point is that Marcuse, in defending the idealist view that we ourselves are responsible for "the facts," cites Hegel as inspiration. He includes a clear and unmistakable reference to a famous passage from *The Phenomenology of Spirit*. In that passage, the seeker of truth is described as looking behind a curtain in search of the fundamental bases of the world of experience: for example, laws of nature or fundamental forces (Hegel 1979: 103, Hegel 1970: Bd. 3 135). Yet behind the curtain is nothing but the human mind itself, rather than a force or entity independent of us. This passage from the *Phenomenology* effects the transition from a broadly scientific realist perspective of the standpoint Hegel treats under the heading "Force and the Understanding" to the idealist one he calls "self-consciousness." Hence it will be important to consider the role of Hegel in Marcuse's idealism, especially the Hegel of the *Phenomenology*. For this, I will urge that we turn to Marcuse's 1941 study of Hegel *Reason and Revolution*, where the same passage is emphasized and expanded upon at length.

A third point concerns the ambiguity in the idealist doctrine that the world we know depends on us. Which aspect of us, exactly? As Marcuse asks: "What exactly is the subject under whose aspect idealism views reality?" Marcuse is careful here to distance himself from certain other possible idealisms which he think emphasize the wrong facet of the subject. It is neither as the possessor of consciousness, nor as the speaker of a language, nor as a scientific knower, that the human being figures in Marcuse's idealism, as other idealisms would have it ("linguistic idealism," "transcendental idealism," "Berkeleyan idealism," etc.). Rather, it is (he writes) "as the subjects and objects of the historical struggle between man and nature." Certainly, this passage implies an association to more pragmatic forms of idealism, those in which it is our interests and activities that determine how the world shows up for us. Yet beyond this vague association, it is difficult to tell exactly what form of idealism Marcuse intends to defend. Of course, the idea that humanity as a whole is involved in a historically ongoing attempt to master nature is familiar from Marx and Engels. Yet it is not typically taken to imply a form of idealism. Why, then, does Marcuse regard it as relevant to understanding knowledge?

This phrase in the passage from *One-Dimensional Man* which defines the subject of idealism as "the subjects and objects of the historical struggle between man and nature" is worth dwelling on further. Per idealism, "the facts" are constituted by human beings—but not by us alone. Rather, they are constituted by the interaction between us and nature. How might the facts be products of that process of constitution? Like tools or techniques, the facts are means devised by us in order to dominate the natural world more effectively. Importantly, the idea that the facts are products of an interaction between mind and nature limits the extent to which nature itself can be deemed mind-dependent. As one pole of the process that constitutes the facts, it must have a reality that goes beyond them. An obvious question we will need to take up is whether this doctrine slights the importance of natural science, and instrumentalizes its findings in an overly crude way.

At this point, a problematic form of relativism or historicism seems to be in the offing. If the attempt to overcome nature is an extended historical process, then presumably the facts it generates are historical as well. As Marcuse puts it, the very "factuality" of the facts—their being facts at all—is due to history. When this endeavor enters a new historical phase, redundant facts will be eliminated and new ones will emerge. It is not just that facts which already obtained are now discovered. Rather, new facts concerning nature will come into being, a somewhat paradoxical idea but one that seems to follow from Marcuse's idealism. We will have to discuss this somewhat rebarbative implication of Marcuse's position later.

A further element of the doctrine: for Marcuse, human beings are not simply the subjects or movers of this process, but also its objects, meaning they are, in turn, profoundly shaped by it.[4] This extends to their cognitive and other capacities, which develop in the course of the attempt to dominate nature. The idea that we are both subject and object is important. If our minds both affect and are affected by this process, then this would be a point in favor of the historicism Marcuse recommends. Human beings would think, perceive, and imagine differently in different phases of history. This might extend concepts and mental representations they employ, the words and language in which they think and speak, their self-conceptions and conceptions of the world around them, and so on. Clearly, we will want to attend to how Marcuse fills in the details of this suggestive view, since it remains abstract and skeletal.

Yet it may be misleading to characterize Marcuse's position as the one that human beings (plural) are engaged in an ongoing struggle with nature which involves scientific knowledge only as a means. In speaking of the struggle between "man" (singular) and nature, Marcuse may seem to be endorsing a version of the Hegelian idea of a collective subject; but this is difficult to discern clearly. Marcuse is well aware of the idealist credentials of this concept, which he discusses elsewhere, once more in the piece "Positivism and Idealism":

> What exactly is the subject under whose aspect idealism views reality? It is not an individual, although it is realized only in a

totality of individual thoughts, actions, and relations. In other words, it is a universal ... the Transcendental Consciousness in Kant, the Mind in Hegel. It is called a subject because it "exists" only in self-conscious knowledge and action, and because it becomes actual only in the knowledge and practice of men.

(CPHM 5: 93)

The idealist's collective subject has advantages, even in a materialist context. The ongoing project of mankind's struggle with nature is in an important sense a collective one, not one carried out by isolated individuals. Even when I, this particular person, struggle to overcome the resistance of the natural world, I am typically engaged in a cooperative enterprise with others currently living. I rely on the previous efforts, as well as the technological innovations, of others now dead. My efforts will survive me and form the preconditions for those of my descendants. This is what renders the struggle continuous across historical epochs and social forms. Spelling out the interconnections between my activity and other people's need not require any recourse to Kant's transcendental subject or Hegel's Geist. The collective subject Marcuse describes could be one whose members are collected by the way production is organized, consciously or unconsciously. It would not be Kant's transcendental subject or Hegel's Geist, but Marx's species-being.

It is perhaps from these commonsense facts that Marcuse concludes (skipping a number of logical steps, unfortunately) that it is a collective subject, "the human species," which struggles with nature. Its ongoing efforts to master nature seem difficult to capture with a fully nominalist ontology in which we only recognize individual subjects but not a collective one embracing them. No sooner have we referred to the efforts of an isolated individual than we seem to invoke those of an indefinite array of others. Significantly, Marcuse draws an association between the idea of a collective subject and Platonism, wherein there are not simply good things but also the Good. Given Marcuse's sympathy with the latter ontology, it seems hard to resist the implication that he is embracing the former as well.

There are numerous problems with the idea of a collective subject, but I will restrict myself to one here. The notion of a collective subject can seem to affirm the present state of the social world in a manner anathema to Marxists. Hegel may have believed that he and his contemporaries had succeeded in ordering life under the intentions of a collective subject, but for Marx, the closest we come under modern capitalism to doing so is by being ruled by capital—a mechanical or automatic subject. If society is ever to be organized by "the general will," then this will have to await the coming of a centrally planned economy. The anarchy of unplanned capitalist production, and the role in it of class antagonisms, seems impossible to reconcile with the language of collective subjectivity. I therefore want to leave the question of the individual or collective subject open. Later I will argue that Marcuse is interested in rehabilitating this Hegelian idea.

A further point requiring emphasis is that Marcuse appears to claim his idealism extends to nature, and not just the social world. It is not only the values we endorse as a society, but even the scientific facts concerning nature which are historically relative. This is an eyebrow-raising anti-realist doctrine whose counter-intuitive implications Marcuse does not always fully acknowledge. As we will see, Marcuse often focuses on facts concerning society. He is especially interested in the way social facts are constituted so as to benefit the powerful and preserve the status quo. He argues that mainstream social science is complicit in this process. However, the idea that facts of nature are historically constituted seems more extreme. Do they, too, exist to serve the interests of the powerful?

A final point in this paragraph that I wish to emphasize is found in its opening sentences (I have proceeded out of order). It concerns the consequences of deviating from Marcuse's Hegelian-Marxist form of idealism. Marcuse tells us that the only way to go beyond a "pragmatic" orientation to the status quo is to accept his idealism. The implicit suggestion seems to be that failing to adopt the idealist doctrine that Marcuse recommends consigns one to a form of conservatism.

This might seem to be a somewhat Manichean view, or inference. Surely it is possible to be a scientific realist *and* a political radical, rather than either/or? However, Marcuse does not seem to countenance this possibility. As we will see, he thinks positivism is inherently conservative. This is a view that might seem to be falsified by the large numbers of left-wing, politically radical positivists, to say nothing of naturalists or other more moderate proponents of scientific philosophy. Yet Marcuse could counter that they achieved political radicalization in spite of and not because of their philosophy of science.

2. The opening arguments of Hegel's *Phenomenology*

Having described Marcuse's Hegelian-Marxist form of idealism, we must now ask what arguments support it. Here I think it may be helpful to turn to Hegel's *Phenomenology*, an obvious source of inspiration for Marcuse. As we saw, Marcuse refers to a famous passage from the *Phenomenology* using the metaphor of a curtain—but this is not much to go on in forming an account of Marcuse's debt to Hegel. However, Marcuse does offer an interpretation of the *Phenomenology* in his 1941 *Reason and Revolution*. There, he proclaims that "The first three sections of the Phenomenology are a critique of positivism" (RR 112). Hence, I propose that we consider in detail Marcuse's interpretation of these opening arguments in our effort to understand his idealist alternative to positivism.

For Marcuse, Hegel is of more than merely historical interest. Writing in 1941, Marcuse insists that Hegel is a vital source of inspiration for the global struggle against fascism (RR vii). Marcuse also presents the nineteenth century in terms that unmistakably reflect the intellectual context in which critical theory arose: as a dispute between the "negative" philosophies of Hegel and Marx and "positive" philosophies, like Comte's (we will clarify this distinction presently). In this way, the critical theorists' own rejection of logical positivism in favor of a more activist approach to philosophy and social theory is shown to have deep roots in the nineteenth century. Clearly, then, Marcuse would reject as false the choice between offering an interpretation of Hegel and defending views of his own. My proposal then is that Marcuse adopts into his own critical theory Hegel's case for idealism.

In claiming that the opening arguments of the *Phenomenology* are a critique of positivism, Marcuse is thinking especially of Hegel's critique of "sense-certainty" (this becomes clear when one examines Marcuse's discussion of the chapter).

First, some background. "Sense-certainty" is one of the many standpoints Hegel calls "configurations of consciousness" [*Gestalten des Bewußtseins*] (1970: 38). Each of them embodies a conception of knowledge, and each such conception is tripartite.[5] Each is composed of i) a conception of the subject, ii) a conception of the object, and iii) a conception how the two must relate if knowledge is to be possible. All three elements are necessary components of a conception of knowledge, or "configuration of consciousness." Hegel adopts this structure from Reinhold, who had made it the "first principle" of a reconstituted version of Kant's critical philosophy, one in which all of the central claims of the critical system derive inexorably from a single foundational claim.[6] Yet in Hegel, Reinhold's "principle of consciousness" is put to a distinct, un-Kantian use, as we will soon see.

"Sense-certainty," the first configuration of consciousness, is essentially a form of empiricism, though Marcuse would likely call it positivist. The knowing subject is conceived as exclusively using its senses, rather than its capacity for conceptual thought, as passive and reliant on the given rather than spontaneous and reflective. The object known is a sensible particular, which is directly presented to us. The direct contact between the senses and their objects is a sensible impression, which this standpoint identifies as knowledge, indeed certainty. At least from an ordinary, pre-philosophical standpoint, the fact that one perceives some object by means of one's senses can appear indubitable (or "certain"). The *Phenomenology* begins with this conception of knowledge because it seems like the most obvious one, favored not just by the empiricist philosopher but by the ordinary person in the street.

Hegel gives the following argument for why sense-certainty is self-undermining (Hegel 1979: 60; 1970: 84). When the subject of sense-certainty is asked to convey in language its sensible impression of the world, its response is a form of ostensive definition: "this, here, now."[7] This is fitting, given that the object of sense-experience is a particular with which I am in contact via my senses. Yet no sooner have I indicated that I know "this, here, now," than the rug is pulled out from under me. "This" is no longer the same "this," "here" no longer the same "here," "now" no longer the same "now" (in Hegel's example, "now" was formerly day but is now night). The object itself may change, if only in a subtle way. It may move from one place to another, if only slightly. A small amount of time may pass. What appeared to be a well-founded claim to knowledge has turned out not to be one at all.

While Marcuse finds in Hegel an argument against a particularly radical form of empiricism, far more is required if he is to build upon it an argument against realism and for idealism. It would stand to reason that this remaining part of the argument would be given in the next two sections of the *Phenomenology*: "Perception" and "Force and the Understanding." Indeed, these sections culminate in the discovery voiced in the "curtain" passage Marcuse finds so important. Unfortunately, Marcuse is somewhat cursory in his review of the details of the argument. This is understandable, since the path Hegel follows is long and winding.

Still, let us see if the makings of an argument against realism, and for idealism, may already be present in this first section—conceding that we will be taking certain liberties with the text. Sense-certainty has taught us that nothing like knowledge can be achieved on the basis of sensible representations of the particulars that affect us. Yet the correct statement of the problem is already a clue to the solution. In Kantian terms, we have learned that not only the intuitions of sensibility, but also the concepts of the understanding are required. Not only sensible representations of particulars, but general concepts which apply to wide ranges of them. What we know is not the particular qua particular, but qua instance of a universal. It is a specific thing, at a specific time and place, brought under the general concepts "this," "here," and "now."

However, the argument soon takes an idealist turn: these concepts, which structure the object, are contributed by the mind, rather than read off of reality.[8] In and of itself, the world of particulars that affect our senses does not come to us already carved up according to a conceptual scheme. This would be the rationalist metaphysical view, on which reality has an intelligible structure we intuit intellectually. Yet Hegel does not seem to endorse such a view, which would be incompatible with Kant's Copernican turn—his revolutionary discovery that fundamental features of the world cannot be naively assumed to exist independent of us but must instead be traced to their origins in the human mind. In any case, it would be illicit to presuppose such a rationalist metaphysical view at this early stage.

The knowing subject is responsible for the conceptual structure of the world. The passive reception of sensible impressions must be supplemented by the active application of concepts on the part of the subject. Accordingly, the sense-certainty discussion has undermined not only a form of empiricism, but also an accompanying realism. It has, further, provided initial motivation for a form of idealism that emphasizes the contribution of the knowing subject to the object known.

For Marcuse, another crucial part of Hegel's critique of positivism in the sense-certainty section lies in the realization that it is not the individual subject, but rather a collective one (society), which is the bearer of knowledge. Here I present, but will not evaluate, Marcuse's interpretation of the remainder of the sense-certainty chapter (one could question whether a collective subject makes its entrance so early, but I leave this question to one side). A collective subject appears to be invoked when the protagonist attempts to fix the referent of "this here now" by invoking its own point of view. It is the "this here now" of which I am conscious. Unfortunately, this simply raises the same problem again one level up. "I" is no less general a term than those others, i.e., "this," "here," and "now." The I who avows knowledge at one moment may not be the I who does so at another. Here too the statement of the problem implies the solution. It is not on behalf of myself qua this particular individual (JM) that I claim to know but, rather, on behalf of everybody: "If I say I see a house here and now, I imply that everyone could take my place as subject of this perception" (RR 105). It is not, then, this individual person (JM) who knows, but always a we, a group or collective: "Just as the Here and Now are universal as against their individual content, so the I is universal as against all individual I's" (RR 105).

What is this "everyone" on whose behalf I claim to know? For Hegel, it cannot be a mere aggregate or sum. Certainly, I am not in a position to add together the knowledge of all individual persons. It is rather a whole that is more than the sum of its parts. It is not the sum of knowing subjects as a further subject, a collective one that they all comprise. Admittedly, this idea can seem extravagant, but Hegel himself thinks it follows naturally from reflections on the nature of knowledge: in particular the fact that in knowing, I do not claim the standpoint of any particular individual. Later, Hegel famously describes Spirit as "the 'I' that is 'We', and the 'We' that is 'I'" (Hegel 1979: 110). Hegel clearly holds that spirit does not appear until later in the argument, but if Marcuse's analysis is correct, then this structure of the I is prefigured earlier. Indeed, Marcuse confirms that this is his interpretation of the *Phenomenology* when, decades later, in the "Jerusalem lectures," he locates in the sense-certainty chapter an argument for "the social content of sense-perception" (CPHM 4 154–55).

While I have offered only a cursory and incomplete account of the *Phenomenology*'s opening arguments, it is hopefully clear why they constitute a critique of positivism and a defense of idealism. The facts are not passively received by us via our senses, but actively shaped via the concepts we deploy. Moreover, this is always a collective or social project. We have focused only on the first chapter of the *Phenomenology*, "Sense-certainty," omitting the second and third. Nonetheless we should be in a position to understand why Hegel would, in the conclusion, declare the discovery that Marcuse refers back to in *One-Dimensional Man*. This is the discovery that it is we ourselves who reside behind the curtain of reality. However, we have not yet arrived at a full and complete statement of Marcuse's position, which incorporates a Marxist dimension. Thus far, there has been scarcely a hint of Marxist reconstruction of Hegel's *Phenomenology*. Where, then, does historical materialism enter the story?

3. Idealism and conceptual realism

While Marcuse appears to endorse the opening arguments of the *Phenomenology*, there must be more to his position. These arguments defend idealism, but Marcuse is no ordinary idealist. His idealism is meant to be combined with critical theory. One component of critical theory is its interest in the revolutionary overthrow of capitalism. I therefore propose we consider the association Marcuse sees between idealism and revolution. Admittedly, the connection may seem superficial, even tenuous. The German idealist doctrine that the world of experience is constituted by Hegel's collective subject or Kant's apperceiving I seems to have little to do with the Marxist, revolutionary credo that human beings make, and must often re-make, their (social) world. Yet Marcuse believes there is a connection between idealism as doctrine and idealist activism already in Hegel, and not just when his thought is supplemented by Marx.

One way that Marcuse connects Hegelian idealism to revolutionary practice is via a third doctrine: conceptual realism, the idea that it is not just particular things but also general concepts or universals which are part of the world of experience.[9] Marcuse's opponent, the positivist, denies this on the grounds that general concepts or universals are not given to us in sense-experience. Hence, Marcuse turns to Hegel for support, but it soon becomes clear that it is politics and not just epistemology that motivates Marcuse's embrace of conceptual realism:

> The positivist attack on universal concepts, on the ground they cannot be reduced to observable facts, cancels from the domain of knowledge everything that may not yet be a fact. In demonstrating that sense-experience and perception, to which positivism appeals, in themselves imply and mean not the particular observed fact but something universal, Hegel is giving a final immanent refutation of positivism. When he emphasizes time and again that the universal is pre-eminent over the particular, he is struggling against limiting truth to the particular "given." The universal is more than the particular. This signifies in the concrete that the potentialities of men and things are not exhausted in the given forms and relations in which they may actually appear; it means that men and things are all they have been and actually are, and yet more than all this.
>
> (RR 113)

Why might an epistemological dispute between realism and nominalism about universals have political stakes? Let us unpack Marcuse's interpretation of Hegel. Hegel's idealism, as set forth in the opening arguments of the *Phenomenology*, consists in the claim that the knowing subject contributes to the character of the object known: more specifically, the object is structured by concepts or universals. Among Hegel interpreters, this is sometimes referred to as Hegel's conceptual realism, the doctrine that concepts are part of the structure of reality as we experience it. (Admittedly, and as already noted, conceptual realism may not seem consistent with Hegel's idealism.

Hegel interpreters differ among themselves on this issue, but we will leave it to one side. Hegel, like Kant, is a thinker who wants to reconcile idealism with a form of realism.)

Next comes an important step. As Marcuse reminds us, concepts or universals often serve as normative standards. When I classify this particular as a member of a universal kind, I can then ask whether it is a *good* (or *bad*) member of its kind: for example, a good knife, a good work of art, a good human being, a good institution. We can ask, as Aristotle does, whether the thing actualizes its potential. Or, as Plato does, how well it exemplifies its form. These, and other normative distinctions, become available when concepts or universals are recognized as real. Hence, Marcuse believes that Hegel's idealism, understood as conceptual realism, provides a basis for normative evaluation. From here, it is a small step to the idea that they provide the basis for a critique of one's society and of the conditions in which its members live, i.e., whether their potential is realized or thwarted. Hence, I think we can see how Marcuse connects idealism to activism via conceptual realism: this latter doctrine provides the basis for a normative evaluation of one's circumstances. For example, one might offer evaluation of a group of human beings, and their institutions and practices, as falling short of whichever concept, essence or kind is the relevant one. Yet it is one thing to evaluate and another to intervene ("philosophers have hitherto only interpreted the world, the point is to change it") (MER 145). We must therefore turn to the volitional component of Hegel's idealism, as Marcuse interprets it.

The connection between idealism and practice is also made via agency, the will or practical reason. This is evident in a passage from *Reason and Revolution* that is worth quoting at length. Marcuse begins by arguing that scientific and common-sense realism are inherently conservative, or anti-revolutionary:

> Common sense and traditional scientific thought take the world as a totality of things, more or less existing per se, and seek the truth in objects that are taken to be independent of the knowing subject. This is more than an epistemological attitude; it is as pervasive as the practice of men and leads them to accept the feeling that they are secure only in knowing and

handling objective facts. The more remote an idea is from the impulses, interests, and wants of the living subject, the more true it becomes.

(RR 112)

The passivity of the realist, who believes the world exists and has the character it does independent of human beings, seems here to parallel the passivity of the conservative, who is intent on leaving existing social arrangements intact. However, the reason for the connection is not spelled out, meaning we will need to do some work on Marcuse's behalf to explain it.

Having said that common-sense or scientific realism is conservative, Marcuse insists on the radical revolutionary character of idealism:

> And this, according to Hegel, is the utmost defamation of truth. For there is, in the last analysis, no truth that does not essentially concern the living subject and that is not the subject's truth. The world is an estranged and untrue world so long as man does not destroy its dead objectivity and recognize himself and his own life "behind" the fixed form of things and laws. When he finally wins this self-consciousness, he is on his way not only to the truth of himself but also of his world. And with the recognition goes the doing. He will try to put this truth into action and make the world what it essentially is, namely, the fulfillment of man's self-consciousness.
>
> (RR 112–13)[10]

While the passage is obscure, it does contain a clue concerning how Marcuse connects idealism with activism. He does so by placing the emphasis not on theoretical reason, but on practical reason, agency, or the will. As he writes, "The realization of reason is not a fact but a task. The form in which the objects immediately appear is not yet their true form" (RR 26). In other words, idealism here does not simply refer to i) the mind shaping the world of experience but also to ii) the will intervening in that world so as to make it rational and good. This is an idealism not so much of knowledge, but rather of ethics and politics. The sense of idealism at issue is the one we have in mind when we say that a person who wants to change the world for the better is idealistic.

However, this is not meant to be a simple change of topic from theory to practice. Marcuse's implicit suggestion seems to be that theory and practice are connected, and that idealism in sense i) is a prerequisite for idealism in sense ii). It is as if realizing that the world (natural, social, or otherwise) is constituted by the mind justifies us in attempting to make the world (this time, surely, the social world) conform to our will. Unfortunately, Marcuse does not frequently clarify the association he sees between the two senses of idealism.

Admittedly, the implication of ii) by i) is not usually thought to hold. Realists too may act in the world and attempt to make it a better place, and idealists (like the counter-revolutionary Hegel himself) may demur. However, Marcuse does seem to hold that the positivist is committed to a type of political conservatism. Most of the positivists were, of course, socialists, but this is not mentioned— presumably because it is merely biographical. For Marcuse, the positivist is a realist, rather than an idealist, at least in the following sense. The positivist denies that the mind actively contributes to the world of experience as we know it. For the positivist, the mind passively receives sensible impressions. Because these are only ever impressions of particulars, the positivist rejects conceptual realism. This means that the positivist cannot engage in the type of normative project Marcuse advocates. The positivist cannot look upon their society and its members as inadequate instances of their kind. Positivism's empiricism commits it to nominalism about universals, and therefore blocks the form of realism about them that Marcuse thinks is a prerequisite for revolutionary change.

Admittedly, there are other forms of social criticism open to the positivist. He or she may express disapproval, but this will be non-cognitive. Marcuse insists that social criticism be cognitive. It is important for him that it constitute knowledge, and not simply a declaration of desire. Hence Marcuse says of positivism that it courts relativism when

> It converts social interest into something personal. The nature of this interest is something merely accidental and of no consequence whatsoever. Every interest of whatever kind can be

refined into a "pure fact" and as such it can be set down in protocol sentences. Scientific philosophy has no capacity to make a critical judgment among differing interests: they are all "facts" in the same way.

(CPHM 5: 78)

Positivism only recognizes statements of empirical fact, and expressions of personal taste or preference. Because of their total-izing and normative character, the claims of the social critic cannot be neatly fit into the first category, and so appear to be condemned to the second. Yet social critique should not be arbitrary in the way that claims of taste or preference are. Rather, social criticism should reflect knowledge, and it can only do this if it invokes concepts that are understood to structure our world. It is perhaps for this reason that Marcuse denies that truths of common sense and natural science, those stressed by the positivists, are the only truths there are. There are also the truths reflected in our efforts to remake the world so that it becomes better. These would be, I suggest, truths about the concepts or universals that things fall under, and the normative claims we are able to make about these things in consequence.

While I have characterized the dispute between Marcuse and the positivist as one between an idealist and a realist, an idealist and an empiricist, and finally (and perhaps confusingly) a *conceptual* realist versus a nominalist, there is another description Marcuse also employs: Hegel is a *negative* philosopher who opposes positivism:

Hegel's critical and rational standards, and especially his dialectics, had to come into conflict with the prevailing social reality. For this reason, his system could well be called a negative phil-osophy, the name given to it by its contemporary opponents. To counteract its destructive tendencies, there arose, in the decade following Hegel's death, a positive philosophy which undertook to subordinate reason to the authority of established fact.

(RR vii)

Why is Marcuse's Hegelian Marxism a negative philosophy in oppos-ition to positivism? Here we should recall that the Hegelian insists on the reality of universals or concepts, whereas the positivist denies that they are part of the world of experience. Next we should remind ourselves of a point of Hegel's from the opening of the *Phenomenology* that Marcuse himself stresses: the universal is defined in terms of its negative relation to the particular; specifically, the relationship of non-identity or difference between the universal and the particular. For example, "now" is not identical with day or night or any particular thing, but is rather the general concept under which all its possible referents can be brought together by a thinker. Once we see this, the dispute with the positivist takes on a different character. The positivist, we may suppose, not only focuses exclusively on the particulars given to us in sense-experience, but also focuses exclusively on positive facts about them: "the cat is on the mat." The Hegelian idealist rejects this approach, not simply because it focuses only on sensible impressions of particulars rather than conceptual thought's grasp of universals, but more fundamentally because it leaves out negative facts in consequence: for example, "the cat is not in the kitchen." These facts, facts concerning what is not the case but could be, only come into view when we take account of universals. These negative facts are crucial to critical theory, because they tell us about the unrealized potential of human beings and their societies.[11] A negative philosophy, then, makes room for negative facts, and in this way distinguishes rigorously between how things are and how they could be. For Marcuse, a philosopher like Quine, who eliminates merely possible entities from his ontology, participates in a politically reactionary project (Marcuse sees this reflected in Quine's comparison of his project to the clearing of a slum) (ODM 221).[12]

While we have explored the connection Marcuse discerns between conceptual realism and activism, an ambiguity needs to be addressed. Does conceptual realism inspire people to make change because they realize that things in the world fall under concepts and therefore under normative standards they do not yet meet? Or is it instead that people realize that they themselves and their social institutions fall under such concepts? At times, Marcuse implies that the answer is both: for Hegel, he writes, "the mind has attained the self-consciousness of its freedom, and become capable of freeing nature and society."[13] Through revolution, things will realize their potential, and Marcuse's Hegel does not seem to distinguish between things in nature and those in society: "The form in which the objects immediately appear is not yet their true form. What is simply given is at first negative, other than its real potentialities ... *All forms* are seized by the dissolving movement of reason which cancels and alters them until they are adequate to their notion" (RR 26, my emphasis). Yet while Marcuse does speak of the way revolution will unlock the potential of nature, tools, artifacts, etc., he more often emphasizes that we ourselves, human beings, will have our potential actualized. If that is so, then there is a conceptual transition not only from theory to practice, but from changing the world to changing ourselves. The knowledge idealism gives us via conceptual realism is self-knowledge, and the change it inspires is self-change. Here we come full circle, as Marcuse's activism reunites with the foundational methodological commitment of the *Phenomenology*. This is Hegel's conviction that conceptions of one's self, of the world, and of the relationship between them stand or fall together.

To sum up, Marcuse derives 10 points from the opening arguments of the *Phenomenology*:

1. Anti-empiricism. Sensible impressions of particulars passively received by the mind are insufficient for knowledge.
2. Idealism. Some active (conceptual) contribution on the part of the mind is required.
3. Collective subject. It is a collective rather than individual subject that is the source of the world's structure.
4. Conceptual realism. The world has a conceptual structure, and entities fall under concepts.
5. Normativity. The concepts things fall under are the source of normative evaluation.
6. Negativity. Concepts are also the source of negative facts about the world, which are distinct from the positive facts.
7. The primacy of practice. Apprehending the conceptual structure of reality is not so much a feat of theoretical knowledge as the practical process of changing it.
8. Truth. This practical process of changing the world is cognitive, a form of knowledge, and therefore reflects an understanding of truth.
9. The inseparability of self-knowledge and object-knowledge. What is more, this knowledge is self-knowledge, inasmuch as it

is we ourselves who are the things whose internal purposes are meant to be realized.

10. The inseparability of self-change and world-change. Since our self-knowledge, and knowledge of the world issues in change, this change will be simultaneously self-change and world-change.[14]

4. Forms of sensibility

Given Marcuse's case against positivism, it might seem as if he leaves little to no room for the senses to contribute to human knowledge. This impression is reinforced by Marcuse's appropriation of Hegel's critique of sense-certainty. Elsewhere, however, Marcuse attempts to provide a more nuanced account, arguing that a place for the senses needs to be preserved even in an otherwise uncompromisingly anti-positivist epistemology:

> We do not think that the split is final, and that philosophy has no longer any existential import. All genuine philosophy contains idealism as well as positivism. As for the positivist element in idealism, we may point to the empiricist, nay, sensualist basis of Kant's Critique of Pure Reason, and to the vast empirical material mastered in Hegel's philosophy.
>
> (CPHM 5: 99)

Understanding just how Marcuse integrates the senses into his picture of human knowledge will require us to set aside his debt to Hegel and consider his debt to a different idealist: Kant.

Overemphasizing Marcuse's debt to Hegel risks slighting the role of the senses. After all, Hegel consistently denigrates "sense-certainty," judging it inferior to "pure thought" or "the Concept." By contrast, it is Kant who regards the senses as making an ineliminable contribution to human knowledge, insisting that "concepts without intuitions are empty." Kant respects this empiricist insight, and rejects the rationalist idea that conceptual knowledge, all on its own, could yield knowledge. Therefore, understanding how Marcuse finds a place for the senses in his epistemology requires taking seriously his debt to Kant: in particular the doctrine of the transcendental aesthetic in the first *Critique*. As with Hegel, however, Marcuse is no simple acolyte of his idealist predecessor, seeking instead to unite Kant's critical philosophy with Marxism.

Marcuse is indebted to Kant for the idea that the faculty of sensibility has a priori forms of its own: space and time. Any content must conform to these if it is to be representable by us in sensible intuition. Kant posited these forms because he thought they were necessary for explaining the possibility of synthetic a priori knowledge. Only invariant structures of the human mind could explain a form of knowledge that always and everywhere holds good; in particular, the knowledge found in Euclidean geometry.

However, it seems clear that Marcuse, like other twentieth-century Kantians, finds Kant's insistence on the historical invariance of the a priori to be unacceptable. What to Kant appeared invariant truths of mathematics and natural science, grounded in the human mind, seemed to his twentieth-century successors to be fallible, revisable, and mutable.[15] Marcuse proposes a "historical a priori," explicitly invoking a concept more often associated with Foucault or Husserl:

> "Radical sensibility": the concept stresses the active, constitutive role of the senses in shaping reason, that is to say, in shaping the categories under which the world is ordered, experienced, changed. The senses are not merely passive, receptive: they have their own "syntheses" to which they subject the primary data of experience. And these syntheses are not only the pure "forms of intuition" (space and time) which Kant recognized as an inexorable a priori ordering of sense data. There are perhaps also other syntheses, far more concrete, far more "material," which may constitute an empirical (i.e., historical) a priori of experience. Our world emerges not only in the pure forms of time and space, but also, and simultaneously, as a totality of sensuous qualities—objects not only of the eye (synopsis) but of all human senses (hearing, smelling, touching, tasting). It is this qualitative, elementary, unconscious, or rather preconscious, constitution of the world of experience, it is this primary experience itself which must change radically if social change is to be radical, qualitative change.
>
> (CR 63)[16]

For Marcuse, as for Kant, there are sensible conditions on the possibility of experience. For both, these are understood as "syntheses," ways of combining parts of what we experience through the senses into the larger wholes we experience as objects. For both, this synthesis is an unconscious matter, since it takes place prior to any conscious experience. Here, however, the parallels cease. Unlike Kant, Marcuse insists that these conditions are socio-historical. What is more, Marcuse clearly thinks that the possibility of change for the better depends upon challenging the way human sensibility is structured under capitalism. The revolution will mean breaking with the frameworks our senses bring to bear on experience—and instituting new ones.

We need to clarify one further dimension of Marcuse's Kantian-cum-Marxist idea that there are a priori conditions of sensibility which are socially and historically significant: the way in which the faculty of sensibility is both theoretical and practical. Reflecting on the term "sensuousness" (Sinnlichkeit), Marcuse reminds us that sense perception, as a source of knowledge, is just one face of sensibility (EC 182). There is, in addition, sensible desire and aversion, which play a role in action.

Kant too noted this point, discussing sensible intuition in his theoretical philosophy, and desire, inclination, etc. in his practical. But whereas Kant asks about sensibility's relation to conceptual thought in each domain, he does not seem interested in the relationship between the two forms of sensibility: impressions and desires. Marcuse regards the latter as, in some sense, prior in importance to the former, an ordering that no doubt reflects a psychoanalytic orientation (the pleasure principle governs not only desire, but also perception). Marcuse's idea seems to be that our sense-perceptions are influenced by our efforts to pursue pleasure and avoid pain. This becomes somewhat more plausible when we expand our conception of sense-perception in the way Marcuse urges. As he notes, among the senses are not only seeing and hearing, but also touch, taste, smell. Scarcely anybody needs reminding of these other sense-modalities—but they are often effaced in austerely epistemological accounts of the mind, where seeing and hearing predominate. Presumably, Marcuse's reason for listing these sense modalities is to remind us that for some, the idea of the sense-organ being trained to perceive in ways conducive to our practical purpose is quite plausible.

5. Hegelian Marxism?

Marcuse has interpreted Hegel in such a way as to bring him as close to Marx and critical theory as possible. However, there remains (at least) one major discrepancy. The elementary facts of economic life emphasized by Marx do not appear to be part of Hegel's account. These would include the need for human beings to labor on nature, as well as the fact that they do so using the available stock of tools and techniques, and within a class structure that is suited to this form of life (the "forces and relations of production"). Clearly, these doctrines would need to be integrated with the above points if Marcuse is to fully develop his Hegelian Marxism.

Although I will not pursue the point, it is interesting to note that Marcuse attempts to show that the rudiments of historical materialism are present in the *Phenomenology*. He does so by analyzing the opening of the self-consciousness chapter, where Hegel famously declares that self-consciousness is desire itself. Desire manifests itself in working on nature, but this proves unsatisfying. Social relationships, relationships of recognition, are required. The relationship between master and slave provides us with our first rudimentary class structure. Marcuse believes the presence of this idea in Hegel's *Phenomenology* indicates a proto-Marxist standpoint. It is, in the language of Marx's "commodity fetishism" chapter in *Capital* I, a relationship between people but mediated by things. Hegel is not only insisting on the primacy of practice over theory in effecting a transition to self-consciousness but, more fundamentally, on the primacy of social labor. He finds a further Marxist doctrine reflected in Hegel's inclusion of stoicism and skepticism in the self-consciousness chapter. This reflects Hegel's belief that each of these philosophical schools instantiates a form of thought that is parallel to a form of laboring and a class position: stoicism is masterly; skepticism, slavish. The mode of thought derives from the mode of labor whose structure it parallels.

Such are the lengths to which Marcuse is willing to go in finding materialist motifs in Hegel's *Phenomenology*. Interesting as it might be, this final part of Marcuse's interpretation of Hegel brings us to an impasse. If Hegel does, in the *Phenomenology*, move from an idealist to a materialist standpoint, then his reasons for doing so can only be gleaned from a long and complex trail of argument. This is a trail we can have no hope of summarizing, let alone adequately defending, and Marcuse's treatment of it is fairly cursory. In the next section, I suggest a way out of the impasse, albeit one which requires leaving Hegel behind and considering Marx's contribution to Marcuse's project.

Ultimately, Marcuse's reasons for moving beyond Hegel's idealism and into materialism are not primarily philosophical—at least not in Hegel's sense of that term. Accordingly, they do not require anything like the final phases of the *Phenomenology*'s argument. Ultimately, they do not reflect the acceptance of a rigorous dialectical argument at all. Rather, they reflect what Marcuse considers an anti-philosophy, one which urges us to turn our backs on certain ambitious projects in philosophical argumentation and instead attend to basic facts. I am referring to the rejection of philosophy implicit in Marx's critique of Hegel's idealism and his insistence on the need to consider political economy. As Marcuse writes, "Even Marx's early writings are not philosophical. They express the negation of philosophy, though they still do so in philosophical language" (RR 258). Marcuse emphasizes the way in which Marx begins from certain empirical facts, a procedure that would be anathema to Hegel who employed a "presuppositionless" a priori method. Among these facts, Marx tells us in the Paris manuscripts, are the existence of the proletariat and the fact that it becomes poorer even as its labor enriches the world (1978: 70). However, I think it is fairly obvious that the facts with which Marx begins also include those on which the science of political economy is based: the existence of human needs; the requirement that human beings work on nature to meet their needs; and the existence of social relationships which facilitate this work. Like other critics of traditional philosophy, Marx insists on the transition to a standpoint more in keeping with empirical science. Yet the science in question is not a natural but a social one (political economy). It is to this different route to Marcuse's end-goal of a Hegelian Marxism that we now turn.

Marcuse is intent on supplementing Hegel's idealism with materialism. While he believes this occurs already in Hegel's thought, there can be no question that it is ultimately Marx's critique of Hegel that is decisive. The question facing us is how Marx himself segued from Hegel's idealism to materialism.

In explaining his own approach to Hegel's idealism, Marcuse refers us to Marx's treatment of Hegel in the Paris manuscripts. There, in a well-known passage that Marcuse refers to in passing (RR 115), Marx expresses an ambivalent relationship towards Hegel:

> Let us provisionally say just this much in advance: Hegel's stand-point is that of modern political economy. He grasps labour as the essence of man—as man's essence in the act of proving itself: he sees only the positive, not the negative side of labour. Labour is man's coming-to-be for himself within alienation, or as alienated man. The only labour which Hegel knows and recognizes is abstractly mental labour. Therefore, that which constitutes the essence of philosophy—the alienation of man in his knowing of himself, or alienated science thinking itself—Hegel grasps as its essence; and he is therefore able vis-à-vis preceding philosophy to gather together its separate elements and phases, and to present his philosophy as the philosophy. What the other philosophers did—that they grasped separate phases of nature and of human life as phases of self-consciousness, and indeed of abstract self-consciousness—is known to Hegel as the doings of philosophy. Hence his science is absolute.
>
> (Marx 1978: 112)

On the one hand, the young Marx credits Hegel's *Phenomenology* with an understanding of history reminiscent of Marx's own in the Paris manuscripts. History, understood in this way, is a story of alienation and its overcoming. On the other hand, Marx insists that Hegel's philosophical system cannot be taken at face value. Rather, its concepts need to be translated into the idiom of another science entirely: political economy. At least in this moment, he presents himself as a kind of anti-philosopher, insisting that philosophy's concepts and insights, if there is to be any hope for them, must be adopted by the most advanced (social) science. Obviously, this is not the way Hegel intends his philosophy to be understood, but the Marxist claim is that Hegel does not understand the true character of his own discoveries. They appear to the idealist Hegel as if through a fog that only the materialist Marx can dispel.

Approached from the standpoint of political economy, Hegel's idealism is revealed to be one-sided. Political economy regards labor as essential to human beings, but Hegel has only partially heeded the teaching of this new science. He has focused exclusively on one type of labor, and far from the most important one: *intellectual* labor. This focus is arbitrary, and can only be explained by bias: in particular, the fact that Hegel is himself (like all philosophers) an intellectual laborer. To be sure, intellectual labor has overcome the division between itself and its objects, chiefly in modern natural science. Yet Hegel has ignored manual labor, the ongoing effort of human beings to physically master nature and use its powers to benefit us. According to Marx, the latter project is more fundamental than the former. It is for the sake of physically mastering nature that we attempt to master it intellectually. Though it claims to be Absolute knowing, Hegel's idealist philosophy turns out to be a partial grasp of the whole of human society and history.

Marcuse further claims that Hegel's idealism, when translated into political economy, turns out to prefigure the Marxist idea of reification: "Hegel hit upon the same fact in the domain of political economy" (RR 112). Marcuse elaborates:

> We borrow the term "reification" from the Marxist theory, where it denotes the fact that all relations between men in the world of capitalism, appear to be relations between things, or, that what in the social world seem to the relations of things and "natural" laws that regulate their movement are in reality relations of men and historical forces. The commodity, for instance, embodies in all its qualities the social relations of labor; capital the power of disposing over men; and so on. By virtue of the inversion, the world has become an alienated estranged world, in which man does not recognize or fulfill himself, but is overpowered by dead things and laws.
>
> (RR 112)

Reification is an error we commit when we treat the economy as if it were subject to the same unchanging laws as nature. Consider, for example, the commodity. It has a value and can be exchanged for others of the same value. This property can seem like something fixed and unalterable about it, like the fact that a material body has weight. Yet unlike the weight of a body, the value of a commodity is conferred on it by a social arrangement. Under such an arrangement, things are exchanged for one another at ratios determined by the average number of labor-hours required to produce them. We not only become habituated to treating value as a property of a thing, on a par with its other properties, but also to treating value as authoritative over our conduct. Accordingly, we feel we must simply adapt our behavior to the assigned values (prices) of things, as we do to gravity. The courses of our lives are dictated by the rise and fall of prices. Perversely, these things (prices, values), which are the creations of human beings, come to rule over us, their creators. The theory of fetishism, in political economy, possesses its philosophical counterpart in Hegel's idealism, which shows that the world of things we inhabit, taken to be real and existing independently of us, turns out to be a "spiritual" product.

An orthodox Marxist might respond that, while Hegel may have hit upon the same fact in philosophy that Marx did in political economy, this is not to Hegel's credit. Hegel's Absolute Idealism is false, whereas Marx's doctrine of reification ("fetishism") is true. The former idea may be the latter in a different medium—but that is a way of discrediting the former. Far from being some minor discrepancy, the difference of medium is everything here. Hence, there is no need to consult Hegel's *Phenomenology* for anticipations of Marx's *Capital*. We can simply begin with the latter. Clearly, this is not Marcuse's view, however. Marcuse embraces both Hegel's idealism and Marx's critique of political economy, rather than treat them as alternatives.

It would be legitimate to ask if this is a coherent combination. Marxists, of course, accuse Hegelians of reversing subject and predicate, placing thought before being when, in fact, being is prior to thought. On the orthodox Marxist view, Hegelianism regards reason, the mind, or spirit as the producer of nature, when actually the reverse is the case. Nature, without us and within us, preexists and conditions thinking. So too does economic production. How Marcuse deals with this last objection from orthodox Marxism is less clear, and it does seem to threaten his proposal to reconcile Hegel's idealism with historical materialism.

Sometimes, in explaining the transition from Hegel's idealism to Marx's materialism, commentators present Marx as having "naturalized" Hegel—but everything turns on what, exactly, this means. In this connection, Marcuse draws an interesting distinction between two types of naturalism. The first is empiricism, which regards sense-experience as the source of all legitimate claims to knowledge. Hedonic utilitarianism would also be a form of naturalism in this first sense, since it regards the desire for pleasure and aversion to pain as the source of human motivation. In classical German philosophy, both sense-perception and desire are considered forms of sensibility. As Marcuse correctly notes, Feuerbach was a proponent of this first type of naturalism, stressing the sensible, affective dimension of human existence.

Yet it would be a mistake to conclude that, in attempting to naturalize Hegel, Marx took recourse to empiricism of this kind. As Marcuse reminds us, Marx is closer to Hegel than to Feuerbach in this regard, at least if Hegel's insistence on the primacy of social labor in the self-consciousness chapter is borne in mind. For both Hegel and Marx, the deliverances of the senses are "mediated," either by spirit or by social labor:

> Marx upholds Hegel on this point, as against Feuerbach. Hegel had denied that sense-certainty is the final criterion of the truth, on the ground that, first, the truth is a universal that cannot be won in an experience that conveys particulars, and, second, that truth finds fulfillment in a historical process carried forward by the collective practice of men. The latter is basic, with sense-certainty and nature alike drawn into the movement so that they change their content in its course.
>
> (RR 271)

> Hegel's point was that labor brings sense-certainty and nature into the historical process. Because he conceived human existence in terms of sense, Feuerbach disregarded this material function of labor altogether. Not satisfied with abstract thought, Feuerbach appeals to sense-perception [*Anschauung*];

but he does not understand our sensuous nature as practical, human-sensuous activity.

(RR 272)[17]

Marx's naturalism derives from political economy, not philosophical psychology, and insists on the fundamentality of labor, class, and technology, not on sense-experience and desire. If Hegel is thought of as an Absolute Idealist for whom all of reality is reason, then Marx naturalizes Hegel. Yet if we consider Hegel's self-consciousness chapter, as Marcuse interprets it, then Marx's effort to naturalize Hegel is one already undertaken in part by Hegel himself. For Marcuse, Hegel, Marx, and Kant are all closer to one another, in embracing a form of transcendental philosophy, than any of them is to the naive empiricism of Feuerbach.

6. The critique of positivism

I have attempted to clarify Marcuse's Hegelian Marxism, but doing so requires us to take account of the position Marcuse treats as the antithesis of his own: positivism. As a preliminary, Marcuse takes this term to encompass more than the Vienna circle. Positivism is a tendency running throughout the history of modern philosophy. It is a tradition that includes Saint-Simon, the late Schelling, Comte, and others.[18] Nevertheless, the Vienna circle are, in some sense, paradigmatic. Even so, Marcuse treats positivism less as a philosophical school than as an ideology, in the following way. Whether or not they consciously adhere to it, it influences ordinary people's thinking and conduct, especially in modern scientific and technological society. Indeed, Marcuse believes that a positivistic orientation is characteristic of the members of modern capitalist societies, something that might come as a surprise to the Vienna circle themselves, many of whom were committed socialists. Marcuse's approach may involve an oversimplified account of positivist ideas, but to object on this score is to miss the point somewhat. Like Christianity, positivism is not just a doctrine but a broader orientation. It is not found exclusively in canonical texts, but in the habits of thought of individuals and groups. Marcuse is as interested in the latter as he is in the former.

As we have seen, Marcuse characterizes the positivist as somebody who believes that the facts are already out there waiting to be apprehended by us, as opposed to the idealist who regards facts as constituted by us. As Marcuse admits, this is something of an oversimplification:

> It might be objected that positivism too, at least its most recent form, takes account of the essential relation to the subject, particularly in the formulation of the elementary propositions which Neurath suggested. This is correct, but the positivist subject has nothing to do with the idealist subject. The subject of the elementary propositions is simply one fact among others, but in no case does it transcend or constitute the facts. It merely registers them, and in this function it can be exchanged for and perhaps even replaced by other apparatuses of registration.
>
> (CPHM 5: 96)

Of course, Marcuse is aware that positivism, especially in its more empiricist varieties, inevitably invokes the standpoint of the subject. The Protokolsätze which form the foundation of every science are observational reports, and there can be no such reports without a subject.[19] However, this subject's role is limited to passively "registering" facts, so much so that its place could conceivably be taken by a machine or recording device. By contrast, the idealist subject herself constitutes the facts, something which is meant to justify a willingness to actively intervene in the world and change it.

As we have already seen, Marcuse, perhaps unfairly, accuses positivism of being inherently conservative. Here he elaborates on this claim, explaining its rationale. One source of conservatism is the positivist view that scientific knowledge is a matter of description, rather than evaluation. As Marcuse explains in his essay "Concept of Essence," positivism warns against

> a confusion of the "evaluative viewpoint with the logical viewpoint," the proton pseudos or false premise of a scientific theory. Positivism adheres to the bourgeois ideal of presuppositionless, pure theory, in which the absence of "ethical neutrality" or the commitment of taking a position signifies delinquency in rigor.
>
> (N 48)

As we have seen, Marcuse profoundly disagrees with the positivist ideal of presuppositionless knowing shorn of ethical commitments. He believes our commitment to a better world reflects a claim to knowledge, not an arbitrary preference or desire. Truth is achieved in action for the sake of a better world, not in knowledge of the way the world is already constituted.

Admittedly, it can seem here as if Marcuse is just arbitrarily redefining the word "truth." Yet Marcuse's "practical" conception of truth has some resonance with the Kantian idea that reason is no less practical than theoretical. On this conception, doing good is as much a manifestation of successful reasoning as is believing what is true. Doing bad is as rationally criticizable as is believing the false. Though Kant does not take this step, one could argue from this that there must be such a thing as practical truth, in addition to theoretical. Whatever exactly Marcuse's rationale for defining truth in this way, it seems clear that it is not a conception the positivist would share. The positivist adheres to a more standard definition, involving correspondence between our thinking (or language) and the facts.

Ultimately, Marcuse's belief that ideals are cognitive may be rooted in his conviction that there are concepts, universals, or essences which prescribe normative standards to things. However, this belief is denounced by positivism as unsupported by the facts, at least those that can be apprehended by sense-perception. Turning again to his classic essay "The Concept of Essence," we see Marcuse emphasizing the anti-metaphysical outlook of positivism:

> The positivist opposition to the "metaphysics" of the doctrine of essence conceived itself primarily as an epistemological critique: our experience of reality (reality by no means being identified with the immediately given) does not at all justify the assumption of two ontologically different "worlds," an assumption presupposed by the opposition of thing and appearance ...
>
> (N 47)

For Marcuse, then, the most threatening positivist teaching is that everything true or real is on a par, so to speak. The totality of facts which make up the world does not include an essence of which these facts are appearances. This leads Marcuse to denounce positivism as "one-dimensional," an interesting choice of words in light of his later work:

> With this contention, positivism takes a decisive step beyond epistemological empiricism. For with its concept of fact, the facticity of an object of knowledge establishes not only its "reality" but simultaneously its cognitive equivalence to every other reality. With respect to knowledge, all facts are as such equivalent. The world of facts is, so to speak, one-dimensional. The real is "absolutely (*schlechthin*) real" and as such precludes any metaphysical or critical transcendence toward essence.
>
> (N 47)

As we will see in a subsequent chapter, when we turn to philosophy of science, Marcuse regards positivism's "one-dimensional" view of reality as inadequate even from the perspective of natural science. Science, as Marcuse conceives it, attempts to explain the facts on the basis of something more fundamental: laws, forces, kinds, essences. Yet it seems fairly clear that Marcuse's principal objection to positivism is the complacent perspective it encourages on social life. By refusing to inquire into the essences of which the facts that surround us are simply appearances, positivism precludes effective social critique.

A final objection Marcuse levels against positivism is that it is relativistic, a commitment he finds politically problematic: "A theory that wants to eradicate from science the concept of essence succumbs to helpless relativism, thus promoting the very powers whose reactionary thought it wants to combat" (N 32). Marcuse attributes the relativism inherent in positivism to its rejection of the concept of essence. Unfortunately, it is unclear why this implication should follow. Would it not be possible for the positivist to remain an absolutist about "the facts," even while refusing to accept the idea of a more fundamental underlying reality that explains them? Evidently, Marcuse believes that without this more fundamental reality, knowledge is threatened with relativism. Perhaps his meaning is that it will be relativized to the perspective of the scientific inquirers themselves.

A form of relativism does seem to be inherent in Carnap's idea that scientists, though not free to choose their own facts, are free to choose the language or the concepts in which they capture those facts. Indeed, Carnap depicts this choice as almost radically unconstrained: "In logic, there are no morals" (1937: 52). Carnap would elsewhere observe that the choice of framework is in the final instance pragmatic. This claim contains the germ of Quine's thesis in "Two Dogmas" that a more thoroughgoing pragmatism results from rejecting the analytic/synthetic distinction, i.e., the distinction between framework and content. Once framework questions, which Carnap thought were settled pragmatically, become inseparable from empirical questions, these too come to be adjudicated in accordance with our interests. Both Carnap's position and that of Quine in "Two Dogmas" are sometimes suspected of relativism.

Whatever other doubts one has about Marcuse's position, this criticism would not extend to it. One could imagine Marcuse responding that the choice of conceptual scheme could be constrained by the introduction of essences into ontology. Then there would be a privileged conceptual scheme to employ, and this would thwart the possibility of relativism.

7. Objections and replies

A potential problem with Marcuse's Hegelian Marxism concerns its core idea that facts are constructed. This doctrine may seem to reject the possibility of truth and objectivity. If the facts are constructed by society, doesn't that mean we are incapable of knowing the world as it is independently of the way society constructs it? There are a number of related worries that follow from this one. If society constructs the facts, does this mean there are many equally legitimate ways of constructing them, varying between societies?

Another concern is that Marcuse's position, in addition to being relativistic, might seem self-undermining. If his Hegelian Marxism gives us reason to think the facts are constructed by society, then it is only natural that we ask whether this is true of the facts that make up the Hegelian-Marxist theory itself: for example, the fact—if it is one—that human beings are involved in a historically ongoing project of mastering nature. If the facts making up Hegelian Marxism are not constructed, then the theory is falsified. If they are, then they seem no more trustworthy than the facts that surround us.

One possible qualification is that not *all* facts are constructed in a way that renders them suspect. I infer that this may be Marcuse's view from his willingness to invoke certain facts in his polemics:

> And yet, the facts are all there which validate the critical theory of this society and of its fatal development: the increasing irrationality of the whole; waste and restriction of productivity; the need for aggressive expansion; the constant threat of war; intensified exploitation; dehumanization. And they all point to the historical alternative: the planned utilization of resources for the satisfaction of vital needs with a minimum of toil, the transformation of leisure into free time, the pacification of the struggle for existence.
>
> (ODM 256–57)

If not all facts are socially constructed in a way that makes them ideologically suspect, then critical theory faces the challenge of sorting the wheat from the chaff. Marcuse would then not deny truth and objectivity, but simply identify a pervasive threat to them. For Marcuse, critical theory just is the procedure of identifying whether and to what extent the facts have been presented to us in a way that is mystifying: "This intellectual dissolution and even subversion of the given facts is the historical task of philosophy and the philosophic dimension." Although this proposal may seem vague, Marcuse clearly understands the task of interrogating alleged facts as following a particular procedure. In short, the facts are to be restored to their context in the whole of the social life-process, and not viewed in isolation:

> The trouble is that the statistics, measurements, and field studies of empirical sociology and political science are not rational enough. They become mystifying to the extent to which they are isolated from the truly concrete context which makes the facts and determines their function. This context is larger and other than that of the plants and shops investigated, of the towns and cities studied, of the areas and groups whose public opinion is

polled or whose chance of survival is calculated. And it is also more real in the sense that it creates and determines the facts investigated, polled, and calculated. This real context in which the particular subjects obtain their real significance is definable only within a theory of society. For the factors in the facts are not immediate data of observation, measurement, and interrogation. They become data only in an analysis which is capable of identifying the structure that holds together the parts and processes of society and that determines their interrelation.

(ODM 195)

Crucially, the larger social context in which the facts appear is not something that can be measured. The institutional framework is not so much the data, as its underlying source. Thus, Marcuse's thought on this point has an anti-empiricist dimension. Positivism, because of its empiricism, cannot allow us to invoke the idea of "society," understood as a non-empirically perceptible source of empirical facts.

A related question concerns Marcuse's insistence that not only facts concerning society but also those concerning nature are, in some sense, constructed. At least in the passage with which we began, Marcuse is fairly clear that neither set of facts is mind-independent. However, it seems much more plausible that social facts are constructed than that natural ones are. Does Marcuse maintain that such things as the laws of physics are, in some sense, products of humanity's ongoing attempt to master nature? Is this not in tension with the idea that these laws are true, "carving reality at the joints," and were present on the scene long before human society arose? Of course, Marcuse may argue that it is necessary to consider the larger context in which facts emerge. However, all of his examples in this connection concern society. It is unclear whether he intends his analysis to extend to nature.

One possible line of response might be to reinterpret Marcuse's doctrine of the relativity of facts so that it does not seem as objectionably subjectivist. One clue to how this can be done is found in the German idealist appeal to practical reason, or the will. Marcuse at one point indicates that an important lesson of idealism is that nature may be viewed from either of two perspectives. On the one hand, it may be viewed from the perspective of theoretical reason, as an object of natural-scientific investigation. Alternatively, it may be viewed from the perspective of practical reason, and therefore as an arena in which we can realize our aims or purposes through action. The idealist's claim that nature is relative to the subject turns out to be ambiguous. It could be a subject of either theory or practice. Crucially, relativizing nature to the will or practical reason is also a form of idealism, albeit a somewhat less familiar one:

> The subject which, in idealism, determines the objective world is not merely the knowing ego, and idealism is not limited to the thesis that the epistemological consciousness shapes the world (Hegel called this Kantian form of idealism an incomplete and spurious idealism). He denotes at another place the subject as the "free will" which does not accept things as they are but takes the world as material that is to be altered and adapted to the free subject's interest. In other words, idealism holds that the given reality must be transformed according to the knowledge and action of the free subject, and that reality attains its true form and content only through this transformation.
>
> (CPHM 5: 93)

Next comes the crucial step. Marcuse argues that nature, seen from the perspective of practical reason, differs from nature as characterized in natural science. It is not the object of theoretical investigation we passively undertake but rather an object we actively alter through our volitional activity:

> For example, idealism would look upon nature not as physical science does, that is, as a quantitative totality of objective phenomena, but as the arena of the subject's development. Idealism takes nature in relation to the unfolding potentialities of the subject, in relation to its freedom.
>
> (CPHM 5: 93)

Does Marcuse, then, regard science's perspective on nature as subordinate to that of moral and political activity? This is an issue I cannot pretend to resolve here, especially because the project of this chapter is incomplete. We have considered Marcuse's conception of knowledge in general, but not that of natural-scientific knowledge in particular. Marcuse's philosophy of science is a topic for a later chapter.

Summary

Though not centrally concerned with issues in contemporary, Anglophone epistemology, Marcuse does take sides in the longstanding dispute between realists and anti-realists, or idealists. He intends to reconcile idealism, inspired by Hegel and classical German philosophy, with the historical materialism of Marx and Engels. Whether such a position, at once materialist and idealist, will turn out to be so much as coherent is doubtful. Yet understanding it fully requires taking account of Marcuse's relationship to positivism.

Marcuse's materialist idealism, expressed in *One-Dimensional Man*, treats "the facts" concerning reality as constituted in the course of humanity's historically ongoing conquest of the natural world. In presenting his position, Marcuse alludes to Hegel's *Phenomenology*, providing a clue to understanding Marcuse's materialist idealism. Turning to Marcuse's interpretation of the *Phenomenology* in *Reason and Revolution* clarifies the arguments for his materialist idealism. Particularly important is the argument of "sense-certainty" which Marcuse refers to as an "argument for the social content of sense-perception." This argument also turns out to clarify the role of a collective subject in Marcuse's Hegelian Marxism. Yet Marcuse is no mere disciple of Hegel. Marcuse reads Hegel against the grain, taking his cue from Marx's idea that Hegel's *Phenomenology* occupies the standpoint of political economy. This equips Marcuse with the criticism that Hegel's Absolute idealism results from one-sidedly focusing on intellectual labor and ignoring manual labor. Finally, Marcuse also incorporates another Hegelian teaching into his materialist idealism: conceptual realism, or realism about universals. The conceptual structure of the world, as well as that of the subject, turns out to imply norms with reference to which society can be criticized as inadequate. Positivism, a form of empiricism reminiscent of sense-certainty, makes no provision for such universals, and does not allow for critique. Yet Marcuse does preserve a role for the senses in his idealism, drawing on Kant's doctrine of a priori forms of sensibility. In Marcuse's hands, this becomes a historicized a priori, as well as one that is dictated by our practical interests and not just our scientific theories.

Marcuse's materialist-idealist position could be questioned on a number of grounds. It could be accused of an objectionable subjectivism and relativism, or even of circularity: relying on the independence of certain facts about nature to establish that nature is dependent on us. A more definitive verdict on Marcuse's epistemological position will have to await consideration of his philosophy of science.

Notes

1 Some have imputed a form of idealism to the early Marx, based on the first of his theses on Feuerbach where he describes his position as a further development of German idealism: specifically an attempt to render it less abstract (MER 143).

2 In preparing this chapter, I have benefited from Kellner's account of Marcuse's reading of Hegel, especially his focus on the theme of anti-empiricism (1984: 130–40).

3 "The factuality of a fact does not yet justify its appropriateness to serve as starting point and principle of theory. The facts are not undifferentiated material, they are in and of themselves structured ... by the fundamental interests of the theory and practice that 'apprehend' them" (CPHM 5: 77).

4 Here, once more, we might refer to "Theses on Feuerbach": "The materialist doctrine that men are products of circumstances and upbringing ... forgets that men change circumstances and that it is essential to educate the educator himself" (MER 144).

5 This is meant to summarize the relevant sections of the Introduction (Hegel 1979: 52–53; 1970: 76).

6 An overview of Reinhold's approach to reconstituting the Kantian system on the basis of the "principle of consciousness" can be found in Neuhouser (1991: Ch. 1 "Origins of Fichte's Theory: The Notion of the Unity of Reason").

7 In fact, the notion of ostension or pointing out does not come up until later, but I am here offering a compressed version of the argument.

8 Admittedly, this may seem to contradict what is sometimes called Hegel's "objective idealism" or "conceptual realism." At least on certain readings, Hegel is thought to maintain that the world itself has a conceptual structure, independent of the activity of the knowing subject. In this he differs from Kant, who insisted that the categories apply to the world of appearances because they are, in effect, imposed upon it by the knower (in the act he calls "synthesis").

72 Epistemology

This is one of the many subtleties of Hegel's position that might come to light if we considered the opening arguments at greater length.

One small point in favor of the more "subjective idealist" reading that seems to be adopted here is that Marcuse emphasizes the turn to the subject within the standpoint of sense-certainty:

> Sense-experience holds it self-evident that the object is the essential, "the real," while the subject is unessential and its knowledge dependent upon the object. The true relation is now found to be "just the reverse of what first appeared" or the universal has turned out to be the true content of experience. And the locus of the universal is the subject and not the object.
> (RR 104)

9 I here follow Feenberg (2023: 161), who also attributes conceptual realism to Marcuse.
10 This passage is also discussed by Feenberg (2023: 98).
11 Russell and Wittgenstein famously disagreed about negative facts. Russell insisted upon them (2010: 41–42) whereas Wittgenstein did not think they were necessary. His stance is reflected in the following passage from the *Tractatus*: "2.05 The totality of existing states of affairs also determines which states of affairs do not exist" (2001: 9).
12 Quine, "On What There Is" in *From a Logical Point of View* (1961: 4).
13 I here follow Feenberg, who calls this "the Double Structure of Potentiality" (2023: 98–99).
14 Once again, I am indebted to Feenberg's idea of "the Double Structure of Potentiality" (2023: 98–99).
15 This story is told in greater detail in Friedman's *Dynamics of Reason* (2001).
16 Feenberg (2023: 54) also discusses Marcuse's debt to Kant's idea of a priori forms of sensibility.
17 Here Marcuse repeats Marx's first thesis on Feuerbach (MER 144).
18 Marcuse's critique of Schelling is discussed by Dews (2018: 399).
19 I thank Fred Rush for this point concerning observation reports.

Further reading

Anderson, K. B. (1993) "On Hegel and the Rise of Social Theory: A Critical Appreciation of *Reason and Revolution* 50 Years Later," *Sociological Theory*, Vol. 11, No. 3: 243–67. [Overview of Marcuse's Hegel-interpretation, as well as its initial reception. Deals with Sidney Hook's critique of Marcuse's book.]
Kellner, Douglas. (1984). *Herbert Marcuse and the Crisis of Marxism*. London: Macmillan. [Ch. 5 offers a very thorough overview of *Reason and Revolution*, focused especially on anti-empiricism and anti-positivism.]

Three
Metaphysics

1. Introduction: the problem of universals

As a critical theorist, Marcuse seems unlikely to have a metaphysics. Critical theorists are followers of Marx and Freud who share their teachers' suspicion of traditional religious and metaphysical worldviews: in particular, doctrines about such things as the immortality of the soul, the origin of the world, and, of course, the existence and nature of God. Yet as I hope to show in this chapter, Marcuse does appear to engage in one age-old metaphysical controversy. This is the so-called "problem of universals," a problem concerning whether, and in what sense, such general features as goodness, redness, or humanity have a real existence independent of the particulars that instantiate them.

Ancient philosophy is integral to Marcuse's reception of the problem of universals, so it may be helpful to review this background briefly at the outset. Plato's theory of forms is one of the most ambitious versions of the view I have called "realism about universals." Plato's doctrine holds that universal concepts denote forms: immaterial, unchanging archetypes of which the material, sensible, changing things in our world are just so many pale imitations. Aristotle's idea of substantial form, understood as a thing's essence or nature, or the potential it strives to fulfill, can be understood as a descendant of this Platonic view—though Aristotle's picture is divested of a separate intelligible world in which the forms reside.[1] Rather than exist separately, forms inhere in things as the ideal they strive to achieve. An acorn growing into an oak realizes its essence, yet this essence was always present in it as a potential, or its "form."

DOI: 10.4324/9781003307075-3

Nominalists, by contrast, deny the reality of universals, insisting that the only things that exist are concrete particulars. One characteristically modern motivation for nominalism is a form of naturalism that maintains that the world contains only those entities which are described by our best science. Forms would be impossible to locate in the natural world thus conceived. Moreover, the scientific revolution famously banished the older Platonic–Aristotelian idea of a "great chain of being," a hierarchy in which different types of entities behave according to their natures. Instead, it pictured a universe in which every material thing, whether an apple or a planet, obeys the same universal laws. Another source of motivation for nominalism might be empiricism. Universals, like humanity, goodness and redness, do not seem to be part of our perceptual experience, even granting that the particulars which instantiate them are.

Though it might seem irrelevant to a critical theory of society, the problem of universals was clearly of great interest to Marcuse. He says so in no uncertain terms: "Far from being only an abstract question of epistemology, or a pseudo-concrete question of language and its use, the question of the status of universals is at the very center of philosophic thought" (ODM 207). Marcuse treats the problem extensively, describing its origins in classical philosophy as well as its treatment among analytic philosophers (ordinary-language philosophers, positivists, naturalists, etc.). What is more, Marcuse appears sympathetic to a form of realism about universals, and unpersuaded by modern philosophical critiques of this doctrine that seek to show that it is outmoded and incompatible with the modern scientific worldview.[2] Since "Platonist critical theory" may seem to be a contradiction in terms, we will need to tread carefully here.

In One-Dimensional Man, Marcuse repeatedly voices support for the classical doctrine, insisting that a distinction between the essences or natures of things and the contingent ways they happen to exist is vital for social critique. What is more, Marcuse clearly rejects the anti-realism about universals he associates with logical positivism and the analytic philosophy of his time. Just as he insists that a distinction between the potential and the actual is crucial for critique, so too does he regard the contemporary rejection of this distinction as lending support to a repressive society.

One indication of the centrality that the problem of universals has in One-Dimensional Man is its bearing on the book's main topic: the distinction between two-dimensional and one-dimensional societies.[3] The universe of the classical philosophers, whose worldview includes universals, is "two-dimensional," meaning there are standards, norms or ideals that things may (fail to) embody. In a world without such measures, critique lacks a normative basis, and we succumb to a "one-dimensional" conformist existence. Seen in this light, the empiricist or positivist rejection of Platonism appears to be a form of ideology, a false view maintained because suited to the preservation of the status quo.

Still, it is unclear just how far Marcuse's sympathy with the classical doctrine of realism about universals extends, and there is clearly a spectrum of possibilities: for example, Marcuse might fully endorse the Platonist view on theoretical grounds; alternatively, he might simply regard it as politically expedient, or else as (in some more philosophically sophisticated way) justified on practical grounds; and between these extremes there are various intermediate possibilities. This chapter, however, is less devoted to deciding whether and to what extent Marcuse was a realist about universals than to investigating the difficulties his (favorable) statements concerning that doctrine raise.

In the first section of the chapter, we will canvass some of the reasons to be wary of attributing the realist doctrine to Marcuse. Orthodox Platonism would seem to be antithetical to critical theory. There is its otherworldly metaphysics and disdain for this world, its belief in an immaterial soul, its mistrust of the senses and of sensible desires, its emphasis on the life of contemplation over the life of action, and so on. Then there are its more direct political implications. The "great chain of being" of the Platonic–Aristotelian tradition seems to have its counterpart in a belief in the naturalness of hierarchy. And in the *Republic*, Plato appears to be an authoritarian, insisting on a rigidly hierarchical, militarized society in which everyone adheres to his assigned role. The prospects for a Platonist critical theory therefore seem fairly dim.

A more obvious problem is that Marcuse's sympathy towards Plato is not tantamount to endorsement. Marcuse seldom if ever avows the doctrine personally, but rather expresses his approval of other thinkers who do. This comes through in the narrative of decline Marcuse offers in his recounting of the history of philosophy. He describes how realism about universals in classical philosophy gave way to the anti-realism of modern positivism. By itself, however, this narrative does not entail that Marcuse himself is a full-blooded Platonist (or Aristotelian) who rejects the modern scientific worldview as we know it in favor of an outmoded earlier one. Indeed, this anti-scientific point of view looks like an extreme position which we might hesitate to attribute to Marcuse simply on grounds of charity. Among other things, it suggests a conservative or even reactionary outlook alien to him. Marcuse is well aware of the neo-scholastic or Aristotelian attempts to revive the realist doctrine. Yet he appears to regard such doctrines as hopelessly anti-scientific: "no resuscitation of some kind of Aristotelian or Thomistic philosophy can save the situation," he writes, "for it is a priori refuted by scientific reason" (ODM 151).

Still, Marcuse clearly thinks that universals underwrite the possibility of criticizing society in terms of ideals it fails to achieve. He claims at various points that doing away with universals in the way that positivist critics of metaphysics advocate would deprive critique of a vital resource: "The unscientific character of these ideas fatally weakens the opposition to the established reality; the ideas become mere ideals, and their concrete, critical content evaporates into the ethical or metaphysical atmosphere" (ODM 151). For Marcuse, the obsolescence of the classical doctrine is no cause for celebration, but a symptom of decline.

Hence the dilemma for an interpreter interested in understanding Marcuse's realism about universals: if Marcuse is a fully convinced proponent of the doctrine, then he risks an unacceptably backward-looking conservatism, whereas if he is not, then he risks succumbing to the one-dimensional outlook he criticizes in the analytic tradition.

While I am unsure whether the texts settle the issue, I will suggest in the concluding section that Marcuse is neither straightforwardly a Platonic–Aristotelian realist, nor some type of positivist or empiricist skeptic about universals, but something else entirely. I base this conjecture on the distinction Marcuse draws between the classical dialectic of Plato and Aristotle, on the one hand, and what he calls the "historical" dialectic (presumably of Hegel and, especially, Marx), on the other. Marcuse's version of realism about universals is meant to respect the materialist insight that philosophy must be seen in a wider context, namely as an aspect of mankind's historically extended project of attempting to master nature. How exactly these doctrines can be reconciled is the puzzle I hope to have resolved, or at least made progress on, by the end of this chapter.

2. Plato as critical theorist?

Although *One-Dimensional Man* is predominantly devoted to a critique of late capitalist society and culture, it contains a surprisingly thorough treatment of ancient philosophy (see especially "The Historical Commitment of Philosophy").[4] Marcuse's aim in discussing this material is to explain how Western culture has moved from a "two-dimensional" outlook to a "one-dimensional" one.

Given the incompatibilities between Plato's theory of forms and critical theory (Marcuse's or anyone's), the prospects for a rapprochement might seem dim. However, Marcuse's interpretation breaks with the received view of Plato as an otherworldly metaphysician, a denigrator of the body and the senses, and a political authoritarian. Marcuse attempts to find revolutionary tendencies in Plato, even if he concedes that these remain implicit. The result is a novel interpretation of the *Republic* and the theory of forms, one undertaken for the sake of critical theory.

For Marcuse, the theory of forms is revolutionary rather than reactionary. This is for the simple reason that it allows people to envision a world better than the one they presently inhabit: "The search for the correct definition, for the 'concept' of virtue, justice, piety, and knowledge becomes a subversive undertaking, for the concept intends a new polis" (ODM 138). On this understanding, Plato's Socrates aims to critically scrutinize the received understandings of virtue, justice and piety. In doing so, he uncovers truths that might be incompatible with the social and political status quo. Indeed, Plato's Socrates demonstrates that the received understandings of these concepts are self-contradictory. Common sense is thus shown to be internally inconsistent. What is more, the correct understanding of any given term is said by Marcuse to have implications beyond the inquiry itself. It is said to furnish us with knowledge of a new and better social world: "the concept," he says, "intends a new polis." Only in a new polis could our revised understanding of the key terms be adequately realized.

Of course, Plato's Socrates interrogates received understandings of numerous philosophical concepts, but it is clear that Marcuse thinks that it is the ethical ones which are of decisive importance; in particular, concepts concerning human life and the normative standards guiding it:

> Analyzed in the condition in which he finds himself in his universe, man seems to be in possession of certain faculties and powers which would enable him to lead a "good life," i.e., a life which is as much as possible free from toil, dependence, and ugliness. To attain such a life is to attain the "best life": to live in accordance with the essence of nature or man.
>
> (ODM 130)

One might wonder why Marcuse is primarily interested in moral and political views from Plato's Socrates, rather than in mathematical or scientific ones. Here, it seems to me Marcuse is invoking a common view of Socrates, stemming from the latter's own self-presentation in the Phaedo. There, Socrates presents himself as a figure who came to reject the earlier philosophers' interest in nature and instead turned towards human life. Plato's cosmology, then, does not figure in Marcuse's effort to recover classical thought for critical theory.

A potential problem with this effort to rehabilitate the theory of forms is that it still seems fairly utopian. So long as the ideal (form) belongs to another world, so too does the better society. It is a utopia or "no place," as More put it. Critical theorists since Marx himself accuse utopian socialists of being unable to legitimate their conceptions (or, less charitably, fantasies) of a world that might exist. The only solution, according to Marx and his followers, lies in attempting to discern in the present the possibility of a better social order.

Though Marcuse does not explicitly address the issue, there is no hint of a belief in otherworldliness in his reconstruction. At one point, he approvingly cites Russell's suggestion that forms or universals are the "stuff of this world," a formula we will attempt to clarify later (ODM 176). A tempting explanation might be that it is some other figure, perhaps Aristotle or Hegel, who furnishes Marcuse with his this-worldly version of the theory. But before resorting to such an explanation, let us examine what resources there may be for interpreting even Plato in this manner—for constructing a Platonist critical theory.

Note first that Marcuse would not be alone in interpreting Plato in this way. From the Neo-Platonists to Hegel, there is a long tradition of attempting to divest Plato's theory of forms of any stark dualism between the sensible and intelligible worlds.[5] The key idea here is that the world of forms and the everyday world are one and the same, apprehended from different points of view, namely those of the senses and the intellect respectively.[6] If the form is the essence of the thing, then it is part of it—indeed, its most important part. It is in virtue of the essence that the thing truly exists and is what it is, meaning that in order to grasp its identity, we must grasp its essence, which only the intellect is capable of doing.

Another argument for this view would be that insurmountable difficulties arise when we try to explain the separateness of the form from the thing. It cannot be a matter of spatial apartness, since this is a relation that only obtains between things (not between forms and things). To the extent that we think of the form as separate from the thing, we may be being misled by our imagination, which wants to picture the form as an object in space, apart from others. Ironically, the very attempt to distinguish in a radical way the form from the thing may start out from a conception of the form that fails to respect its uniqueness.

Yet while universal properties like beauty or goodness are possessed by the particular things we perceive, they must also transcend these things. Each form encompasses not just all the actual instances, but all the possible ones; for example, possible future instances of justice such as might be found in a society better than our own. In fact, it is often held that no particular fully meets the standards constituted by the form. The difference in modal status between thing (actual) and form (potential) is thus closely tied to the normative status of the latter.

But there are further obstacles to recovering Platonism for critical theory. One lies in its methodological limitations. Platonism has often seemed to its critics to rely on a faculty of rational (intellectual) intuition. It is as if reason itself and not only the senses were capable of being presented with objects. Yet this philosophers' version of the mystic's "third eye" would seem to be a fiction. The familiar five senses are the only senses there are, and though there may be some role for reason to play in our grasping the spatial world, it is not likely to be intuition, i.e., direct contact with objects that present themselves to the faculty.

Marcuse is well aware of the controversial status of Plato's method: "Classical Greek philosophy relies largely on what was later termed (in a rather derogative sense) 'intuition'" (ODM 130). As a follower of Kant and German idealism, Marcuse would have known full well the criticisms of rationalism and its idea of rational intuition. Still, he persists in his view that Plato's original theory does not rely on anything as "mysterious" or "strange" as rational intuition:

> It is not a mysterious faculty of the mind, not a strange imme-diate experience, nor is it divorced from conceptual analysis. Intuition is rather the (preliminary) terminus of such an analysis—the result of methodic intellectual mediation. As such, it is the mediation of concrete experience.
>
> (ODM 130)

As Marcuse correctly points out, essences are not intuited at a single stroke, but are, rather, "the terminus of an analysis," "the result of intellectual mediation." For an example of this analysis, we need look no further than the Platonic dialogues themselves. There we find that the forms are reached through a process of dialectic. In this pro-cess, Socrates teaches his interlocutors the difference between par-ticular beautiful (or pious, just, etc.) things and the beautiful (or the pious, the just, etc.) itself. Ultimately, then, the discovery of essences is a result of a fairly elementary form of intellectual reflection on our experience of the world. This is a process that starts with the objects of experience—as he says, it is "the mediation of concrete experience"—but then culminates in an intuition of that which these objects all have in common (the universal, "the terminus of an analysis").

Another potential obstacle to the recovery of Plato in a modern context is the latter's bias towards contemplation over action. Even within a Platonic framework, Marcuse denies that the forms are exclusively objects of contemplation. For him, they are intended to issue in action:

> Dialectical thought understands the critical tension between "is" and "ought" first as an ontological condition, pertaining to the

structure of Being itself. However, the recognition of this state of Being—its theory—intends from the beginning a concrete *practice*.

(ODM 137)

Marcuse invokes a Socratic doctrine that effectively erodes the dichotomy between contemplation and action. On this "intellectualist" doctrine, virtue is knowledge. Knowing the good motivates one to actualize it: "If man has learned to see and know what really is, he will act in accordance with truth" (ODM 129). Unlike Aristotle, Plato's Socrates does not seem to allow the possibility of *akrasia*, at least when defined as knowing the good but failing to act in accordance with it. (This is a point of difference between Plato and Aristotle that Marcuse does not note.)

It is one thing to seek a life of virtue and wisdom, another to seek the revolutionary transformation of society. The former may seem to be an aspiration for private life in contrast to the latter, which requires some type of public intervention at the very least. Still, Marcuse insists that the radicalism of the dialectic not be gainsaid. So urgent is the practical import of knowledge of the forms that it may drive the philosopher to risk public censure, punishment or even death. The true significance of philosophy is thus illustrated in the life and death of Socrates, who was executed by his countrymen for the crimes of impiety and corrupting the youth. Equally illustrative is the allegory of the cave, which tells us that the wise risk persecution from the very people they wish to liberate from ignorance and bondage. "In Plato," Marcuse writes, "the extreme concepts which illustrate this subversion are: death as the beginning of the philosopher's life, and the violent liberation from the Cave" (ODM 136).

Alongside its dismissal of the senses as sources of knowledge, Platonic rationalism supposedly demotes bodily desires as sources of motivation. Virtue is attained partly by resisting our animal instincts and urges—in fact, per the *Phaedo*, through the separation of the soul or intellect from the body that we achieve when we die. Against this otherworldly, anti-materialist strand in Plato, Marcuse draws our attention to the erotic dimension of knowledge in Plato's thought. For Plato, what truly is (i.e., the forms) is the object of love, not merely the object of knowledge. Marcuse also finds this conviction in Aristotle, a figure whom he generally treats as his (and Plato's) opponent:

> The philosophic quest proceeds from the finite world to the construction of a reality which is not subject to the painful difference between potentiality and actuality, which has mastered its negativity and is complete and independent in itself—free. *This discovery is the work of Logos and Eros.*
>
> (ODM 131, my emphasis)

In Marcuse's retelling, this classical Platonic–Aristotelian doctrine assumes an unmistakably Freudian–Marxist form. The pursuit of knowledge and erotic desire are inextricably intertwined. They conspire to propel the individual beyond the confines of the mode of thought and existence prevalent in their society.

This joint reference to Platonic and Aristotelian doctrines marks a rare moment in the text where Marcuse refers approvingly to both figures. In Plato, he has in mind Diotima's speech from the *Symposium*, while his sources in Aristotle are the central books of the *Metaphysics*. There, Aristotle tells us that all things are engaged in a form of loving imitation of divine self-sufficiency. I shall devote greater attention to the Platonic half of the discussion, because it is Plato whom Marcuse prioritizes.

The central idea of Diotima's speech is that Eros leads the lover on a journey that culminates in a sort of knowledge. The love of beautiful things (boys, songs, etc.) inspires an ascent to love of the beautiful itself (210 b–e, 211). Hence, there is more than one route from things to the forms in which they participate. One such route is through philosophy—in particular, Socratic dialectic. There, the interlocutors are brought to realize that such things as the pious or the just cannot be identified with particular pious or just acts. Another route, however, is Diotima's erotic ascent. Hence, Marcuse finds within Plato's own outlook the resources to defend a Freudian view of human beings as driven by love in the expanded Platonic sense. In this regard, Marcuse is following Freud himself, who famously referred approvingly to Plato's concept of Eros.

So far, we have not discerned any connection between this doctrine and the central topic of Marxist critical theory, namely economic activity. But Marcuse does trace such a connection. Applying the metaphysical concepts of becoming and being, particular and universal, and existence and essence, to human beings, they take on economic meaning. If people are constantly engaged in toil, they are not free to realize their essential virtues and therefore incapable of living well:

> There are modes of existence which can never be "true" because they can never *rest* in the realization of their potentialities, in the joy of being. In the human reality, all existence that spends itself in procuring the prerequisites of existence is thus an "untrue" and unfree existence.
>
> (ODM 132)

Here Marcuse may also be thinking of Aristotle's idea that the highest good, the life of contemplation and virtue, demands at least some measure of freedom from the struggle for existence. Plato's and Aristotle's Greece was according to Marcuse

> a society based on the proposition that freedom is incompatible with the activity of procuring the necessities of life ... and that cognition of the truth and true existence imply freedom from the entire dimension of such activity. This is indeed the pre- and anti-technological constellation *par excellence*.
>
> (ODM 139)

Traditional philosophy and critical theory have generally been adversaries, but in the context of the ancient world they find one point of agreement: the conviction that the good life requires freedom from toil.

Yet as Marcuse also notes, "this activity is the 'natural' function of a specific class"—a small elite. Hence there is a seemingly insurmountable obstacle to providing a sympathetic interpretation of Plato from the perspective of critical theory. After all, it remains the case that Plato did not advocate freedom from toil for all, but only for those deemed worthy. How, then, can we reconcile Marcuse's affinity for Plato with Plato's elitism? Here, Marcuse displays a perhaps excessive degree of interpretative charity. He effectively offers an excuse on Plato's behalf, namely that during the period in which Plato wrote, the forces of production were in an immature state of development: "If truth presupposes freedom from toil, and if this freedom is, in the social reality, the prerogative of a minority, then the reality allows such a truth only in approximation and for a privileged group" (ODM 133). During Plato's era, freedom from toil, and a life devoted to the pursuit of wisdom and virtue, could only ever be possible for a few. The many were consigned to lives of toil producing what society needed to provide for its members' needs. Today, Marcuse thinks, matters are different. In modern society, with science, industry and technology, the possibility of freedom from toil is available to all. This is the possibility that would be realized under socialism with public ownership of the means of production. However, it is also a possibility thwarted by capitalism, which ensures that wealth is concentrated in the hands of a particular class.

3. Marcuse's Plato in question: MacIntyre's critique

Later on in the book, however, Marcuse suggests a further explanation why Plato and his followers did not pursue theory to its practical conclusion: socialism. Marcuse seeks to explain why they did not succeed completely in acting in accordance with their notion of the good, contrary to the doctrine that knowledge is virtue, that theory entails practice. His thought is familiar from left-Hegelianism. On Marcuse's view, there were powerful impediments to a just, egalitarian society. Hence energies which could not find expression in a revolutionary transformation of Greek society instead found expression in utopian thinking:

> For philosophy, the contradiction is insoluble, or else it does not appear as a contradiction because it is the structure of the slave or serf society which this philosophy does not transcend. *Thus, it leaves history behind, unmastered, and elevates truth safely above the historical reality.* There, truth is preserved intact, not as an achievement of heaven or in heaven, but as an achievement of thought—intact *because its very notion expresses the insight that those who devote their lives to earning a living are incapable of living a human existence.*
>
> (ODM 133–34, my emphases)

For Marcuse, then, Plato's imagined utopia is an exercise in alienation, much in the same way that the Christian's idea of heaven is according to Marx ("the heart of a heartless world," "the sigh of the oppressed creature"). Plato's fantasy of an ideal society serves as compensation for the very real pain of existing in a non-ideal one and being unable to change it in the way that philosophy demands.

Ultimately, then, Marcuse does not take Plato's utopianism at face value. The Platonic idea that the just society is impossible reflects his inability to see that the barriers to its realization were historical: "Here, the historical barrier arrests and distorts the quest for truth; the societal division of labor obtains the dignity of an ontological condition" (ODM 133). For Marcuse, what stands in the way of justice is not some invariant feature of the human condition, like self-interest or partiality, the instinct to give preferential treatment to one's family over one's neighbors. Rather, it is the immature state of the productive forces that makes socialism as-yet impossible. Clearly, Plato would not have been in a position to grasp this point, which is only available to a historical materialist.

Alasdair MacIntyre has charged Marcuse with misrepresenting Plato's political views, in particular by imputing to the ancient thinker an egalitarianism he would have rejected. While we will later consider a number of objections from MacIntyre that pertain directly to Marcuse's (Platonic, Hegelian) dialectical logic, we here sample just one of these objections concerning Marcuse's interpretation of Plato. Commenting on one of the above cited passages, MacIntyre writes:

> Marcuse's statement is plainly false. Plato never envisaged the equality of men and he did not think that it was because most men had to spend their lives in procuring the necessities of life that they lacked access to truth; Plato believed that some men were genetically incapable of rising to the truth.
>
> (1970: 84)

MacIntyre's diagnosis of this interpretive error is that Marcuse has an ulterior motive. Marcuse is interested in condemning modern capitalist societies, as well as the reigning "one-dimensional" philosophies, i.e., logical positivism, logical empiricism, and analytic philosophy more generally. For dialectical and rhetorical purposes,

Marcuse must present an overly rosy picture of the ancient Greek polis and its "two-dimensional" philosophy, i.e., Platonism: "It is difficult to resist the conclusion that Marcuse actually minimizes the ideological content of 'classical philosophy' in order to draw the contrast with recent philosophy that his thesis requires" (1970: 84).

Yet while it is true that Marcuse prefers the two-dimensional outlook of ancient philosophy to the one-dimensional outlook of modern, it would be a mistake to conclude that he completely idealizes the past. Marcuse's attitude towards Platonism is more subtle, and MacIntyre's objection rests on a oversimplified characterization of it. Marcuse's position is not that egalitarianism was Plato's considered view of human beings as well as his recommendation for how they ought to live together. His point is instead that there was a repressed egalitarian dimension to his thought.

While fully acknowledging the inegalitarianism propounded in Plato's *Republic*, Marcuse calls our attention to an egalitarian dimension that he detects in other works. Thus in the *Meno*, it is shown that anybody, even a slave boy, can in principle achieve knowledge of the forms (ODM 113). It would follow from this that anybody could, in principle, live a good life.

I am not denying that Marcuse's interpretation of Plato is questionable. Plainly, it is not a disinterested, scholarly reading which is meant to find favor among classicists and specialists in ancient philosophy. On the contrary, it presupposes the truth of Marcuse's outlook, which combines Freudian psychoanalysis and Marx's historical materialism and theory of ideology. What is more, it relies on the perhaps arrogant idea that critical theorists understood great figures from the history of philosophy better than they understood themselves. Certainly, it would be legitimate to argue that this interpretation is question-begging, over-clever, or tendentious. However, MacIntyre goes too far when he denounces it as straightforwardly false, and moreover when he charges Marcuse with offering this interpretation in bad faith.

4. Analytical philosophy 1: positivism

If Plato and Aristotle are Marcuse's allies in defending a "two-dimensional" outlook in which universals are real and serve as normative standards, then his foes are those contemporary analytic philosophers who reject realism about universals. Marcuse's treatment of the views of his opponents is not particularly nuanced, and he can often seem to be running disparate schools of thought together. He criticizes positivists, behaviorists, ordinary-language philosophers, and naturalists alike. Whatever the disagreements between them, Marcuse regards all of these movements and figures as united in one respect: all take a reductionist approach to universals.

As background: Marcuse clearly understands most modern thought to be under the sway of a doctrine about scientific theories he calls "operationalism" (ODM 90). This is a doctrine concerning the meaning or significance of the concepts invoked by our best scientific theories. It urges that, instead of understanding such concepts in terms of what they refer to in the world, we should understand them in terms of what behavior someone who possesses them performs. Our commitment to the concept "electron" is not based on the certainty that this concept "carves reality at its joints." Rather, our commitment to this concept is a matter of our commitment to certain acts of measurement that have been borne out by the theory. Marcuse cites modern scientists themselves in his account of operationalism, and believes they are primarily motivated by problems raised in the theory of relativity. Yet he clearly also thinks operationalism has transcended the sciences and come to influence analytic philosophy. For Marcuse, there is a close connection between operationalism and the philosophical doctrine of behaviorism, and he often refers to them in the same breath: "operationalism in the physical, behaviorism in the social sciences" (ODM 14).

Marcuse is especially critical of a broadly behaviorist approach that reduces universal concepts to something more tractable. He understands this approach to be based on the idea that the meaning of a universal concept can be specified in terms of a disposition to act on the part of the person whose thought and speech it informs. Marcuse is skeptical: "not a single one of these reformulations, nor their sum-total, seems to capture or even circumscribe the full meaning of such terms as Mind, Will, Self, Good" (ODM 208). Marcuse insists that we distinguish universals themselves "from the various modes of behavior or disposition that, according to the analytic philosopher, fulfill their meaning" (ODM 208). The master thought in his engagement with analytic philosophy is that no proposed reduction will capture what was meant to be reduced. As he writes, "This description is of precisely that metaphysical character which positivistic analysis wishes to eliminate by translation, but the translation eliminates that which was to be defined" (ODM 215). And he elaborates on the reasons why no reduction can succeed:

> No snow is pure white, nor is any cruel beast or man all the cruelty man knows—knows as an almost inexhaustible force in history and imagination. Now there is a large class of concepts—we dare say, the philosophically relevant concepts—where the quantitative relation between the universal and the particular assumes a qualitative aspect, where the abstract universal seems to designate potentialities in a concrete, historical sense. However "man," "nature," "justice," "beauty" or "freedom" may be defined, they synthetize experiential contents into ideas which transcend their particular realizations as something that is to be surpassed, overcome. Thus the concept of beauty comprehends all the beauty not yet realized; the concept of freedom all the liberty not yet attained.
>
> (ODM 218)

One of the reasons Marcuse gives is surprisingly Platonic: the universal will always be more perfect than the particulars that instantiate it. Other reasons reflect a more modern philosophical context and are likely to remind readers of Hume and the problem of induction (or Nelson Goodman's distinct but broadly analogous problem concerning natural kinds and the projections they enable). A universal like goodness, justice, or redness encompasses all its instances: past, present, and future; possible or actual. Yet we human beings only know of those instances we have actually encountered.

One obvious line of response available to Marcuse's opponent is the following. If the universal cannot be reduced to operations, behaviors, dispositions, etc., then so much the worse for universals. The reductionist need not claim to have a perfect replacement for the universal. She is only claiming to have recouped as much of the function of this area of discourse as is possible. Here Marcuse's final line of response must simply be that "no mode of thought can dispense with universals" (ODM 114). The reductionist who believes

she can make do without universals and replace them with a nom-
inalistic vocabulary is deluded.

Another school Marcuse considers is ordinary-language philosophy, which he understands as a critique of traditional philosophy
and metaphysics. The ordinary-language philosopher aspires to show
that traditional philosophy uses words in a manner that goes beyond
their ordinary, accepted usage. In so doing, the traditional philosopher courts nonsense, though he or she will claim to have achieved
an especially ambitious kind of knowledge. Here as before, Marcuse's
strategy is to insist that the materials with which the ordinary-
language philosopher wants to replace universals are inadequate to
the task. He also makes the interesting point that it is precisely the
job of philosophy, poetry, and other ambitious areas of culture to
innovate our language and expand our conceptual universe, and that
there is nothing inherently illegitimate in going beyond our current
vocabulary and usage. Behind this argument lurks Marcuse's suspicion that ordinary-language philosophy and other related schools
encourage conformism:

> In its exposure of the mystifying character of transcendent
> terms, vague notions, metaphysical universals, and the like,
> linguistic analysis mystifies the terms of ordinary language by
> leaving them in the repressive context of the established uni-
> verse that the behavioral explication of meaning takes place—
> the explication which is to exorcize the old linguistic "ghosts"
> of the Cartesian and other obsolete myths.
>
> (ODM 196)

For Marcuse, the threat posed by ordinary language philosophy is
that it will be unwittingly complicit in the degradation of speech
and writing by consumer culture and late capitalism. In ignoring the
"repressive context of the established universe," it misses the opportunity to be critical of accepted ways of speaking. As a counterweight
to ordinary-language philosophy, Marcuse recommends figures like
Kraus, Barthes, and Lenin who focus on the institutional backdrop
against which language use takes place.

A broader objection Marcuse makes to the procedures of ordinary-
language philosophy is that it is procrustean. It insists that philosophy

conform to ordinary language and common sense, when the reverse would be preferable. Ordinary language and common sense should be encouraged to rise to the level of philosophy. The "common stock" of our language includes not just ordinary language but also the extraordinary languages of philosophy, literature, and other forms of discourse that challenge the everyday:

> What is this "common stock"? Does it include Plato's "idea," Aristotle's "essence," Hegel's Geist, Marx's Verdinglichung in whatever adequate translation? Does it include the key words of poetic language? Of surrealist prose? And if so, does it contain them in their negative connotation—that is, as invalidating the universe of common usage?
>
> (ODM 192)

5. Analytical philosophy 2: Russell and Whitehead

Most of Marcuse's discussion of the problem of universals takes place as part of readings of other figures. He offers a sympathetic overview of classical philosophy and its realism about universals, and a much less sympathetic one of the reductionist treatment of universals found in analytic philosophy. When we consider the few statements Marcuse makes in his own voice, however, his allegiances become relatively clear. To anticipate, he favors a "deflated" version of realism about universals. They are real but not immaterial—not "mysterious." Ironically, Marcuse draws support for this deflated realism from two analytic philosophers who are not reductionists in the sense Marcuse objects to: Russell and Whitehead.

While the doctrine of realism about universals is often seen as philosophy at its most ambitious, Marcuse presents it (rather surprisingly) as a matter of ordinary common sense. In Marcuse's view, realism about universals is straightforwardly implied by our everyday experience of the world. Here, in one of the few passages in which he seems to endorse the position while speaking in his own voice, Marcuse notes its common-sense appeal:

> Talking of a beautiful girl, a beautiful landscape, a beautiful picture, I certainly have very different things in mind. What is

common to all of them—"beauty"—is neither a mysterious entity, nor a mysterious word. On the contrary, nothing is perhaps more directly and dearly experienced than the appearance of "beauty" in various beautiful objects.

(ODM 214)

Here, Marcuse envisions real universals like beauty as the subject-matter about which we disagree when we argue over the definition of beauty. It is important to him that there is an underlying fact of the matter and not simply the variety of definitions given by different people in different roles for different purposes:

The boy friend and the philosopher, the artist and the mortician may "define" it in very different ways, but they all define the same specific state or condition—some quality or qualities which make the beautiful contrast with other objects.

(ODM 214)

Admittedly, this might seem to be insufficient evidence on which to base the claim that Marcuse is some type of realist about universals, rather than a nominalist. Even supposing we grant the already questionable idea that everyday experience and ordinary linguistic practice in some way reflect a widespread belief in the reality of the universal, this would not be sufficient to resolve the philosophical dispute. The dispute concerns whether these (alleged) facts of everyday experience and linguistic practice limn the underlying structure of reality. What is more, we should note that Marcuse, in this passage, says something that could be taken as a rejection of the conception of universals as otherworldly: beauty "is neither a mysterious entity, nor a mysterious word." This raises the problem that will occupy us for the remainder of the chapter: whether Marcuse's apparent affinity for the doctrine of realism about universals commits him to anything like an orthodox Platonist view.

Before doing so, however, we must consider the two other sources of support for Marcuse's deflationary realism: Russell and Whitehead. Though analytic philosophers are typically Marcuse's opponents when it comes to the problem of universals, Russell and Whitehead are allies since both are realists rather than anti-realists.

At two critical junctures in One-Dimensional Man, Marcuse alludes favorably to these thinkers' views on the matter. The first is a quotation from Russell's My Philosophical Development, where Russell puts forward the idea that universals like whiteness or sweetness are simply "the stuff of the world" (ODM 216). Universals, on this conception, are the objects we relate to by means of the senses. One can see why this conception would be appealing to Marcuse. Rather than treat the universal as an object of intellectual intuition, this doctrine allows that it is (in some way) sensible. Rather than place it in a world beyond experience, this doctrine situates the universal in the everyday. The second is a quotation where Whitehead speaks of the universal as an "eternal object" and every particular as "the occasion" for its realization (ODM 220). The upshot is that, contra orthodox Platonism, the universal depends on the particulars and vice versa. Without an occasion for its realization, there would be no eternal object. Here too, then, the otherworldliness of orthodox Platonism is avoided.

From these passages, it seems clear that Marcuse, though a realist about universals, attempts to avoid the associated idea of a purely intelligible world beyond this one. His realism about universals is domesticated, tamed—but is not yet nominalism. Still, if we are to fully understand Marcuse's engagement with this classical doctrine, we have to consider his appropriation of Plato at greater length.

6. Universals and the productive forces

Up until this point, I have assumed that Marcuse's defense of realism about universals can be taken at face value, and that he is sincere in advocating this doctrine. However, it may be that there is more to the story, and that Marcuse is not so much taking sides in this philosophical debate as commenting on it from a position well outside of traditional philosophy. As Marcuse tells us at one point, in a passage that is difficult to reconcile with many of his subsequent comments, "The following discussion does not claim to enter into the 'problem of universals', it only tries to elucidate the (artificially) limited scope of philosophic analysis and to indicate the need for going beyond these limits" (ODM 212). If this is so, then we ought to consider the possibility that Marcuse, though sympathetic to realism, understands the problem of universals in a wider context. Another sign that Marcuse is not actually engaged in this philosophical debate is that he is extremely selective in his treatment of it, choosing to ignore universals that are not politically relevant. At any rate, this politically focused approach seems to be implied in his criticism of academic philosophers for their technical and abstruse treatment of only those universals relevant to mathematics and natural science. Even if we were to grant reality to political universals, he asks,

> do not all the other universals have a very different status? They do, but their analysis is all too easily kept within the limits of academic philosophy. The discussion will again be focused on substantive as distinguished from logico-mathematical universals (set, number, class, etc.), and among the former, on the more abstract and controversial concepts which present the real challenge to philosophic thought.
>
> (ODM 212)

A clue to the unusual vantage point from which Marcuse addresses the problem of universals: Marcuse sometimes speaks of his interest in translating the ontological dialectic into the historical—the Platonic dialectic into a Marxist one. I interpret this to mean that he is interested in taking realism about universals and giving it a historical materialist interpretation:

> The transformation of ontological into historical dialectic retains the two-dimensionality of philosophic thought as critical, negative thinking. But now essence and appearance, "is" and "ought," confront each other in the conflict between actual forces and capabilities in the society.
>
> (ODM 146)

What becomes of realism about universals when it is understood against the backdrop of historical materialism? By "materialism," I mean the Marxist theory that a society's philosophy, religion, and morality are conditioned by its class structure and the tools, techniques, and instruments it uses for production. The former are part of the society's ideological superstructure, the latter making up its economic base. Seen in this light, all metaphysical doctrines—realism, nominalism, etc.—are ideological in that they are mystifications of reality that prevent it from being seen with full clarity. However, realism is to be preferred, because it reflects, if only obscurely, a contradiction inherent to capitalism. This is the contradiction between the great potential to alleviate poverty which arises under capitalism through its development of the productive forces, and the way capitalism also thwarts this possibility by its class structure. The contradiction between the productive forces and their employment finds its counterpart in the philosophical one concerning essence and existence, the forms and the particulars, the potential and the actual.

The difference between the classical realist doctrine and the historical materialist one is brought out when we dwell for a moment on a phrase from the last passage, where Marcuse says that "'is' and 'ought' confront each other in the conflict between actual forces and capabilities in the society" (ODM 146). The prominent empiricist Hume contested this ancient view when he argued that there could be no deriving an "ought" from an "is." In a sense, though, this is precisely what the classical philosophers tried to do when they argued that insight into the nature of something, e.g., the human being, could tell us how that thing ought to behave—what would be good for human beings; what exactly it is we should be pursuing as we pursue virtue and flourishing. A famous instance of this is found Aristotle's *Nicomachean Ethics*, in particular in the function argument. Just as it is by looking to a tool's designated function that we understand what the tool ought to do, so too must we look to the nature of human beings to understand how they ought to live.

Yet Marcuse characterizes the realist doctrine in terms that suggest Aristotle's reference to tools is no mere illustration. For Marcuse, the conflict between is and ought, existence and essence, proves to be as much a product of the state of development of the productive forces as it is of the underlying metaphysical structure of reality. Does this imply that Marcuse does not in the end accept the classical, Platonic–Aristotelian doctrine, embracing instead a historical materialist one? Or does he end up with a hybrid view? I will leave this question unanswered here, but Marcuse's ambivalence about the classical doctrine will be discussed repeatedly in the chapters to follow.

Summary

Though not a traditional metaphysician, Marcuse is intensely preoccupied with the problem of universals. He repeatedly expresses sympathy with the classical, Platonic–Aristotelian doctrine that not only particulars but also the universals they fall under must have a place in our worldview. He is also critical of the positivist, empiricist attempt to eliminate universals from our ontology in favor of a reductive nominalism. Marcuse reinterprets Plato's Socrates as a figure whose theory of forms is a politically subversive doctrine. By interrogating those who were thought wise in his society about their conceptions of justice, virtue, and piety, Socrates aims not simply at wisdom but at "a new polis." This dialectical ascent to knowledge of the forms has both an erotic and a rational dimension.

Yet Marcuse's case for realism about universals does not rely on classical sources alone. He also finds inspiration for a more modest form of realism about universals in some of his philosophical contemporaries, like Russell and Whitehead. This version of the doctrine is in no way otherworldly, and treats universals as part of the contents of the world we experience: they are "the stuff of this world." Marcuse also makes some effort to integrate Platonism with historical materialism, arguing that the gap between existence and essence, is and ought, has something to do with the state of development of the productive forces. Yet it remains unclear how this rapprochement between Plato's metaphysics and Marx's historical materialism is supposed to take place.

Notes

1 It may be for this very understandable reason that Feenberg (2023: 66), in his interpretation of Marcuse, focuses more on Aristotle and his category of "potential," than on Plato (though Plato is present). One could also defend Feenberg's approach on the grounds that a) the notion of potential, and b) the organic, are far more important for Aristotle than for Plato. Another respect in which Feenberg's approach differs from the one I will take in this chapter is that he locates an important amendment to Marcuse's Aristotle-inspired essentialism in the early study *Hegel's Ontology and Theory of Historicity*. Interestingly, Plato does enter Feenberg's account at one point, though in a different connection: as a thinker of *techne* (2023: 94–95, 130).

2 I here follow Feenberg (2023: 161), who describes Marcuse as embracing "conceptual realism," a view I regard as equivalent to realism about universals.

3 I here, once again, follow Feenberg (2023: 84–85). As Feenberg usefully notes, the "two-dimensional" ontology is in place long before One-Dimensional Man. It can be found in *Reason and Revolution*, the essay on essence, and elsewhere. It is a mainstay of Marcuse's thought.

4 This is the title of a recent study by Thakkar (2018).

5 Hegel mocks the "two-worlds" conception, accusing it of preceding as if forms were "things that exist but in another world or region, and a world of actuality were to be found outside them" (SoL 29–30; W 5: 43)

6 Thakkar, a modern author who interprets Plato as a critical theorist, adopts a "one-world" view as well (2018: Ch. 1).

Further reading

Cobb, W. M. (2004) "Diatribes and Distortions: Marcuse's Academic Reception," in J. Abromeit and W. M. Cobb (eds.), *Marcuse: A Critical Reader*, Abingdon/New York: Routledge, 163–87. [Contains a helpful overview of MacIntyre's critique of Marcuse, and responds to its shortcomings.]

Feenberg, A. (2023) *Towards a Ruthless Criticism of Everything Existing*. London: Verso. [Ch. 3 offers an account of Marcuse's essentialism, though one that differs from mine in its emphasis Aristotle's category of "potential" and Hegel's "real possibility."]

MacIntyre, A. and Truitt, W. H. (1971) *Herbert Marcuse: An Exposition and Polemic*, London: Fontana. [An overcritical but comprehensive and philosophically sophisticated treatment. Criticizes Marcuse's interpretation of Plato.]

Rush, F. (2006) "Conceptual Foundations of Early Critical Theory," in F. Rush (ed.), *Cambridge Companion to Critical Theory*, Cambridge: Cambridge University Press. [Discusses Marcuse's concept of essence, and the role of this category in his form of critical theory.]

Whyman, T. (2023) "Two Sorts of Philosophical Therapy: Ordinary Language Philosophy, Social Criticism and the Frankfurt School," *Philosophy and Social Criticism*. Online First. https://doi.org/10.1177/01914537231203525.

Four

Philosophy of science

1. Introduction: Marcuse and technology

Marcuse devoted considerable attention to understanding the role of science and technology in Western capitalist countries during the twentieth century. Recent treatments of Marcuse's views in this area of philosophy focus primarily on Marcuse's thinking about technology. This focus is entirely justified, and there are many good reasons for it. Yet the present chapter differs in focusing exclusively on science, rather than on technology. I do so not to minimize the importance of technology but to confirm it (ODM 149). The approach I adopt allows us to see that, for Marcuse, even pure, non-applied science is already informed by our interests and practices.

The focus on technology, by Feenberg and other commentators, is entirely understandable. For one, technology represents a concrete, applied side of science with a clear connection to everyday life. Hence, technology is more immediately relevant to questions in critical social theory about how we ought to live. One is more curious to know Marcuse's perspective on nuclear weapons, television and radio, and computing than on the theory of relativity or quantum mechanics.

What is more, Marcuse's particular view of the relationship of technology to pure (non-applied) science entails that the former should have priority. Marcuse characterizes the conception of science that is the very antithesis of his own as follows: "Pure science is not applied science; it retains its identity and validity apart from its utilization" (ODM 158). For Marcuse, then, practical application is

DOI: 10.4324/9781003307075-4

already internal to theory. This is a theme in much pragmatist philosophy of science, and, to this extent at least, Marcuse would agree with this tradition.

This stance concerning the primacy of practice reflects the more general idea that science must always be understood in terms of its role in society, usually via technology. Once again Marcuse sets himself against a dualistic view that separates what should be united. It assumes, he says,

> two separate realms and events that meet each other, namely, (1) science and scientific thought, with their internal concepts and their internal truth, and (2) the use and application of science in the social reality. In other words, no matter how close the connection between the two developments may be, they do not imply and define each other.
>
> (ODM 158)

Of course, Marcuse's opponents might acknowledge that pure and applied science are often difficult to separate in practice. They could, however, argue that this distinction can and should be drawn when we theorize science. Yet here Marcuse appears to be taking a more extreme position, denying that it is even conceptually possible to distinguish the two. With this radical rejection of the dichotomy between pure and applied science, Marcuse follows Marx and certain authors in the pragmatist tradition.

At one point, Marcuse refers to the "internal instrumentalist" character of science, a phrase worth dwelling on. For him, it is not just that science admits of instrumentalization, but that it is always already a type of instrument. To this extent, Marcuse's philosophy of science is not only pragmatist but also instrumentalist, though he may not accept every doctrine that has gone by that name.

In just the same way that Marcuse denies that pure science can be distinguished from applied science, so too does he seem to deny that technology should (or can) be considered in abstraction from its current role in society—though he is not always consistent on this score.[1] Like Marx, Marcuse believes in the importance of "productive forces," the means by which a society produces its economic output. Hence, technology together with science come to be conceived of as productive forces, in Marcuse's outlook. Yet while this may sound like vulgar Marxism, Marcuse's account of science and technology turns out to be far more nuanced.

As Feenberg shows, Marcuse's theory of technology draws on phenomenology and existentialism to understand science and technology as modes of world-disclosure (2023: 104–5). It is not technology per se, but rather what Marcuse calls the "techno-logical a priori" which makes a vital contribution to capitalism by "projecting" a world (ODM 157). It does this by ensuring that the natural world and our fellow human beings show up to us in ways conducive to domination and control. It is, Marcuse tells us, a vehicle of reification, leading us to view nature and one another as mere things to be instrumentalized.

Though the nature and extent of Marcuse's debt to Heidegger is contested, it is undeniable that "The Question Concerning Tech-nology" plays an important part in the chapter on technology in *One-Dimensional Man* (ODM 157). Heidegger provides Marcuse with the idea that the essence of technology is not anything inherently technological, but rather a more abstract stance towards nature and the world: specifically, a view of them as so much raw material to be exploited by human beings. If before it seemed as if Marcuse's thinking about technology and science was vulgar Marxism, it now seems to be virtually the opposite, a quasi-idealist doctrine that affirms the way in which "scientific-technological rationality" affects our mode of engagement with the world.

Crucially Marcuse acknowledges, as many Marxists have, that certain technologies transcend the role they happen to have under capitalism. They might conceivably be employed under socialism as well, where they would be used primarily for the aim of satis-fying human needs and not maximizing corporate profits. Indeed, it has often seemed that socialism would be impossible without the technological achievements of capitalism, and that many of these would survive the transition to a future socialist society. Marcuse himself considers this position: "An electronic computer can serve equally a capitalist or socialist administration" (ODM 157).

Still, Marcuse discerns an especially close connection between technology and post-Fordist capitalism, devoting much of his ana-lysis to the ways technology stabilizes this system. This it does by creating an enormous and powerful apparatus of production to which individuals must submit if they are to earn their livelihoods. It also placates its would-be critics among the working classes and other potentially subversive segments of society with the expanded opportunities for leisure and entertainment it provides.

Marcuse's thought confronts difficult questions concerning the relationship of modern technology to the capitalist mode of production.[2] Is technology biased towards capitalism's relentless drive to maximize profit and power, often by exploiting the natural world? Or is technology instead neutral and therefore in principle capable of being used to promote a world organized by the principle "from each according to his abilities, to each according to his needs"?

Feenberg at one point suggests the intriguing possibility that these possibilities are by no means mutually exclusive, and that, for Marcuse, technology's bias is its neutrality (2023: 138). This last claim seems promising, and to encapsulate Marcuse's ambivalent but by no means inconsistent position. On one hand, modern technology is useful for any and every purpose one might have, and not tied to any particular enterprise. On the other hand, this flexibility and adaptability is precisely what capitalism requires of us. Technology's "purposiveness without a purpose" must therefore be seen as benefitting the capitalist class and the regime of relentless profit-seeking over which it presides.[3]

While I agree that Marcuse regards science and technology as inseparable, the science-focused approach I take in this chapter differs from the technology-focused one. I adopt this approach because I am interested in recovering Marcuse's philosophical legacy and presenting his thought to a contemporary philosophical audience. Focusing on science will allow us to explain Marcuse's perspective on classical issues in twentieth-century philosophy of science: in particular, the controversy between scientific realists and anti-realists. Far from contradicting the technology-focused approach, this science-focused one will complement and confirm it. It will do so by clarifying Marcuse's case for the idea that modern science is proto-technological, showing that even abstract theories anticipate their concrete, practical applications.

At one point, Marcuse even seems to imply that this is true of logic, and the basic operation of forming concepts: "Long before technological man and technological nature emerged as the objects of rational control and calculation, the mind was made susceptible to abstract generalization" (ODM 142). I will leave these and other claims about technology to one side, but Marcuse's idea that even logic is proto-technological suggests the possibility I want to explore here. I mean the possibility that his thinking about science and technology can be reconstructed from the top down, in an effort to show that even pure science anticipates its own application.

A casualty of this approach is that I will not be able address the many difficult questions concerning Marcuse's philosophy of technology: for example, whether and to what extent modern technology might be pervasive in a future socialist society. For this approach, and these questions, I refer the reader to the work of Feenberg and others, which I include in the Further Reading section at the end of the chapter.

How, then, do we characterize Marcuse's philosophy of science? While I acknowledge countervailing tendencies in his thought, and even a certain fundamental ambiguity at the core of it, I propose to interpret Marcuse as a scientific anti-realist. I have already indicated Marcuse's affinities with instrumentalist and pragmatist theories, but "anti-realism" remains the best heading under which to consider his thought. Marcuse is a figure who rejects as naïve the conviction that our scientific theories describe a reality that exists and has the character it does independently of them.

Ironically, much of Marcuse's support for his anti-realist position is drawn from modern science itself, which he thinks has rendered untenable the idea of a reality that exists and has the character it does independent of a human perspective. Beyond modern science, Marcuse also derives support for this tradition from two unexpected sources, the genetic psychologist Piaget and the phenomenologist Husserl. Both supply him with an account of origins of scientific and mathematical concepts that roots them in the embodied experience of socially and historically situated human beings. Marcuse adapts the Piagetian and Husserlian theories to a historical materialist framework, arguing that the determinant of theory-choice is in the last instance the prevailing mode of production.

Since Marcuse advocates a return to the Aristotelian view of nature and of human beings as having essences, potentialities, or natures, rather than the Galilean view of them as matter in motion, we will need to consider the question of whether Marcuse's position is regressive. We will also need to treat his idea that science in a future socialist society might be very different from bourgeois science. Finally, it will be vital to see how not only the natural sciences, but also the social sciences, serve to uphold the status quo and perpetuate the one-dimensional society.

2. Dissolving matter in relations

In attempting to define Marcuse's anti-realist outlook concerning science, we should first note a conviction of his that is non-realist (if not straightforwardly anti-realist). This is Marcuse's conviction that the outlook of modern science itself renders realism untenable. Marcuse says of this outlook that it has dissolved physical matter in relations:

> [it] finds its extreme form in some conceptions of contemporary scientific philosophy, according to which all matter of physical science tends to dissolve in mathematical or logical relations. The very notion of an objective substance, pitted against the subject, seems to disintegrate.
>
> (ODM 151)[4]

Marcuse here invokes the idea that modern science is (pan-) dispositionalist. In other words, modern science, in contrast to its pre-modern counterparts, focuses on the relationships between things or events, but not on the underlying substance, essence, or nature of the things themselves. Marcuse cites a range of figures and doctrines, but the underlying thought is the same. All that we know of things, according to modern science, consists in their dispositions to behave in certain ways under certain conditions. Especially significant are the ways objects behave in relation to us—to our behavior towards them, or our use of measuring instruments on them. As to what the things themselves are, independently of their dispositions to behave or interact with us in these ways, we cannot have the slightest idea.

To capture the contrast between modern science and its predecessors, it may be helpful to invoke a formula of Cassirer's: "substance versus function" (1910). For Cassirer, modern science has moved from the older, Aristotelian idea of substances, each having a distinct essence, to the modern scientific idea of functions, which define a thing solely in terms of relationships. Of course, we refer to substances, in some colloquial sense of the term—protons and electrons, electro-magnetic and gravitational forces, acids and bases. Yet Marcuse thinks this is merely shorthand for the dispositions these things have been observed to have when treated in certain ways. As Marcuse writes, this development "strengthens the shift of theoretical emphasis from the metaphysical 'What is...?' ... to the functional 'How ...?'" (ODM 155)

Swiftly and crudely summarized, Marcuse's idea is then that dispositionalism entails a certain vacuity in the natural world, as if it were a network of relationships, but without genuine nodes. However, it is not yet clear how this point serves Marcuse's project in critical theory. After all, the anti-realist point that concerns us here has been made by numerous philosophers and analysts of modern science, often in the context of very different philosophical projects. It forms part of the basis of Schopenhauer's distinction between the world as will and representation, as well as for the "neutral monism" of Russell (1978: 25), and, finally, for contemporary views like "structural realism" in philosophy of science (views which maintain that it is relations, and not entities, which represent the best hope for scientific realism; Ladyman 2023). Diverse conclusions have been reached from the premise that modern science de-substantializes the world; our task here is to understand how Marcuse's critical theory could be among them.

Before doing so, it is important to qualify Marcuse's view in one respect. The crucial upshot for the controversy between realists and anti-realists is that modern science has rendered vacuous the question of what truly exists out there in the world independently of our perceptions, our interests, and practices: it "denies or even questions the reality of the external world but that, in one way or another, it suspends judgment on what reality itself may be, or considers the very question meaningless and unanswerable" (ODM 154). Yet Marcuse is careful to distinguish this from an outright denial of the reality of the external world. Rather, his point seems to be that modern physics calls into question our ability to know the intrinsic character of nature. While I have described Marcuse as an anti-realist, this is misleading in one respect. Marcuse's position is not that we can definitively say that modern science fails to capture nature's inherent qualities. His position is the more subtle one that whether or not science is successful on this score is unresolvable.

The second development Marcuse sees at work in modern science is the replacement of quality by quantity. To some extent, the way is paved for this development by the passage of substance into function. Essences, natures, and kinds, understood in teleological and normative terms (purposively and in terms of norms of good or healthy functioning), are replaced by dispositions, which operate by efficient causation alone. However, several further steps are needed before a qualitatively defined universe is replaced by a quantitatively defined one:

i.   The first step is to realize that these dispositions are one and all those of matter, and not of unique types of entity. Everything in the Newtonian universe, from a falling apple to a planet, plays by the same set of rules, something not true of the Aristotelian cosmos with its hierarchy of being where the entities on each level possess a distinct nature that dictated a distinct set of goal-directed behaviors.

ii. A second step concerns the properties that remain of matter, properties that lend themselves to quantification. In another context, Marcuse alludes to the early modern distinction between primary and secondary qualities, whereby features like color, taste, and smell are relegated to the domain of the subjective and mind-dependent and only things like shape, size, and motion remain mind-independent and fully real (ODM 142). Yet even this already sparse characterization of the universe will undergo further pruning.

iii. A final step eliminates the last vestige of quality in nature. To be sure, size, shape, and dimension are geometrical (spatial) features, and in that sense qualitative. Yet with the nineteenth-century "algebraization" of geometry, which Marcuse invokes at a key point in the argument (ODM 151), even these last remaining qualitative features evaporate: this development "replaces visible geometric features with purely mental operations" (ODM 151). The reduction of quality to quantity is complete. Not only do

substances give way to functions, but these functions are themselves relations between quantities. Although function is not an
inherently quantitative notion (it simply refers to an operation
on one set of objects yielding another set), its connection to
algebra is not irrelevant in this context either.

In sum: for Marcuse, science has taken us from a world of qualities,
chiefly the essences, kinds, or natures of the substances surrounding
us, to a world of quantities, those figuring in the mathematical
equations that describe relationships and dispositions.

The third development Marcuse detects in modern science,
which is less obvious than the previous two, concerns a growing
dependence of the world on the observing subject—and it is here
that Marcuse's anti-realism verges on a form of idealism. This
subject-dependence does not seem to be entailed by the other two
developments in modern science, de-substantialization and the
transformation of quality into quantity. Yet Marcuse offers a hint
when he refers to "the role of the subject as point of observation,
measurement, and calculation" (ODM 150).

Once substances give way to functions, and these relate quantities,
rather than qualities, there remains a further question concerning
how these quantities themselves arise. A realist would maintain that
they are, in some straightforward sense, in the world. Based on the
reference to measurement, Marcuse would likely object that nothing
in the world comes to us in units of measurement. The conviction
that numbers and mathematical entities are not in any straightforward way found in nature is the inspiration for Hartry Field's *Science
Without Numbers* (1980). The unit of measurement must be stipulated,
Marcuse argues. He further infers that this is a process that reflects
human interests, practices, and capacities.

A more subtle realist could rejoin that it is not the quantities,
measured in units, which are found in the world, but rather the
corresponding unit-free magnitudes. This is the response to Field
given by Peacocke (2019). There may not have been kilometers
before the metric system, but there was the corresponding magni-
tude in nature.

To find resources for a response in Marcuse's writings, we have to
delve more deeply into Marcuse's study of modern science. In this

connection, it is noteworthy that Marcuse's discussion seems to be informed by two developments in modern science: the theory of relativity and quantum mechanics. Marcuse seldom if ever explicitly discusses these scientific theories, but they are in the background of much of the philosophy he cites; for example, passages from Born and Heisenberg. It therefore seems warranted to ask how both of these developments might lend support to an anti-realist view. I take each in turn, mindful that I am elaborating on what are little more than suggestions in Marcuse's text.

i. Special relativity plausibly shows that simultaneity is relative to an inertial frame of reference, and therefore dependent on an observer. Among the consequences of this are length contraction (or "Lorentz transformations"), the phenomenon in which a moving object's length is shorter than in its own frame of reference. Marcuse acknowledges the perspective of Born and others who argue that there is nothing especially observer-relative about relativity. Instead, quantities of motion are relative to certain other quantities of motion. Yet Marcuse points out that this relationalism itself yields a form of dependence upon an observer who determines which quantities will serve as a privileged standard. In this framework, then, quantities of motion "can be meaningfully objective only for a subject" (ODM 153). Here, Marcuse allows for a qualification to the idea of observer-relativity, a qualification introduced by Reichenbach: observer-relativity need not mean relativity to any particular observer, but rather to a kind of generic observer (ODM 152).

ii. Quantum mechanics can plausibly be said to have shown that, before the location of a particle is measured, all that we have is a cloud of probabilities. This is an idea contained in a passage Marcuse cites from the physicist Werner Heisenberg, the father of the "uncertainty principle" (ODM 153). Here too there is potential observer-dependence, since it is the observer whose activity of measurement causes the cloud of probabilities to resolve into a single value (or cause the "wave-function" to "collapse"). Of course, the question of how best to interpret quantum mechanics is controversial, and the quasi-idealist notion that observers affect the world by measuring it, though embraced by members of the Copenhagen school, has been rejected by many scientists philosophers of science. Judging by the figures he cites, e.g., Heisenberg and Born, Marcuse is likely sympathetic to this interpretation.

Another theme in Marcuse's philosophy of science is the role of abstraction in science. For Marcuse, the abstraction introduced into the world by modern science is not limited to the object of natural scientific inquiry, i.e., nature. Rather, the abstraction undergone by the object occasions a corresponding abstraction undergone by the observing *subject*. As we have seen, nature is understood in modern science according to purely quantitative terms, abstracting from quality; moreover, this presupposes a subject who conducts measurement. Yet if that is so, then this subject too must be abstract in the following sense. It is reduced to its measuring capacity—or, at any rate, to the cluster of capacities relevant for it to fix the abstract quantitative character of nature. The subject too is divested of its qualitative characteristics, since all of these are irrelevant to measurement: "In science, the medium is the observing, measuring, calculating, experimenting subject divested of all other qualities; the abstract subject projects and defines the abstract object" (ODM 190). Crucially, this will include individuality, inasmuch as it effaces many of the qualities that mark one human being as different from the rest. All that is left is a generic inquirer.

The rise of the abstract object has thus been accompanied by the rise of the abstract subject. This figure will be recognized as the protagonist of much of the philosophy of the early-modern period: Descartes' cogito, Kant's "I think," Husserl's transcendental consciousness, and so on—none of whom are the concrete individuals with distinct identities whom we encounter in our day-to-day lives. Yet as we will soon see, Marcuse clearly thinks of this abstract subject as corresponding not only to innovations in philosophy but also to the capitalist economy that is taking shape at this time. The abstract subject of scientific inquiry prefigures the abstract subject of capitalist exchange, the buyer or seller whose name, history, and background we need not know so long as they are willing and able to buy and sell. Finally, it is important to recall that human beings, like the natural world, constitute objects of scientific inquiry. Therefore the abstraction characteristic of our conception of the subject, like that of the object, threatens to distort our image of the world at both poles.

Marcuse's idea of a parallelism between the scientific knower and the world that is scientifically known has another dimension. Marcuse shares with Weber and other theorists of modernity the idea that it is an epoch in which value and fact have become distinguished, and this separation is particularly extreme in modern science. Indeed, this separation of fact from value Marcuse sees as occurring on the side of the object as well as on that of the subject.

On one hand, the mathematization of nature by Galileo banishes final causes, goals, and natures, and together with them the values in terms of which entities can be judged: "The quantification of nature, which led to its explication in terms of mathematical structures, separated reality from all inherent ends and, consequently, separated the true from the good, science from ethics" (ODM 150).

On the other hand, the subject who scientifically studies nature is one that has had to leave aside its ethical or political commitments, in the name of objectivity: "no matter how constitutive may be the role of the subject as point of observation, measurement, and calculation, this subject cannot play its scientific role as ethical or aesthetic or political agent" (ODM 150). Though more effective at scientific investigation of nature than its predecessors, this subject is also likely to be less effective at resisting the social order. This subject is the protagonist of a one-dimensional (conformist) society.

To sum up, Marcuse finds in modern science four decisive developments:

i.   The dissolution of material substances in webs of relations.
ii. The replacement of qualitative features, such as the essences of these substances, by quantitative ones, such as the primary qualities of shape, size, and number.
iii. The growing dependence of nature's quantitative features on the observer who measures them.
iv. The abstract nature of this observer, who constitutes an equally abstract world of objects.

3. Structuralism and phenomenology: Piaget and Husserl

While I have suggested that Marcuse is embracing an idealist view of science, this designation is potentially misleading. This is not only because, at one point, Marcuse takes pains to differentiate the value-laden idealism of his hero Hegel from the one-dimensional universe of modern science. It is also because, in insisting that the world described by science depends on us, Marcuse does not necessarily mean to refer to each of our individual minds. His is not Berkeleyan idealism, nor even Kantian idealism if this is understood as the thesis that reality depends on something partially transcending particular individuals: human reason. Rather, as soon becomes clear, the world of modern science is said to depend upon other dimensions of the human being than its cognitive apparatus. Seeing these other dimensions requires us to take a wider view of human beings, looking beyond their capacity for scientific inquiry.

The first of these is practice, and it is foregrounded in Marcuse's use of insights from the developmental psychologist and structuralist Jean Piaget. In Marcuse's retelling, Piaget is credited with the idea that even basic mathematical concepts are abstractions from types of action undertaken by a subject on an object.[5] For example, take the concept of a set (or a number, operation, etc.). Suppose that one discovers that it cannot be employed by children who do not first master certain bodily movements, i.e., grouping items together. Next comes the crucial step. One can argue, on this basis, that the concept of a set constitutively involves these bodily movements. In other words, the claim is not just about the genesis of a concept in the mind of the child, but about the nature of the thing that concept denotes. It is fundamentally opposed to the Platonist idea that a set is an abstract object, subsisting in some non-physical realm. It is further opposed to the nominalist or reductionist idea that sets are convenient fictions, imaginary, etc. The upshot is that the context for our most fundamental scientific and mathematical concepts is not theory but practice, even if this is not reflected on the surface of the concepts themselves. Although we will not dwell on it here, an important point in Piaget that Marcuse also picks up on is the idea that reality, though it depends on us, cannot be exhausted by us either. In other words, there is a contribution by the subject and the object, and neither can be eliminated from the analysis. To this extent, realism and idealism are each one-sided. This is an ambiguity we have seen surface in Marcuse's position before. Though his position is not straightforwardly realist, he does, to some extent, refuse the choice between realism and idealism.

Yet while Marcuse accepts Piaget's claim that scientific and mathematical concepts have an inherent connection to human action, he disagrees about the nature of those actions. Marcuse detects in Piaget an effort to limit the scope of human actions to only those immediately relevant to science and mathematics; for example, the rotation and transformation of shaped objects as a precursor to knowledge of geometry. Marcuse thinks this is question-begging, and seems to propose a more ecumenical account wherein all manner of human actions enter into the constitution of scientific and mathematical concepts:

> granted that all scientific knowledge presupposes coordination of particular actions, I do not see why such coordination is "by its very nature" logico-mathematical—unless the "particular actions" are the scientific operations of modern physics, in which case the interpretation would be circular.
>
> (ODM 166)

Obviously, Marcuse's is a more thoroughgoing pragmatism than Piaget intends, since Marcuse wants science and mathematics to be seen in the context of a potentially unlimited field of possible human actions and therefore of the human interests these actions serve. This interest in going beyond Piaget doubtless informs Marcuse's turn to another figure: Husserl.

While Marcuse approves of Piaget's pragmatic version of subject-dependence, he deems another theory superior because of the importance it attaches to the socio-historical milieu in which the human being finds herself: the later Husserl's account of science. Here, we must recall that it is the need for measurement above all which figures in Marcuse's case for the anti-realist thesis that the world of modern science depends on human beings. At least in Marcuse's retelling, measurement is also the later Husserl's main theme: in particular, measurement figures in an attempt to show that the world of Galilean science reflects the practical, everyday context in which human life is ordinarily lived (the *Lebenswelt*—"life-world").[6]

In particular, Husserl claims that the core concepts of modern science are abstracted aspects of the practical activities of land-surveying and measurement (ODM 167; Husserl 1970: 28, 49).[7] These practices involve a number of idealizations. For example, they presuppose a form of consistency on the part of the world that makes possible stable expectations. One assumes that the standards of measurement and the corresponding properties of the things measured do not change in some subtle way.[8] These practices also presuppose the possibility of various types of projections and anticipations (expectations) concerning as of yet unmeasured spaces to be encountered only in future times.

The justification for these presuppositions is above all pragmatic. In other words, they are legitimate because they are required by the practice itself, and cannot be justified in any other way. They certainly cannot be empirically verified. For example, when we are guided by these presuppositions, we are assuming that our instruments and the world do not change in certain ways. Yet sensory perception would not register the relevant type of change.

For Husserl, these unavoidable presuppositions of our practices of measurement and land-surveying are fateful. They are the unacknowledged basis of the scientist's belief in the stability of nature, at least insofar as it is characterized in quantitative terms. This means that science and mathematics are unavoidably rooted in the human life-world. We cannot say that beings with a radically different form of life than our own would employ these tools. We cannot use them to speculate about the world as seen from a fundamentally different perspective. Of course, they may allow us to rise above certain parochialisms; for example, our view of the world in terms of tastes, smells, threats, and opportunities. Yet they do not allow us to achieve anything like a view from nowhere. They always reflect the human standpoint, that of creatures who have certain of our interests and practices. Marcuse clearly agrees with Husserl, at least to this extent.

A final implication of Husserl's account is that science, no matter how often and how radically it revolutionizes our conception of the universe, remains "static" and "conservative" in one crucial respect: it cannot transcend the society (the life-world) that forms its unacknowledged condition of possibility:

> With respect to the institutionalized forms of life, science (pure as well as applied) would thus have a stabilizing, static, conservative function. Even its most revolutionary achievements

would only be construction and destruction in line with a specific experience and organization of reality.

(ODM 169)

Hence Marcuse qualifies the Enlightenment idea that scientific progress is a progressive force which leads to social and political change. For Marcuse, there is an upper limit to the progress that can be achieved in this way. Science cannot overturn the life-world in which it is rooted, one which Marcuse thinks is the world of modern capitalism. Since this Marxist claim is not obviously entailed by Husserl's phenomenological account of science, we need to address this seeming lacuna in Marcuse's argument.

Yet even this consideration of Piaget and Husserl's roles in Marcuse's distinctive version of anti-realism does not get us all the way to his unique view, which has a distinct, "materialist" (Marxist) dimension.[9] We can see this by addressing a lacuna in the Husserlian account just sketched. On this account, the life-world is the hidden presupposition of modern science, and its attempt to reduce nature to abstract quantity. But which life-world, exactly? For all we have been told, the life-world in question might simply be a generic one, present at all times and places, where human beings have dealings with nature that require the practice of measurement. Certainly, this description of the life-world does not help us choose between different Marxist epochs in the history of production: slavery, feudalism, capitalism.

However, it seems clear that Marcuse takes a step beyond Husserl, and is thinking of the *life-world of modern capitalism* as the basis of modern science. Though not spelled out, Marcuse's reasoning is that this is a system in which abstract quantitative metrics are especially vital. This is due to the constant and overwhelming need to generate an abstract form of value: more specifically, exchange value, the abstract numerical ratio in which commodities can be traded for other commodities. It is further characteristic of capitalism to deemphasize use-value, the qualitatively specific and concrete human needs and purposes a commodity fulfills. For Marcuse, then, there is a connection between the perspective of modern science, on one hand, and modern capitalism, on the other:

Individual, non-quantifiable qualities stand in the way of an organization of men and things in accordance with the

measurable power to be extracted from them. But this is a specific, socio-historical project, and the consciousness which
undertakes this project is the hidden subject of Galilean science;
the latter is the technic, the art of anticipation extended in
infinity.

(ODM 168)

In response, an opponent could grant that there is such a parallel
between modern (Galilean) science and capitalism, but deny that
the latter explains the former. Marcuse himself anticipates this perspective: "Between the two processes of scientific and societal quantification, is there parallelism and causation, or is their connection
simply the work of sociological hindsight?" (ODM 161). Marcuse
turns on the idea that scientific inquiry is always situated, occurring
against the backdrop of a given social order and the power-relations
and interests which characterize it:

> The preceding discussion proposed that the new scientific ration-
> ality was in itself, in its very abstractness and purity, operational
> inasmuch as it developed under an instrumentalist horizon.
> Observation and experiment, the methical organization and
> coordination of data, propositions, and conclusions never pro-
> ceed in an unstructured, neutral, theoretical space. The project
> of cognition involves operations on objects, or abstractions from
> objects which occur in a given universe of discourse and action.
> Science observes, calculates, and theorizes from a position in
> this universe.

(ODM 161)

This response seems insufficient. Of course, nobody would deny that
science takes place in a social context, and that it may (on occasion)
serve prevailing interests. Yet this does not by itself undermine the
claim of science to be a true and objective description of the natural world. Here, it would seem that Marcuse has committed a
non-sequitur. From the fact that science serves the ruling class, he
has concluded this is all it does—and that its claims to carve reality
at the joints are exaggerated.

Yet a closer look reveals an intermediate premise; namely, the idea
that science is not primarily and in the first instance a theoretical but

a practical activity. Here we need also to recall the previous steps in Marcuse's argument. These steps involve various claims to the effect that the very concepts in which scientific theories are formulated presuppose the standpoint of an embodied human being in a particular social and historical context. These claims are meant to invalidate the idea that such concepts have been, empirically or otherwise, read off of the natural world. It is not just that we have, on the one hand, an account of the genesis of scientific mathematical concepts, and, on the other, an account of what makes up or constitutes the real phenomena they describe. Rather, the genetic account implies a constitutive one. The view we are left with is one in which the connection between science and society, when spelled out completely, forecloses on the possibility of a realist view whereby our theories and concepts correspond to a mind-independent reality that is isomorphic with them.

4. Re-enchanting nature?

Few contemporary anti-realists intend to reject the modern, scientific worldview, and their position is compatible with the idea that Galilean science is a genuine advance over its predecessors. Yet Marcuse's position differs slightly, and in a way that is somewhat alarming. Marcuse, we may recall, holds a view of nature closer to the traditional Aristotelian one, and this raises the concern that his position is anti-modern, regressive, or retrograde. According to such a view, nature is not homogeneous matter, subject to one set of laws of motion. It is, rather, made up of different types of things, each of which strives to realize distinct goals. Yet Marcuse denies that he is attempting to turn back the clock and "re-enchant nature":[10]

> The preceding discussion seems to suggest not only the inner limitations and prejudices of the scientific method but also its historical subjectivity. Moreover, it seems to imply the need for some sort of "qualitative physics," revival of teleological philosophies, etc. I admit that this suspicion is justified, but at this point, I can only assert that no such obscurantist ideas are intended.
>
> (ODM 49)

These assurances are welcome, but insufficient. One would hope Marcuse could explain why his position, though critical of modern science and sympathetic to Aristotle, does not constitute a relapse into a pre-modern point of view.

Here, we might think of McDowell's treatment of "reenchanting the world." Though himself an Aristotelian, McDowell clearly regards any simple form of re-enchantment as a non-starter. If there is a way to rehabilitate Aristotle, it cannot be by simply turning one's back on the modern scientific world-view and ignoring its achievements. In McDowell's view, re-enchantment will come via the complicated idea that sensibility is always already informed by our conceptual capacities and that conceptual thought therefore has no outer bound. Does Marcuse have a comparably sophisticated proposal? Or is he simply proposing a regression to pre-Galilean science?

We can focus this question with another: what, exactly, does Marcuse mean when he distances himself from any simple "revival of teleological philosophies"? Marcuse may simply mean that, though he is indeed an Aristotelian essentialist, he does not want to be associated with the most extreme versions of such a conservative position. For example, these might include Thomisms, vitalisms, astrology, esotericism, Whitehead's process philosophy, or various mystical and theosophical views. However, Marcuse may mean something more subtle, such as that his essentialist position is not Aristotle's. As we know, Marcuse's thought is fed by other currents, some more idealist or pragmatist. Hence it may be that his essentialism is intended less as a metaphysical thesis intended to "carve reality at the joints" than as an expression of human interests or perspective. Here it is worth noting that Marcuse is fairly reticent about the essences of things in the natural (non-human) world, and he tends instead to emphasize the essences of human beings, institutions, and practices. Hence it is not altogether clear he means to contradict modern science. He can concede the correctness of a physicist's view of such things as matter in motion, but insist on a home for the alternative view of it as answering to human purposes.

One indication that Marcuse's Aristotelian essentialism is not of the orthodox variety comes to the fore in a dispute with Dewey (ODM 171). Dewey also addresses the contrast between modern science and pre-modern worldviews, especially that of the ancient

Greeks. For Dewey, these can be explained in terms of a contrast between contemplative and active stances towards the world (ODM 171). In a way somewhat reminiscent of Marcuse, Dewey regards the modern view of nature, in terms of mathematical quantity, as informed by a desire to dominate and control the natural world (and one another). Yet Dewey goes awry, according to Marcuse, when he argues that the ancient, teleological view of nature, in terms of essences, goals, and purposes, reflects a less active and more con-templative mode—one Dewey praises for the "aesthetic" enjoyment it affords (ODM 171). For Marcuse, both ancient and modern views, teleological and mechanistic paradigms, reflect human interests and purposes. Each world-view, when inspected closely, reveals itself to possess conflicting tendencies, e.g. toward domination and toward liberation: "Classical thought was sufficiently committed to the logic of secular control, and there is a sufficient component of indictment and refusal in modern thought to vitiate John Dewey's formulation" (ODM 171). Crucially for our purposes, it would seem that Marcuse does not regard the ancient teleological view as a purely disinter-ested account of the workings of nature. Rather, this view too is served by human interests.[11]

5. The history of science

Interestingly, Marcuse does not deny that modern science more closely approximates ideals of truth and objectivity than earlier forms of science, and one wonders how he can reconcile this with his claim that even the most advanced science reflects human interests and practices. As he writes:

> contemporary science is of immensely greater objective validity than its predecessors. One might even add that, at present, the scientific method is the only method that can claim such val-idity; the interplay of hypotheses and observable facts validates the hypotheses and establishes the facts.

> (ODM 170)

Marcuse's position is ambivalent. On one hand, he appears to think we can evaluate modern science as superior to its predecessors in terms of the goals of objectivity and truth. On the other, he seems to maintain that even the most objective, truthful science we possess cannot be defended in realist terms; for example, as corresponding to a reality independent of us.

At one point, Marcuse makes a claim that promises to clarify his ambivalence. He endorses a model of historical and intellectual change whereby scientific theories or political institutions give rise to problems they cannot solve, and as a result go under. In other words, they contain within themselves the seeds of their own destruction. As he writes, "Aristotelian science was falsified on the basis of its achievements; if capitalism were falsified by communism, it would be by virtue of its own achievements" (ODM 225). The resonances of this model with Hegel and Marx, in the philosophy of history, and with Kuhn, in the philosophy of science, seem clear. The model hinted at is one in which theories are not simply superseded by others that arise exogenously to them, but rather self-undermine and then produce their own replacements in an endogenous process. On such a model of theories as historically evolving and self-correcting, we have a clear basis for regarding some theories as superior to others. This is so even though we may lack any independent grounds for claiming that one theory corresponds more closely to reality than another.

This is not the final world for Marcuse, as he looks forward to a future science that will improve upon the current one. As one might predict, this is the science of a future socialist society. It is a science freed from the distortions imposed upon it by the imperatives of capitalist production and imperialist expansion. Just what these distortions are and how they will be lifted is difficult to discern, however, and Marcuse is less than transparent on this question. Might Marcuse be saying that it is in its practical application, rather than in its theoretical structure, that science is beholden to either capitalism or socialism? Marcuse seems to intend something stronger:

> The point which I am trying to make is that science, by virtue of its own method and concepts, has projected and promoted a universe in which the domination of nature has remained linked to the domination of man—a link which tends to be fatal to this universe as a whole. Nature, scientifically comprehended and

mastered, reappears in the technical apparatus of production and destruction which sustains and improves the life of the individuals while subordinating them to the masters of the apparatus. Thus the rational hierarchy merges with the social one. If this is the case, then the change in the direction of progress, which might sever this fatal link, would also affect the very structure of science—the scientific project. Its hypotheses, without losing their rational character, would develop in an essentially different experimental context (that of a pacified world); consequently, science would arrive at essentially different concepts of nature and establish essentially different facts. The rational society subverts the idea of Reason.

(ODM 170)

Socialism "severs the link" because, while it continues to "dominate nature" in some sense, it ceases to use this as a pretext for "dominating man." Under such a system, the power we have over nature is used to benefit all mankind, and not just a ruling class. The domination of nature is undertaken for the sake of collective human freedom. So much is familiar. More difficult to decipher is Marcuse's claims about the continuities and discontinuities between bourgeois science and its socialist successor.

On one hand, he claims that hypotheses will be upheld ("retain their rational character"), suggesting that much science would be retained. This is encouraging, since one would hope that Marcuse does not want to jettison Galilean science on the grounds that it arose during the rise of modern capitalism. On the other hand, Marcuse suggests that these same hypotheses will be recast in terms of "new concepts" and "different facts." The explanation Marcuse gives of this is that the "experimental context" will differ. It will be that of a "pacified nature."

Here, I want to propose that Marcuse is invoking the opposition between an ancient concept of nature, in terms of essence, and a modern one, in terms of quantity. The latter is conducive to simple domination, the former a vital resource in the struggle for freedom. If that is so, then one expects the ancient conception to undergo a kind of revival under socialism, such that "new concepts" and "new facts" reflecting an Aristotelian essentialist outlook appear once more. Marcuse is clearly anticipating some type of rapprochement between this traditional outlook and modern science, as he wants to retain its achievements. Yet he does not say more about how this rapprochement would proceed, and it is probably not wise to speculate. Here it is worth remembering Marcuse's Husserl-inspired idea that modern, Galilean science presupposes a particular life-world, implying that a changed life-world would result in a new science.

6. Realist rejoinders

Although I have characterized Marcuse's position as anti-realist, pragmatist, and instrumentalist, there is an occasional countervailing, realist tendency. For example, Marcuse concedes the realist claim that the stars Galileo observed are the same as those Aristotle theorized, seeming to admit that the natural world exists and has the character it does independently of our theories about it. Yet a closer look at the relevant passage reveals that even this realist stance leaves room for an element of idealism:

> The stars which Galileo observed were the same in classical antiquity, but the different universe of discourse and action— in short, the different social reality—opened the new direction and range of observation, and the possibilities of ordering the observed data. I am not concerned here with the historical relation between scientific and societal rationality in the beginning of the modern period. It is my purpose to demonstrate the internal instrumentalist character of this scientific rationality by virtue of which it is a priori technology, and the a priori of a specific technology—namely, technology as form of social control and domination.
>
> (ODM 161)

This passage reveals Marcuse's position to be nothing if not ambivalent. Even if it is the case that nature exists and has the character it does independently of us, there is still room for two respects in which nature might depend on us anyway.

First, our social surroundings and historical situation may influence which dimension of reality we choose to study, even if they do not fundamentally alter the nature of reality itself. A version of this point is familiarly made about the special and applied sciences; for example, strains of AIDS that predominantly affect impoverished people in sub-Saharan Africa were, at least for a period, less well understood, less studied, and therefore less treatable than those affecting wealthier Westerners. One could understand Marcuse's hybrid realist-idealism as a generalization of this point. Reality may exist independently of us, but our interests dictate which aspects of it are likely to feature in scientific research and technological innovation.

Second, Marcuse evidently thinks that history may influence the way data is organized, if not the data itself. It is a truism that scientific theories, rather than simply repeating information we have gleaned from nature in a set of true propositions, present us also with the systematic interrelations between this data. Presumably, Marcuse thinks that these interrelations are, in some instances, underdetermined by the data. Otherwise, there would be no distinct problem of how to link the propositions of a science, as opposed to that of merely discovering and enumerating them. Yet, Marcuse seems to be claiming, a certain perspective-dependence arises in the task of interlinking true propositions about the world. In particular, the techniques available for organizing these propositions, as well as the interests that dictate how this is done, may differ according to the historical epoch in which we find ourselves.

One obvious example of the non-empirical principles dictating how empirical data is organized: logic. Perhaps surprisingly, Marcuse is emphatic that our choice logic is itself something relative to our practical interests and historical situation, and he is interested in the differences among logics:

> However, while all thought stands under the rule of logic, the unfolding of this logic is different in the various modes of thought. Classical formal and modern symbolic logic, transcendental and dialectical logic—each rules over a different universe of discourse and experience. They all developed within the historical continuum of domination to which they pay tribute.
>
> (ODM 171)

Marcuse's position here resembles that of contemporary logical pluralists, at least up to a point. Like them, he does not believe in the one true logic. Unlike them, however, Marcuse does not just regard different logics as suited for different purposes. Rather, he believes each is indexed to a different epoch in the history of production. The throughline in this history is humankind's ever-growing domination of nature, and Marcuse believes that each logic, in some way, reflects the exigencies of a distinct approach to dominating nature: scientifically, technologically, conceptually and so on. To take one example, Marcuse locates in the simple logical procedure of subsuming an object under a concept an attempt to lay in place the conditions necessary for controlling nature: "subsuming particular cases under a universal, in subjecting it to their universal, thought attains mastery over the particular cases. It becomes capable not only of comprehending but also of acting upon them, controlling them" (ODM 171). In the present context, the importance of this point is that it introduces another historically relative ingredient into science. Once again, sciences are not just sets of true propositions, but also ways of connecting these in a system. The principles guiding these connections and resulting in the edifice of science are logical—and logic, for Marcuse, reflects shifting historical interests.

Unfortunately, it is far from clear that the hybrid realist-idealist view Marcuse advocates does not, in the end, reduce to a form of (non-mentalistic) idealism. While it is tempting to maintain that Aristotle and Galileo's stars are the same entities, characterized in different ways, this seems implausible. In short, the profound differences between the Aristotelian and Galilean outlooks are likely to extend to the way stars themselves are understood; for example, Aristotle thought the heavenly bodies were ensouled, something hard to find echoes of in modern physics. Once one acknowledges that not only the laws of nature, but also the entities suspended in them, differ along with the framework, there seems to be little content left to the claim that it is nevertheless the same nature that Galileo and Aristotle described. Nature here is simply an empty placeholder, rather than a substantive category. There is some X that Galileo thought of as matter in motion and Aristotle thought of as a great chain of being. This may qualify as realism, but only in a technical sense. There is something to which our theories are one and all answerable, and serving to disclose—but what it is we cannot say. It is like Kant's unknowable thing-in-itself; and as with the thing-in-itself one is tempted to ask as Kant's earliest critics did: if we cannot know anything about it, then how can we know it exists?

Still, the analogy with Kant may be fruitful. In the final analysis, Marcuse's picture resembles a historical-materialist version of Kant's. Just as Kant's transcendental subject stands over and against a world of things which, though they exist, are unknowable "in themselves," so too Marcuse's "collective subject" of production stands over and against a nature which, though it exists, is unknowable apart from our interests and practices. Kant's immediate followers in the idealist tradition face the difficult question of whether it is consistent to maintain both that this object is unknowable and that it exists. Once one accepts that its properties are not the ones it is seen to have from the human standpoint, one is left with the conclusion that it might as well be nothing. Like Kant's position, as seen by the post-Kantian idealists, Marcuse's conception of nature teeters on the brink of absolute idealism.

7. From natural to social science

So far, we have considered Marcuse's views on the natural sciences, but it is important not to forget his views on social science as well. We will begin by considering Marcuse's critical treatment of the social science of his time and place: America in the postwar era. Marcuse criticizes this social science as complacent. He maintains that it is only capable of improving the functioning of the society in which we currently live, but not of criticizing this society and advocating its replacement with another:

> If the given form of society is and remains the ultimate frame of reference for theory and practice, there is nothing wrong with this sort of sociology and psychology. It is more human and more productive to have good labor-management relations than bad ones, to have pleasant rather than unpleasant working conditions, to have harmony instead of conflict between the desires of the customers and the needs of business and politics.
> (ODM 110)

For Marcuse, the tacit purpose of much social science is administration, not critique. It helps ensure that existing institutions are efficient but does not question their right to exist.

Why, exactly, does social science exhibit this complacency? Why does it tend to serve administration, rather than resistance?[12] Marcuse's answer is that the social science of his day relies on a questionable philosophy of science. In particular, it relies on a questionable "positivist" view of the type of concepts that are admissible in a legitimately scientific theory, namely, those with obvious correlates in the empirical world. One could even say its deficit is semantic, in that it relies on a faulty theory of the meanings that terms in our theories have (or ought to have): specifically, a theory which refuses to admit meanings deemed "unrealistic." As he writes, "once the 'unrealistic' excess of meaning is abolished, the investigation is locked within the vast confine in which the established society validates and invalidates propositions" (ODM 117). Why, though, does this positivistic approach hamper social science?

Marcuse believes the social sciences are limited in their critical potential by their allegiance to a theory of concepts which he calls "operationalist," though the label is somewhat misleading. As usual, Marcuse is less careful than he might be in grouping his opponents. Marcuse associates the operationalist doctrine with a set of opponents from somewhat disparate schools of thought: behaviorism, positivism, the Vienna circle, early Wittgenstein, the naturalism of Quine, and so on. Central to the theory Marcuse opposes is the idea that concepts, as we find them, exhibit features which must be eliminated if they are to serve scientific inquiry. These features are objectionable because they are not empirically verifiable, i.e., cannot be justified on the basis of the observations we make using our sense-organs (or other instruments). One of them is generality, the way in which concepts are universals ranging over a large number of particular objects. This is a feature of concepts first noticed by Plato and made the basis of his theory of forms. Indeed, Marcuse makes favorable remarks about "realism about universals," even seeming to endorse it. Marcuse's opponents are not only empiricists, but also, in a sense, nominalists. They want to reduce concepts to sets of sensible particulars.

When it comes to concepts pertaining to human conduct, these opponents, especially the behaviorists, intend to reduce them to "mental operations." By this, Marcuse really means functions whose input are stimuli, and whose output are responses. He is criticizing a view of concepts like goodness, justice, pleasure, etc. which reduces them to generalizations about what people are in fact disposed to find good, just, pleasurable, etc. In this way, these concepts have their critical potential eliminated. There is no longer room for an idea of goodness that transcends what is found good at a particular time and place. Hence Marcuse is setting a normative understanding of concepts against the neutral one favored by his opponents. Just for ease of understanding, I will refer to these opposing theories of concepts as the "operationalist" and "the Platonic."

Though we have already considered Marcuse's objections to this "operationalist" (positivist, behaviorist) theory of concepts, it remains to be seen how it is he thinks it undermines social science. Here, Marcuse's view is basically that this theory of concepts leads social scientists to misunderstand their subjects, the people they study. It is not the "operationalized" concepts which figure in ordinary people's lives, but rather the more Platonic variety, Marcuse thinks. To illustrate this, Marcuse considers a classic of industrial sociology, a study of relations between owners and workers in a firm: Roethlisberger and Dickson's *Management and the Worker* (1939). This study collected workers' grievances over working conditions and wages. Yet the social scientists misunderstood these grievances. They did so by seeking to replace the concepts used by the workers with others that were allegedly more scientific. The workers' concepts were general and normatively laden, but the researchers viewed them as vague, unverifiable, and subjective. Hence the researchers sought to translate these concepts into scientific ones. To take some examples, workers would complain that washrooms were unsanitary, wages were too low, that conditions were dangerous (ODM 111–14). The researchers translated these statements into ones like "on such and such occasion, I went into the washroom and the washbowl had some dirt in it" or "the piece wages are too low [for] a particular worker whose wife is in the hospital." This retranslation, done in the name of scientific rigor, had the effect of minimizing the workers' concerns and allowing for remedies that were superficial.

Marcuse sees in the workers' lack of precision a certain insight. This is the realization that the problems they face are, indeed, general rather than particular; for example, the plight of all wage earners under capitalism, and not just this (or these) particular one(s) at the factory. In other words, they implicate the entire capitalist mode of social organization, and not these isolated manifestations of it. Marcuse implies that this method of operationalizing concepts has bled into other areas of social life. In our "therapeutic" culture, for example, we are encouraged to translate our general dissatisfaction with society and the world into terms applicable to our particular life-experiences. Marcuse's proposal is that this is not necessarily an improvement in clarity, and that the truth of one's situation may be better captured in general terms rather than in personal ones.

What, then, is the alternative Marcuse envisions to modern social science? Marcuse concedes that this social science may be useful for facilitating the smooth operation of the capitalist system. However, he goes on to add a crucial caveat:

> But the rationality of this kind of social science appears in a different light if the given society, while remaining the frame of reference, becomes the object of a critical theory which aims at the very structure of this society, present in all particular facts and conditions and determining their place and their function.
>
> (ODM 110)

Essentially, Marcuse's alternative to American social science is Hegelian Marxism, which is to say Marxism as Lukács and the Frankfurt School understood it. On this interpretation, Marx's critique of capitalism addresses the system in its "totality," treating it as a structure in which each part can only be understood by being related to the principle of the whole. Contra industrial sociology, a particular worker's wages are not too low because his wife is in the hospital and he has recently had to reduce his shifts. They are too low because he is a member of the proletariat, selling his labor-power for a wage commensurate with the cost of reproducing it. This would include the food, shelter, and clothing he needs in order to be capable of returning to work the following day and performing his role. It might not include healthcare for his dependents, however. Nor would it necessarily include his mental health, upon which his wife's calamity will have taken its toll. The implication of Marx's analysis is that the problems of each worker are those of the working class in general. To the extent we are focused on the particular details of a particular worker's situation, we lose the plot. It is understandable that industrial sociology would be uninterested in this type of analysis. Its aim is reform, whereas Marx sought revolution.

If Marcuse's objection to natural science in the modern world is that it leads us to ignore the essences, natures, or potentials of things in favor of their quantitative characteristics, his objection to social science is that it leads us to ignore the social totality, in favor of the local, contingent happenings in individual people's lives. For Marcuse, these errors are interrelated, as we can only understand the repressed potentials of human beings in the context of the social totality that produces and reproduces them through the labor process. Marcuse's rejection of the natural and social sciences, at least in their more positivistic orientation, amounts to a plea for a Hegelian Marxism infused with Aristotelean essentialist currents. It is not so much a plea for alternative social science as for traditional philosophy, at least whatever of it remains admissible in critical theory.

One might object that Marcuse's critique of modern social science is unlikely to generalize, since he focuses on only one specific type of research: industrial sociology. While I will not go into the rest of Marcuse's critique in detail, it is worth noting that Marcuse attempts to demonstrate that the positivistic tendency he identifies in industrial sociology is at work in other social sciences as well—and to similarly baleful effect. Marcuse considers political science, public opinion polls, market research, and other areas. Admittedly, Marcuse does not consider cutting-edge, academic social science, which one might think is less prone to being exploited by the ruling class for its ends. However, this would be consistent with the Frankfurt School's general position, which is that social science is capable of being carried on in both "traditional" (non-emancipatory) and "critical" ways.

Summary

Though philosophy of technology has formed the focus of many recent treatments of Marcuse, this chapter examines his philosophy of science. For Marcuse, modern science does not, as the realist thinks, "carve reality at the joints." Indeed, it has rendered "vacuous" the question of what reality may be in itself, apart from its relational or dispositional properties. From Piaget, Marcuse inherits the idea that basic logical and mathematical concepts derive from the embodied person's transactions with the world. From Husserl, Marcuse adds to this model the idea that basic equivalences or identities found in science reveal its tacit reliance on our everyday activities; in particular, our practice of measurement. Marcuse's position seems compatible with an element of realism, as when he says that the stars in the night sky were the same for Galileo as for Aristotle.

Marcuse's critique of modern science is undertaken in the service of a form of conceptual realism, which risks rendering his position backward looking or regressive. Yet Marcuse denies that he is simply seeking to "re-enchant" nature in the way that Thomists and others do. Instead, he proposes that this conceptual realism is reconcilable with a historical materialist outlook, though he does not spell out exactly how this is meant to occur. Marcuse is also a critic of contemporary social science, whose positivist presuppositions he thinks encourage a myopic perspective on social programs and prevent an adequate grasp of the social whole.

Notes

1 I am here following Feenberg, who explores Marcuse's ambivalence about technology (2023: Ch. 5). Feenberg is uncertain as to whether Marcuse ever resolves this ambivalence. One of Feenberg's many intriguing ideas is that this ambivalence can be traced to the presence of two disparate strands in Marcuse's treatment of technology: a romantic one from Heidegger and a socialist one from Marx. A similar point is made by Ganesha (2004: 199).

2 See supra n. 1.

3 Cf. Feenberg (2023: 101), though here Feenberg is discussing Weber. As he goes on to explain, Marcuse's position is more subtle, and involves a Marxist critique of Weber.

4 A similar statement, though free of the idea of relations, appears in Marcuse's "From Ontology to Technology: Fundamental Tendencies of Industrial Society" where he writes: "The density and the opacity of 'objects,' and of objectivity as well, seem to evaporate" (CPHM 5: 134).

5 Marcuse primarily relies on a passage from Piaget's *Introduction à l'épistemologie génétique* (1950 III: 287).

6 I am indebted to accounts of Marcuse's relationship to Husserl in Feenberg (2023: 104–5), Alford (1985: 54–55), and the more critical O'Neill (1988).

7 "The art of measuring thus becomes the trail-blazer for the ultimately universal geometry and its 'world' of pure limit-shapes" (Husserl 1970: 28).

8 These uniformities are not found in nature but have to be assumed for the purpose of our practices: "the things of the intuitively given surrounding world
   fluctuate, in general and in all their properties, in the sphere of the merely
   typical: their identity with themselves, their self-sameness and their tempor-
   ally enduring sameness, are merely approximate, as is their likeness with other
   things" (Husserl 1970: 25).
9 Alford (1985: 55) questions the extent of Marcuse's debt to Husserl. Alford bases
   this on a point of Gurwitsch's: for Husserl, even the life-world presupposes a
   transcendental subject and is therefore not ultimate.
10 To use the Weberian idea, memorably reintroduced into contemporary philosophy by John McDowell (1994: 70–71).
11 See also Marcuse's pair of essays "Review of John Dewey's Logic: The Theory of
   Enquiry" and "Critique of Dewey's Theory of Valuation" (CPHM 5: 80–87, 87–92).
12 Feenberg (2023: 96) also discusses Marcuse's critique of management science
   and its positivist presuppositions.

Further reading

Alford, F. C. (1985) *Science and the Revenge of Nature: Habermas & Marcuse*, Tampa and
   Gainesville: University Presses of Florida. [See esp. Ch. 4 for a helpful discussion of Marcuse's ideas concerning the new science that will exist in a socialist
   society.]
Feenberg, A. (2017) *Technosystem: The Social Life of Reason*, Cambridge, MA: Harvard University Press. [Prominent recent text in philosophy of technology. Authored by
   Marcuse's most prominent interpreter, and at least partly inspired by Marcuse's
   thought.]
Feenberg, A. (2023) *Towards a Ruthless Critique of Everything Existing*, London: Verso. [Ch.
   5 "The Critique of Technology" and Ch. 6 "A New Concept of Reason" are perhaps the best treatments available in English of Marcuse's views on science and
   technology.]

Five

Aesthetics

In this chapter, I turn to Marcuse's views on aesthetics, the area of philosophy concerned with the nature and significance of artistic experience. I focus on Marcuse's *aesthetic formalism*, his idea that it is the form of a work of art, rather than the *content*, which is the chief source of the work's value; in particular, both its aesthetic value and its potential to effect social and political change. Of course, formalist views were not uncommon in the philosophical tradition before Marcuse. As Marcuse knew full well, Kant defended such a view in the third *Critique*. Before we are in a position to evaluate Marcuse's formalism, it will be important to ask what makes his version of the thesis unique. (Numerous doctrines have gone by the name "formalism" in the long history of aesthetics and philosophy of art. Here, I only mean to attribute an aesthetic formalism to Marcuse in a fairly narrow and specific sense.)

An obvious if overly general claim would be that, unlike formalist doctrines from the history of philosophy, Marcuse's aesthetic formalism is defended in the context of a critical theory of society. To render this answer more concrete, we must consider two main currents of thought informing critical theory and then ask what resources each of them contributes to the case for aesthetic formalism. It is, I think, uncontroversial that critical theory in many of its forms attempts to unite Marx's historical materialism and Freudian psychoanalysis—and that this characterization, whatever its limitations when it comes to other figures in the Frankfurt School, proves especially apt in the case of Marcuse's project. Reformulated, then, the question we must attempt to answer as we come to grips with Marcuse's aesthetics and its status as a contribution to critical theory is as follows: What becomes of the traditional doctrine of

DOI: 10.4324/9781003307075-5

aesthetic formalism when it is integrated into a (Marxist) historical materialist and (Freudian) psychoanalytic framework?

Marcuse holds that it is chiefly owing to their form that great works of art contribute to the type of revolutionary transformation of society Marxists sought. As Marcuse writes, "the critical function of art, its contribution to the struggle for liberation, resides in the aesthetic form" (AD 8). It is far from clear just why this is so, but Marcuse's proposal to defend formalism on Marxist grounds, already striking on its own, becomes even more controversial when we realize the following: as Marcuse himself is well aware, formalism represents a profound break with much orthodox Marxist theorizing about the arts and their role in society.

In fact, the received view among Marxists is virtually the exact opposite of Marcuse's aesthetic formalism. Most orthodox Marxists are anti-formalist and focus on the content of works of art; for example, whether a work accurately depicts problems of capitalism, such as poverty and exploitation. Formalism, like other traditional philosophical doctrines, is considered by most Marxists to be a form of bourgeois (ruling-class) ideology. We will devote more space below to spelling out why, but even at this early stage, it is not too difficult to see how an excessive focus on style might prove incompatible with the goal of bringing awareness to social problems. Where social problems are depicted, they may seem less serious than they are, owing to the way they are stylized. Or perhaps they are not depicted at all, since experimentation in style does not privilege any particular content. It is as easy for the modernist painter to "defamiliarize" a bowl of fruit as it is to do so to a beggar.

For this reason, Marcuse will defend aesthetic formalism's Marxist credentials by arguing in a two-fold way:

i. It is in virtue of their form, not their content, that great works of art are capable of contributing to the class struggle.
ii. The content of a work of art, far from helping it contribute to the revolutionary transformation of society, renders it counter-productive in this regard.

As we will see, the lynchpin argument for this two-fold thesis is that art operates most effectively on the level of established modes of perception. Yet it can only do so when it is innovative at the level of form. When artists attempt to have a political effect through the selection of content, they fail. This is because their work ceases to function as art, and becomes something else: philosophy, activism, or propaganda. Yet there is no reason to think artists should be especially good at mounting these alternative types of interventions. All that will result is flawed or ineffective philosophy, activism, or propaganda. Even worse, artists risk capitulating to a social order which insists on instrumentalizing everything for practical purposes, and mistrusts anyone and anything that wishes to resist this process.

This brings us to the role of Freudian psychoanalysis in Marcuse's aesthetic theory. If we want to know whether art can inspire people to revolt against oppressive social conditions, we need to know something about human psychology. As we will see, Marcuse's case for his Marxist version of aesthetic formalism will draw on a Freudian theory of the instincts: more specifically, the late Freud's idea that the two fundamental motivations in human life are Eros and Thanatos, the life drive and the death drive, or, more plainly, the sexual and aggressive instincts. Though repressed for the purpose of social harmony, these unruly instincts are stimulated by great, formally innovative art. Such art, Marcuse will say, rebels against "the reality principle." What is more, it does so at the level of its form, not its content. This last idea is among the most challenging in Marcuse's aesthetics, since it is much more natural to think of sexuality and aggression as manifesting themselves in a work's content than in its form.

Here the Marxist and Freudian dimension of Marcuse's aesthetics coalesce, since it is by stimulating the anti-social sexual and aggressive instincts that such art makes its main contribution to the revolutionary overthrow of capitalism. Yet the incorporation of Freud into the theory turns out to place limits on the traditional Marxist aspiration to instrumentalize culture for the class structure. In the final analysis, Marcuse's aesthetics will insist that great art, because of its relationship to unvarying dimensions of human life (Eros and Thanatos), possesses a universal importance which makes it transcend any particular period in history or phase of the class struggle.

1. Form and content

Before proceeding, it will be important to clearly define the terms "form" and "content." We begin with the latter because it is simpler.

In a brief statement of his conception of art, Marcuse writes: "A work of art is authentic ... not by virtue of its content (the 'correct representation of social conditions')" (AD 8). From this, we can extrapolate a definition of content, albeit one that Marcuse never provides. The content of a work of art would seem to be its subject-matter broadly construed: in this case, "social conditions." For example, a literary work's content would include its characters, setting, plot, and so on. As Marcuse writes, "The specific social denominator, that which is 'dated' in a work of art and surpassed by historical development, is the milieu, the Lebenswelt of the protagonists" (AD 23). As if to strike an association with neo-Kantian epistemology, Marcuse will also refer to the content as "data" or even as "the given." This somewhat stilted terminology, I think, conveys that content has its source in sense-experience: either that of the author or that of the society of which she is a part. Accordingly, the content of a work of art will be drawn from the social environment in which the author finds herself. Of course, artists often adopt as their subject-matter a different social or historical world, but then they will be limited to the artifacts of it in their own.

For Marcuse, it is not just that content is drawn from the artist's experience of her surroundings, however broadly these are construed. It is that there is no other source for a work's content. The work "contains nothing that does not also exist in the given reality, the actions, thoughts, feelings, and dreams of men and women, their potentialities and those of nature" (AD 54). Of course, the artist need not have experienced these things for herself (it is often noted that Shakespeare's life experience was much too limited for him to know as much as he evidently did about the lives, careers, and experiences of so many diverse types of people). An author may rely on testimony from others, directly or indirectly communicated. Ultimately, however, the author is limited by the stock of experiences available to her in her surroundings. This means that artists interested in transcending their surroundings have a difficult challenge facing them, one they can only meet with the resources made available by form.

Here an obvious question arises for the theory that is taking shape: can there really be no content that is not invented, created ex nihilo? In response, Marcuse might adapt a well-worn empiricist argument, dating back to Hume, which runs as follows. Although new combinations or juxtapositions of content are possible, the basic elements from which these are composed must, ultimately, come from the author's experience. At least in the aesthetic domain, there are for Marcuse none of the rationalist philosopher's "innate ideas" (whether there is any of the transcendental philosophers a priori representations is another question, which we will confront in a subsequent chapter). Perhaps Marcuse's claim is extreme, but it can be softened somewhat. For our purposes, the crucial point is that it is chiefly at the level of content that society's influence is felt: "society remains present in the autonomous realm of art ... as the 'stuff' for the aesthetic representation which, past and present, is transformed in this representation" (AD 18). How, then, does form alter the content made available by the artist's social surroundings?

In contrast to "content," the form refers to the distinctive way or manner in which the content of a work of art is presented. If content is "data," then form is the way in which this data is "reshaped," "reordered" (AD 8). Marcuse sometimes refers to this process as 'stylization" (AD 8). Typically, it is at the level of form that the unique approach of an artist, school, or even a tradition manifests itself. We can tentatively define "aesthetic form" as the result of the transformation of a given content (actual or historical, personal or social fact) into a self-contained whole: a poem, play, novel, etc. The work is thus "taken out" of the constant process of reality and assumes a significance and truth of its own (AD 8).

Here, Marcuse, in effect, takes up the question of form's significance, the question of why it is so important that content be "reshaped" or "reorganized." His answer is that only in this way will the content become a possible object of the distinctive type of experience we want the arts to give us. Before it is presented to us in a given form, a thing will typically have some other significance; for example, an artifact, like a bowl, is thought of primarily in terms of its typical use. Yet it is only once it is presented to us in a certain form that it becomes a work of art.

Staying with the same example, when the bowl is depicted in a still-life painting, it becomes available for a new type of experience not closely tied to its ordinary use. If content is a source of confinement, then form is a vehicle of transcendence. As we see, content, because it is drawn from experience, links a work to the social environment of the artist. Indeed, content arguably even limits the work to that world, at least in terms of the basic elements from which the work will be constructed. By contrast, form is what enables the work to go beyond that environment and enable us to relate to things in an unfamiliar way. Marcuse refers to the formal dimensions of a work as those "where art transcends its social determination and emancipates itself from the given universe of discourse and behavior" (AD 6). He speaks of a "rupture" between the world of the work of art and the world of everyday life (AD 9). It is as if the work gives rise to a new world, distinct from the world of our ordinary, everyday lives. This is especially straightforward in the case of fiction, whose setting, characters, and plot occur in a realm seemingly separate from our own.

This account of aesthetic form may sound extravagant, as if it only applies to certain especially innovative works; for example, films or photographs that invite one into an altered perceptual state, perhaps using fish-eye lenses or other effects. Yet Marcuse appears to think that this transporting effect is achieved by everything that genuinely deserves the name of art. As he tells us, it is only through the process of taking a subject-matter and submitting it to form that we finally have something that can be called "a poem, a play, a novel" ("A play, a novel become literary works by virtue of the form which 'incorporates' and sublimates 'the stuff'" AD 42). Otherwise, we have simply chosen a subject-matter, not created a work of art based on it. This subject-matter will remain a brute fact in the world or else a choice in the author's mind, but until it has been "reshaped," "stylized," or simply formed in certain ways it will not assume the status of a work of art. Not that this is a simple matter.

Marcuse speaks of "the demands of the art form" meaning it presents a challenge for the artist (AD 7, my emphasis). The challenge of how to form a certain material is essentially that of art itself. Indeed, Marcuse seems to think that, compared with the challenge of finding a form, the challenge of choosing material is trivial—a point that will be important in his dispute with orthodox Marxist aesthetics. Sometimes the stylization of the subject-matter will be minimal, as in realist works. Sometimes it will be more extensive, as in the modernist literature Marcuse prizes. Or perhaps it is naïve to imagine that realism and modernism are simply distinguished by lesser or greater amounts of stylization (as opposed to qualitatively different styles that do not admit of this type of comparison in terms of more and less).[1] However, the element of form or style is always present so long as must we are dealing with art. Here, unfortunately, we must skirt over the diverse and complex set of demands the task of imposing form on matter brings with it: those of the medium; the genre; the artist's own individual style; that of a school; or some other set of conventions. All of these demands are those of form. In relation to them, the choice of subject-matter is only a first step.

This line of argument may seem to suggest that artists would be better off experimenting in the realm of form exclusively, not limited by any particular content. Perhaps there is (or could be) art involving only form and its use in innovative ways. In such art, formal experimentation would occur without resistance of any subject-matter or content. However, Marcuse is not such a radical formalist as this. For him, it is "content in form" that constitutes (great) art, rather than form or content alone. In a passage we have already considered, he writes that

> the critical function of art, its contribution to the struggle for liberation, resides in the aesthetic form. A work of art is great or true not by virtue of its content (i.e. the "correct" representation of social conditions), nor by its "pure" form, but by the content having become form.
>
> (AD 8)

Marcuse's formalism, then, does not advocate form to the exclusion of matter, but rather in addition to it. It is not simply an aesthetic formalism but an aesthetic hylomorphism. Unfortunately, it is unclear which artists or critics he has in mind when he distances himself from an aesthetics of pure form: perhaps the paintings of Pollock and other abstract expressionists as they were understood by Clement Greenberg, i.e., as an achievement in pure form.[2]

This distinction between empty form and the form of content may seem to be an overly subtle one but it serves an important purpose in Marcuse's account. In short, it helps Marcuse distinguish between one type of experimentation with form that he thinks is frivolous, and another which he values:

> Neither is the truth of art a matter of style alone. There is in art an abstract, illusory autonomy: private arbitrary invention of something new, a technique which remains extraneous to the content, or technique without content, form without matter.
>
> (*AD* 40)

Understanding Marcuse's reason for skepticism of this "empty formalism" (to use a phrase of Hegel's from another context) recalls an important fact about content: it is the content which typically connects the work to its social surroundings. Hence, empty formalism will tend to transport us to another world, rather than transforming our relationship to this one. Yet Marcuse thinks that it is only the latter that is genuinely subversive:

> The world intended in art is never and nowhere merely the given world of everyday reality, but neither is it a world of mere fantasy, illusion, and so on. It contains nothing that does not also exist in the given reality, the actions, thoughts, feelings, and dreams of men and women, their potentialities and those of nature.
>
> (*AD* 54)

Great art exists at a midpoint between the poles of pure fantasy and uncompromising realism.

Because Marcuse's account of art in terms of the distinction between form and content is highly abstract, it may be helpful to examine a concrete instance: literature. Language is the medium in which the subject-matter of literature is depicted—"the mimesis in literature occurs in the medium of language" (*AD* 45). Hence, the task of giving appropriate form to the content is a linguistic one. To give an unfamiliar perspective on familiar content—e.g., a setting, character, or plot—the author must break with ordinary modes of speech and writing. Here, Marcuse explains a variety of techniques for effecting this break. Language, he writes,

> is tightened or loosened, forced to yield insights otherwise obscured. Prose is subjected to its own rhythm. What is normally not spoken is said; what is normally spoken too much remains unsaid if it conceals that which is essential. Restructuring takes place through concentration, exaggeration, emphasis on the essential, reordering of facts.
>
> (*AD* 45)

Here, the potential for confusion arises. Although literary language departs from ordinary language, it is not that the former is form and the latter is content. The content is the subject-matter, e.g., a love story. Literary language and ordinary language are two forms in which this content could be recounted, and Marcuse is advocating for the former. Although Marcuse lists a range of ways in which the language of literature is distinct from that of everyday life, no particular one of them seems to be required. What matters is that the break is effected, so that the content that is depicted (the "mimesis") assumes a new form. Consequently, Marcuse is prepared to praise extremely different writers for their experiments with language, so much so that it can seem as if forming content is less an achievement of certain great writers than a sine qua non of literature itself:

> Critical mimesis finds expression in the most manifold forms. It is found both in the language of Brecht, which is formed by the immediacy of the need for change, and in the schizophrenically diagnostic language of Beckett, in which there is no talk of change. The indictment is just as much in the sensuous, emotional language of *Werther* and the *Fleurs du Mal* as it is in the hardness of Stendhal and Kafka.
>
> (*AD* 46)

Significantly, Marcuse here indicates that even literary works which seem to dispense with formal experimentation altogether and employ plain, unadorned language are more formally innovative than they appear. For example, the language in Brecht's writings might seem to be the direct, stripped-down language of political protest and propaganda, rather than the highly stylized language of great literature.[3] For Marcuse, however, Brecht's writing has a literary style of its own, an urgent mode of discourse that reflects the felt need for social change. But what of text that is presented to us untransformed, e.g., quotations? "Even where a fragment of reality is left untransformed (for example, quoted phrases from a speech by Robespierre) the content is changed by the work as a whole; its meaning can even be turned into its opposite" (AD 42). Here, Marcuse's answer is that, simply by virtue of being included in a larger whole, the quoted text is transformed. Hence, even where the text itself is seemingly untransformed, the new context is sufficient to alter it decisively. As before, however, Marcuse believes there are limits to formal experimentation. The point is not to introduce new forms arbitrarily, but to do so with the content firmly in mind. Only in this way does art achieve its mission of transforming the way we perceive our social surroundings. Hence, Marcuse thinks that even the most avant-garde art and literature will preserve some connection to the language we speak: "This is the case even when the words are broken, when new ones are invented—otherwise all communication would be severed" (AD 41).

Marcuse's reference to "wholes" in his discussion of form is not accidental, but reflects his belief that it is the work's form which unifies it into a single thing with an identity of its own. The very limits or bounds of the work are where its form leaves off and ordinary language (or life) takes over. A work's form is what individuates it as a thing standing apart from other things in the surrounding world of ordinary life. Without form, the work would be a mere heap to which parts could be added or subtracted arbitrarily. Form is what gives a work its identity, and distinguishes it from its mundane surroundings.

2. "Another sensibility"

Having defined form and content, we can introduce Marcuse's aesthetic formalism. By this, I mean his idea that it is in the form of a work of art that its value and significance chiefly reside. For Marcuse, the value of aesthetic form is that it facilitates a unique type of perceptual experience not available to us in ordinary life: "The inner logic of the work of art terminates in the emergence of another reason, another sensibility, which defy the rationality and sensibility incorporated in the dominant social institutions" (*AD* 7). It is the form imposed on a content drawn from experience which allows us to perceive the latter in a new and unfamiliar way. This content, when it is encountered outside of a work of art, appears to us in a familiar way; for example, the bowl of fruit when seen on my kitchen table appears as an ordinary household object.

In speaking of the way works of art challenge established modes of perception, Marcuse means to cast an extremely wide net. He refers not only to perceptions in the different sense-modalities of seeing, hearing, touch, but also to perceptions of a more sophisticated (cognitive) kind. Hence, he speaks of changes in "the perception of individuals—in their feelings, judgments, thoughts; an invalidation of dominant norms, needs, and values" (*AD* 8). As this last passage indicates, Marcuse means to include conative as well as cognitive factors under the head of "perceptions." Not only sensible impressions of the world, but also desires to act in it and bring about change come within the ambit of Marcuse's analysis. Even our values appear to be implicated, since they too presumably influence our perceptions of artistic and extra-artistic reality. What is more, Marcuse does not insist that a great work of art can only challenge the form of perception occurring in its own medium; for example, painting, film, or photography challenging received habits of visual perception. He allows that language, for example, may be used to undercut received ways of perceiving the world in a variety sense-modalities, and credits Mallarmé with the most subversive experiments in this area ("the poetry of Mallarmé is an extreme example; his poems conjure up modes of perception, imagination, gestures—a feast of sensuousness which shatters everyday experience and anticipates a different reality principle," *AD* 19). Perception, in Marcuse's sense of the word, encompasses a diverse set of cognitive, desiderative and sensory transactions with the world. In claiming that great art transforms perception, Marcuse means to include all of these modalities. Once perception is defined in this

broad way, it is much easier to see why it is almost as a matter of definition connected to artistic form, understood as the way or manner
something is presented, rather than the thing itself.

How, exactly, do formally innovative works of art challenge
established modes of perception? Marcuse seems to think there are
a range of ways, but the main one he emphasizes reflects a debt to
Freud and psychoanalysis. For Marcuse, great works allow for the
expression of sexual and aggressive instincts that society represses:
"the primary erotic-destructive forces which explode the normal
universe of communication and behavior" (*AD* 20). In expanding on
this idea, Marcuse makes clear his debt not just to this particular psychoanalytic doctrine but to virtually the entire Freudian apparatus:

> The ego and the id, emotions, rationality and imagination are
> withdrawn from their socialization by a repressive society and
> strive toward autonomy—albeit in a fictitious world. But the
> encounter with the fictitious world restructures consciousness
> and gives sensual representation to a counter-societal experi-
> ence. The aesthetic sublimation thus liberates and validates
> childhood and adult dreams of happiness and sorrow.
>
> (*AD* 44)

Here, Marcuse invokes Freud's tripartite model of the mind, as well
as his further idea that the social taboo has its home in childhood
experiences and in dreams. However, these details may distract us
from the simplicity of the core idea, which is simply that of a clash
between unruly sexual and aggressive instincts, on one hand, and
social repression, on the other. Hence, Marcuse also describes art as
contradicting "the reality principle," which tells us to do whatever
is necessary to survive in our natural and social surroundings. ("The
nomos which art obeys is not that of the established reality principle
but of its negation," *AD* 73). Correspondingly, he describes art as
obeying "the pleasure principle," the id's law of seeking enjoyment
even at the risk of death. These anti-social instincts, though permitted an outlet by great art, only express themselves in a fictitious
world. Presumably, it is because they express themselves in this relatively harmless way that they are tolerated by a society which would
not allow them to find expression in the real world. As we will see,

it is difficult to reconcile this Freudian conception of art's role with formalism, since it can seem obvious that sexuality and aggression are principally relevant to a work's content (subject-matter) rather than its form. However, I will argue that these two strands of argument in Marcuse's aesthetic theory are in fact consistent.

If great, formally innovative art has some connection to the psychological forces of Eros and Thanatos, love and death, sexuality and aggression, then an obvious question arises: how, exactly, do the two interact when they are stimulated by great art? Marcuse seems to acknowledge a range of ways, indicating that either Eros or Thanatos can assume priority.

Eros reigns primary in works that are "beautiful." Psychoanalysis furnishes Marcuse with a unique case for the enduring importance of beauty as an aesthetic ideal. It is, one might say, Marcuse's decidedly non-transcendental deduction of the concept of beauty, locating this concept in Eros and not in the faculty of judgment. Marcuse's conception of beauty is based on the thought that artistic beauty gives expression to humanity's erotic instincts, albeit in an indirect or "sublimated" way. What is more, Marcuse draws from this the lesson that beauty is subversive of social norms. This would come as a surprise to those who view standards of taste as instruments of class-based domination and oppression. As we will soon see, this critique of beauty is made by those who think art should focus more squarely on social problems: "it seems difficult indeed to associate this concept with revolutionary art; it seems irresponsible, snobbish to speak of the Beautiful in the face of the necessities of the political struggle" (AD 62). In contrast to the harsh realities of class-based domination and oppression, beauty seems like a frivolous topic—a luxury that socialists cannot afford.

In explaining why beauty is subversive, Marcuse aligns beauty with the pleasure principle and opposes it to the reality principle, which tells us to limit our pleasure-seeking activity to those behaviors that society tolerates. Hence, artistic beauty has the potential to provoke a collision with society and its repressive standards: "As pertaining to the domain of Eros, the Beautiful represents the pleasure principle. Thus, it rebels against the prevailing reality principle of domination" (AD 62). While it would be tempting to conclude that Marcuse is here invoking Freud against Marx, the truth is more complex. Marcuse joins Marx's critique of capitalism to

Freud's analysis of civilization to argue that, under the present mode of production, which is profoundly exploitative, social repression is excessive. Correspondingly, repression could only be lessened sufficiently in a future socialist society where exploitation is eliminated.

Nevertheless, Thanatos (death and aggression) seems to predominate in what Marcuse, following a tradition that goes back to Aristotle, regards as the greatest art: tragedy. Marcuse defends tragic art in terms that recall Freud's pessimistic doctrine that Thanatos is ultimately victorious over Eros, and that "life is a long detour to death":

> If art were to promise that at the end good would triumph over evil, such a promise would be refuted by the historical truth. In reality it is evil which triumphs, and there are only islands of good where one can find refuge for a brief time. Authentic works of art are aware of this; they reject the promise made too easily; they refuse the unburdened happy end. They must reject it, for the realm of freedom lies beyond mimesis.
>
> (AD 47)

This defeatism might seem incompatible with Marcuse's activism, his unflagging lifelong commitment to a revolutionary transformation of society. Marcuse acknowledges the appearance of inconsistency, but attempts to explain it away.

His line of counterargument is the following. Once we are aware that Thanatos prevails over Eros, we will not be reconciled to the status quo. Rather, we will be outraged that, under capitalism, there is so much more pain and suffering than there needs to be. Hence, we will attempt to bring about a future in which pain and suffering are reduced to a minimum, even as we acknowledge that they can never be eliminated entirely:[4]

> Tragedy is always and everywhere while the satyr play follows it always and everywhere; joy vanishes faster than sorrow. This insight, inexorably expressed in art, may well shatter faith in progress but it may also keep alive another image and another goal of praxis, namely the reconstruction of society and nature under the principle of increasing the human potential for happiness.
>
> (AD 56)

A tragic view of life is not only compatible with socialist politics, but complementary to them, inasmuch as our resolve is strengthened to reduce suffering and pain to their necessary minimum. What is more, this tragic view has additional potential concerning the struggle against totalitarianism. This is an important point for Marcuse given his concerns about the communist regimes of the Eastern bloc which he thought had betrayed socialism in favor of a totalitarian form of rule. By identifying certain fixed limits to human progress, tragedy counters the naïve optimism that prevails in some socialist movements and regimes. It reminds us that even "really existing socialism" cannot eliminate the problems of unrequited love or the irreversibility of time.

Marcuse's idea that aesthetic experience involves two phases, "sublimation" and "desublimation," reflects both the similarities and the differences between his doctrine and Freud's. Though "sublimation" is often a technical term in philosophy and psychoanalysis, Marcuse employs it in a somewhat idiosyncratic way. Essentially, he uses it to refer to the way a work of art imposes form on content: the way in which familiar subject-matter is presented in an unfamiliar way and thereby transformed as if to another world beyond the ordinary one in which we live. At times, Marcuse indicates that this will mean "sublimation" in Freud's sense: the redirection of aggressive and sexual instincts away from anti-social activities and towards socially acceptable ones. At others, however, the Freudian associations of the term are absent, and it simply describes a general type of estrangement or defamiliarization.

Yet for Marcuse sublimation is only the first phase in a two-phase process, the second of which, desublimation, suggests a more activist theory than the one Freud develops. In desublimation, the sexual and aggressive instincts that have been aroused seek an outlet beyond the virtual world of the work of art. In other words, the work of art has had a spill-over effect on society at large, and people who have viewed the work are now on a collision course with the "reality principle." In this phase, we witness "de-sublimation on the basis of the original sublimation, dissolution of the social taboos, of the social management of Eros and Thanatos" (*AD* 44). Revolutionary desublimation is to repressive sublimation as precipitation is to condensation.

Without "desublimation," Marcuse's aesthetic theory risks seeming conservative, as if the goal of great art were to provide anti-social instincts with a harmless outlet, a kind of safety valve that allows social members to let off steam. Yet it is clear that Marcuse does not think these instincts can ever be fully satisfied with the type of outlet great art provides. Once stimulated, they will press for satisfaction in the real world, even if this poses a threat to the established order. The sublimation of these instincts through art does not extinguish them. It rather sends them on a detour which could, in the end, lead to a collision with social norms. This is desublimation. Crucially, great art does not simply allow anti-social instincts an outlet in any direct way; for example, the way that very realistic pornography might. For Marcuse, release occurring at the level of content, rather than form, risks co-option by the powers that be. True subversion only takes place via the indirect detour Marcuse describes.

At times, Marcuse describes relief from inhibition per se, and not just the inhibition of sex and aggressiveness, as one of the main tasks of art. This more general sense of relief is reflected in the exaggeration and intensification that is characteristic of great works of art: "Men and women speak and act with less inhibition than under the weight of daily life; they are more shameless (but also more embarrassed) in their loving and hating; they are loyal to their passions even when destroyed by them" (AD 44). Presumably, Marcuse is thinking the relief from repression that occurs here takes place not at the level of content, but, rather, at the level of form. It is not what is said and done, but rather the uninhibited manner in which it is said and done—and presumably the uninhibited atmosphere in which the audience is invited to share. Great art's break with social convention extends beyond human behavior and into the environment itself: "the objects in their world are more transparent, more independent, and more compelling" (AD 45). It is difficult to see how such an altered relationship to objects could be produced by loosened inhibitions against aggressiveness and sexuality. Perhaps it is because objects show up differently under the reality principle than they do under the pleasure principle. Once again, though, it is always a matter of the form rather than the content, the way an object is given as opposed to which objects are given. However, some of Marcuse's examples are ambiguous on this score, suggesting that we need to look harder at the issue of whether it is form or content that is principally subversive.

A potential problem for Marcuse's account I have already hinted at should be considered in greater depth now. It would be natural to wonder if Marcuse's emphasis on tabooed instincts like sexuality and aggression is consistent with his formalism. After all, it is tempting to suppose that the way great art excites these instincts is through its content, not its form; for example, using sexually arousing or anger-inducing subject-matter. Indeed, it is somewhat difficult to understand how Eros and Thanatos could influence a work's form. Of course, it is not so implausible that there could be such a thing as an erotic or aggressive style, but we are far from understanding what such a style would entail. However, the inconsistency is only apparent as it soon becomes clear that Marcuse does, indeed, envision the relief from repression as occurring at the level of form. This emerges from his treatment of two examples of subversive art, one successful and the other less so: Baudelaire's poetry, and pornography. We will consider each in turn.

Following a number of influential essays by Benjamin, Marcuse selects as his main example of this type of art the poetry of Baudelaire. Initially, this might seem inconsistent with Marcuse's formalism, since it is at the level of content that Baudelaire is subversive: more specifically, the sexual subject-matter of the poetry, as well as the interest in death and decay. However, it soon becomes clear that what is central is not the subversive content itself, but rather the approving way in which it is presented. Baudelaire's poetry is characterized by "a pleasure in decay, in destruction, in the beauty of evil; a celebration of the asocial, of the anomie" (*AD* 20). Thus, it is not decay, destruction, evil, etc., themselves, but the attitude towards them which is decisive in Baudelaire and results in a new method of literary depiction for this subject-matter. Incidentally, Baudelaire, as interpreted here, provides a clear example of art informed by Thanatos, the death drive, the aggressive instincts, and so on. The Frankfurt School authors clearly considered such art to be deeply subversive, albeit in a one-sided way. Indeed, they believe an exclusive emphasis on Thanatos is characteristic of the right-wing (fascist) revolt against liberal capitalism, rather than the left-wing (socialist) one.

For an instance of art that is subversive only at the level of its content and not its form, we have to turn from romantic and modernist poetry to a cruder form: pornography (and obscenity more generally):

> The qualitative difference of art does not constitute itself in the selection of a particular field where art could preserve its autonomy. Nor would it do to seek out a cultural area not yet occupied by the established society. Attempts have been made to argue that pornography and the obscene are islands of nonconformist communication. But such privileged areas do not exist. Both obscenity and pornography have long since been integrated. As commodities they too communicate the repressive whole.
>
> (*AD* 17)

Pornography and obscenity are defined by their explicit subject-matter, which may indeed disturb cultural conservatives. Yet it is mistaken to think that the choice of any particular subject-matter is sufficient to produce great art. Even as pornographic or obscene works challenge convention through their content, they capitulate to it at the level of their form. However, because it is formally that works of art are most subversive of established modes of perception this is a losing proposition from the perspective of social critique. As Marcuse notes, obscenity and pornography are more than capable of being "integrated," since they too can be made to serve the interests of the powerful. This occurs when they are made into things whose main purpose is to be bought and sold, commodities. So regardless of how subversive the content of a work of pornography is, its form, being none other than that of the commodity, ensures it will serve the prevailing mode of production. In one instance, Marcuse refers to the eroticism of mass culture as "hygienic," implying that the temporary relief from repression it provides serves the health of the present society, not its revolutionary overthrow and replacement with another.

Once again, it would be legitimate to wonder if this theory is authentically Freudian. Even Freud did not think relief from repression was the unqualified good Marcuse seems to think it is. For Freud, a certain level of repression is necessary for a basic level of social order. In families and in the larger social group, the id cannot be allowed to express itself outside of the constraints imposed by the super-ego. The result would be war and chaos, patricide and incest. Freud refers (approvingly) to sublimation, but not to de-sublimation.

The solution to this puzzle is likely that Marcuse has incorporated Freudian psychoanalysis into a Marxist framework. This sets him up to argue that the level of repression in modern capitalist society is excessive because this society is exploitative. While it may be that some repression is necessary for social order, we suffer repression in excess of this: "surplus repression." Just as, for Marx, we are compelled to produce surplus value, value in excess of what is required to sustain ourselves, so too for Marcuse is there "surplus repression," repression in excess of what Freud thought was necessary for a baseline level of social harmony. Hence the greater urgency of relieving people of their excess repression, a task great art helps facilitate. Crucially, however, Marcuse insists that this relief from repression must occur in the indirect way art facilitates, rather than through simple disobedience.

Marcuse's reliance on Freudian psychoanalysis gives his aesthetics a universalist dimension that does not sit easily with historical materialism. Following the late Freud, Marcuse thinks of human nature, in all periods, as consisting of a delicate balance between two fundamental forces, Eros and Thanatos. While Marcuse respects the Marxist idea that history will change the shape that human nature assumes, he does not think of human nature as infinitely malleable. This leads Marcuse to interpret great works of art as preoccupying themselves with a universal human nature, even if they do so in the context of a particular time and place. As Marcuse writes, "Eros and Thanatos assert their own power in and against the class struggle" (*AD* 24). Even works concerned with the social conflicts of particular historical periods have a dimension that is universal: "Dostoyevsky's *The Humiliated and the Offended*, Victor Hugo's *Les Misérables* suffer not only the injustice of a particular class society, they suffer the inhumanity of all times' (*AD* 23). Marcuse's insistence on a universal human nature may seem philosophically arrogant, but it can be construed in a more modest way. Marcuse simply thinks there are certain universal human problems that no future society, no matter how progressive, can be expected to eradicate: "it is difficult to imagine a society which has abolished what is called chance or fate" (*AD* 24). Other critics of orthodox Marxism invoked an invariant human nature, but Marcuse's position is more subtle than this—and in ways that his aesthetic theory foregrounds. As an example, consider Marcuse's interpretation of Goethe's *Sorrows of Young Werther* as a work that is simultaneously a love story and a chronicle of class struggle (*AD* 26). It is, at once, a tale of the conflict between true love and social custom, and, at the same time, of the conflict between the bourgeoisie and the old nobility.

Marcuse's Freudian idea that great art, through its form, stimulates aggressive and sexual instincts tabooed by society may seem to conflict with the doctrines of a great formalist from the philosophical tradition: Kant.[5] Kant thought that the pleasure we take in great works of art was "disinterested." Whereas our ordinary desires for things like food and sex motivate us to act in ways that satisfy or extinguish these desires, the pleasure we take in great art does not have this effect. It is less a spur to action than one to reflection (on our response to the work). This marks the difference between the ordinary pleasure we take in what is merely "agreeable," and our pleasure in the "beautiful" great art. For Kant, works of art are "purposive without purpose," because, though they are clearly artifacts and products of design, they differ from ordinary tools, etc., in having no particular use ascribed to them.[6]

Yet Marcuse's psychoanalytic account of aesthetic pleasure can suggest that the "beautiful" is simply "the agreeable" in disguise. After all, Marcuse maintains that beauty is sublimated erotic desire. Does this Freudian claim not risk reducing beauty to ordinary, interested pleasure?

In response, Marcuse would likely argue that his theory has a way of marking the distinction Kant draws, even if it is not exactly the way Kant prefers. For Marcuse, there remains a difference between the beautiful and the agreeable, since there is a difference between sublimated sexual desire and the ordinary variety. The former is evoked by form, the latter by content. The former can only be awakened in us by the arts, whereas the latter is part of our ordinary, instinctual lives. Of course, the distinction between sublimated eroticism and the ordinary kind is much less stark than the one Kant draws between disinterested and interested pleasure. Still, it is a version of Kant's distinction adapted to a psychoanalytic framework. In such a framework, the idea of wholly disinterested pleasure appears more dubious than it may have for Kant, who regarded freedom from the rule of instinct as a genuine possibility for human beings. In Marcuse's Freudian-inspired framework, instincts are altered, re-directed, refined—but never ignored entirely in favor of a second, non-instinctual source of motivation.

3. Semblance and reification: Plato v. Marx

In turning to the Marxist dimension of Marcuse's formalism, I will consider his effort to answer an objection to the arts that goes back to Plato. This objection accuses art of trafficking in falsehoods, both theoretical and practical. Art deceives us, both about the world we live in and about how we ought to behave within it. A painting of a chair is a copy of a copy, at a two-fold remove from the form of the chair. More perniciously, tragedy teaches us that suffering and death are evils to be feared, whereas a wise man knows this is not so. Of course, Plato's own metaphysics, epistemology, and ethics are presupposed by his version of the criticism. Still, it should be clear that a version of Plato's worry applies to great art as Marcuse conceives of art, even outside the framework of Platonism.

For Marcuse, it is due to aesthetic form that familiar content appears in a new and unfamiliar guise. Hence, formally innovative work could be seen as distorting reality. This is not simply because art deals with the sensible, rather than the intelligible world, but because it inevitably stylizes its subject-matter. The distortion could be of many different types; for example, an idealized image of the society in which one lives, or simply of the human condition in general. However, the important point would be that art, as Marcuse envisions it, remains guilty of what Plato originally accused it of being: morally corrupting illusion.

Marcuse's response is to challenge the assumption that ordinary modes of perceiving objects allow us to see them as they really are. Marcuse argues that our perception of objects is socially conditioned in ways that distort the truth. Since the image of the world ordinary perception yields is distorted, departure from this image is warranted. What is more, art's departure from the ordinary way of relating to things could, in effect, correct the distortion: "the world formed by art is recognized as a reality which is suppressed and distorted in the given reality." Against the idea that art is a falsification of the world of everyday experience, Marcuse depicts the latter as mystified and the former as the means by which the fog is dispelled. As he writes, form "withdraws art from the mystifying power of the given and frees it for the expression of its own truth" (*AD* 9).

It is in explaining the specific ways aesthetic form addresses distorted perception that Marx's critique of capitalism becomes important to Marcuse's aesthetic theory. The first way, already discussed, lies in art's ability to combat "reification": the reduction of everything in the natural and social worlds to the status of a commodity to be bought and sold. This last idea is worth dwelling upon because it clarifies a potential point of obscurity in Marcuse's account. In particular, it suggests an account of how, exactly, Marcuse envisions the antagonism between prevailing modes of perception and those encouraged by great art. Modern capitalist society encourages us to view everything as a commodity: something useful that is exchangeable for something else of an equivalent quantity of abstract value. By contrast, great art offers us alternative modes of viewing the things that surround us: as a unique individual incommensurable with other things, as defined by its specific qualitative features, as having an idiosyncratic or personal significance, as being "beyond price," and so on.

As indicated earlier, the Marxist and Freudian dimensions of Marcuse's account coalesce here. Art's "de-reifying" role is essentially equivalent to its opposition to the reality principle. Treating things as commodities is one of the principal ways in which we promote our own self-preservation under capitalism. We risk self-destruction when we obey the pleasure principle and relate to things in a different manner, a manner untethered to the logic of the market and more at home in dreams, fantasies, or childhood experience. Of course, the imperative to consume, enjoy, and so on, is integral to the modern market economy. Yet this is not identical to the pleasure principle, which urges us to enjoy even when doing so poses a threat to our survival, under current social conditions. When art de-reifies, it obeys the pleasure principle in this sense. This is the principle of the id's functioning, not the ego's.

Art's role in combating reification extends to human beings themselves, who are also viewed as commodities under capitalism. Seen through the lens of reification, they are just so many bearers of labor power to be exchanged for wages. As Marcuse writes:

> Art is committed to that perception of the world which frees individuals from their functional existence and performance in society. It is committed to an emancipation of sensibility, imagination, and reason in all spheres of subjectivity and objectivity.
>
> (*AD* 9)

Here, too, the contrast is between a view of human beings as commodities, just so many interchangeable workers for purchase and sale, and as unique, priceless individuals. At a more subtle level, Marcuse thinks that art is subversive simply through its intense concern with inner experience, which is difficult to reconcile with the profit-motive:

> With the affirmation of the inwardness of subjectivity, the individual steps out of the network of exchange relationships and exchange values, withdraws from the reality of bourgeois society, and enters another dimension of existence.
>
> (*AD* 4)

As we will soon see, Marcuse's defense of inwardness clashes with the orthodox Marxist view that interiority is a characteristic of bourgeois culture, a convenient distraction from the class struggle.

In defending the role of art in demystifying social reality, Marcuse further invokes the Hegelian-Marxist idea that the laborer inhabits an "inverted world" in which everything appears as the opposite of what it actually is. This may sound obscure, so here is an example: In their exchange of labor-power for wages, the laborer and capitalist appear free and equal, though they are, in fact, the opposite of this. This equality is merely the surface "appearance" of a process whose "essence" is coercion, domination, and exploitation. Far from being transparent, social reality itself may be obscure in ways that art may help clarify:

> As fictitious world, as illusion (*Schein*), it contains more truth than does everyday reality. For the latter is mystified in its·

institutions and relationships, which make necessity into choice, and alienation into self-realization. Only in the "illusory world" do things appear as what they are and what they can be.

(*AD* 48)

Unfortunately, Marcuse does not develop these proposals for how art's demystifying potential can be used for revolutionary ends. For example, it is unclear just how, exactly, a work of art would reveal the apparent freedom and self-realization we enjoy under capitalism to be their opposites. Was this not the role of *Capital*, itself a work of empirical social science rather than formally innovative art? What is more, it is not clear how a work of art would effect this revelation by virtue of its formal structure and not its content. Here, once again, we confront the suspicion that Marcuse's formalism is inconsistent with his Marxism. Certainly, one can envision a didactic piece of propaganda that explains, in a manner reminiscent of *Capital*, why the wage labor contract is deceptive. Obviously, this would not be a work of great art in Marcuse's sense.

In Marcuse's defense, the demystification of capitalist social relations is just supposed to be one example of how great art can provide insight into social life: "Deception and illusion have been qualities of established reality throughout recorded history. And mystification is a feature not only of capitalist society. The work of art on the other hand does not conceal that which is—it reveals" (*AD* 56). Art, far from falsifying experience, can dispel the mists of ideology. True, Marcuse does not explain how this is meant to work in any specific case, such as the wage-contract under capitalism. Yet this may be because he envisions the model as applying more generally to other cases of social deception. It is also presumably true that this is only one way formally innovative art can contribute to experience.

4. Base and superstructure: art in orthodox Marxism

Although Marcuse's aesthetic formalism is Marxist in inspiration, it differs from the received Marxist view which Marcuse thinks of as primarily focused on content.

Unfortunately, Marcuse does not clearly explain who, exactly, his Marxist opponents are meant to be. This may lead one to wonder if his target is unclear at best and a strawman at worst. Brecht is clearly one figure who sometimes espouses the received Marxist view. Simply at the level of its content, a work like The Threepenny Opera, because it is focused on the plight of the urban poor, poses a challenge to bourgeois ideology. However, as Marcuse indicates, Brecht is a more complex figure whose thinking about the arts contains formalist and anti-formalist dimensions. Though his work has realist dimensions, Brecht is also an expressionist, and Marcuse seems to think that this formal innovation is much more subversive than anything Brecht does at the level of content. It might be tempting to suppose that Marx and Engels themselves are the antagonists, but Marcuse suggests that their own views on art and literature are not at all anti-formalist (AD 11). His intent is to denounce contemporary Marxists as untrue to the legacy of the founder. But who, exactly, are these contemporary Marxists?

One possibility I find quite promising is that Marcuse is describing the way art and culture are treated in the Soviet Union. Because no particular figure is named, I think it is reasonable to suppose that Marcuse has in mind some group or movement. Occasionally, Marcuse does associate the anti-formalist view with totalitarian regimes. Clearly, the focus on content and the consequent instrumentalization of art is characteristic of the type of propaganda that proliferates in these regimes. However, I leave the issue of who, exactly, Marcuse's antagonists are meant to be to one side. Their position itself is clear and compelling enough on its own to merit attention. The anti-formalist aesthetic essentially asserts that artists sympathetic to Marxism should further the political aims of this movement in the most direct way possible. In other words, at the level of subject-matter, rather than style.

The Marxist view that Marcuse opposes approaches aesthetic questions from the vantage point of historical materialism: more specifically, the idea that art is part of the social "superstructure," rather than the economic "base." Though the details are complex, the core contention of this perspective on aesthetics is that art has traditionally functioned to uphold the existing class structure. We are here dealing with a "conception of art as performing an essentially dependent, affirmative ideological function, that is to say, glorifying and absolving the existing society" (AD 11). Worse still, stylization has traditionally helped art serve its function of supporting the status quo. Contra Marcuse, not all formally innovative art is subversive.[7] On the contrary, style allows the artist to present her subject-matter in ways that are ideologically suspect: for example, sentimentalizing poverty, idealizing war, or glorifying excessive wealth and political power. Society's evils will weigh on us less heavily once we experience the cathartic release that is great art's classical raison d'être: art "cannot represent this suffering without subjecting it to aesthetic form, and thereby to the mitigating catharsis, to enjoyment. Art is inexorably infested with this guilt" (AD 55). For the orthodox Marxist, art stands accused of a crime that is none other than what Hegel's idealist aesthetics praised it for doing: reconciling us with our (social) world.

While Marcuse believes great art will, at least on a formal level, concern itself with universal human problems like love and death, the received Marxist view denies this. It accuses traditional art of deceiving victims of capitalist exploitation that their problems are ones that would present themselves at all times and places: "this privatization of the social, the sublimation of reality, the idealization of love and death are often branded by Marxist aesthetics as conformist and repressive ideology" (AD 26). Essentially, the received Marxist view is that traditional art has deceived its audiences about the main sources of conflict in human life. These are not problems of human nature, ones affecting every individual in the innermost recesses of her subjectivity. They are, rather, problems specific to class societies and affecting people insofar as they are members of the subordinate class and doing so in concrete, material ways; for example, lack of access to property and resources. The orthodox Marxist need not deny that death, illness, and disappointment are universal problems. Yet she will question whether these problems are as important and pervasive in human life as traditional art seems to think they are. On the orthodox Marxist view, these problems are exaggerated so as to distract from the problems specific to capitalism. Since only the capitalistic-specific problems could be ameliorated by revolution, obscuring them tends to counteract the forces of change. The tragic view of the human condition espoused by much great art deceives people because it ignores the fact that, under capitalism, life is more tragic than it needs to be.

The received Marxist view attempts to reverse the pacifying effect traditional art has had and give it a revolutionary one. On this received view, artists should focus on content, rather than form. More specifically, artists ought to make the class struggle and its history the subject-matter of their works. Quoting a Marxist theoretician, Marcuse writes: "this view demands that the protagonists in a work of art represent individuals as 'types' who in turn exemplify 'objective tendencies of social development, indeed of humanity as a whole'" (AD 12). Perhaps it is impossible to present this subject-matter with no stylization whatsoever, but the orthodox Marxist urges that style be kept to a minimum. In other words, the style, to the extent that there is one, should be that of realism. Socialist realism would be the principal example. As Marcuse notes, Marxists have frequently denounced surrealist and romantic approaches— those focused on events occurring in dreams and hallucinations or else in the innermost recesses of an individual's subjectivity. Finally, the received Marxist view is that both author and recipient should be members of the working class.[8] Here, we have to recall the idea considered above that the content of the work of art must come from the experience of the artist. The orthodox Marxist suspects that only a member of the working class will have the appropriate vantage point on the class struggle. On this view, members of the bourgeoisie, a declining class, can only produce "decadent art." Ultimately, the received Marxist view attempts to reverse the causal role of art in society, so that it is no longer conservative but, rather, revolutionary.

One of Marcuse's main objections to the received Marxist view is that it wrongly assigns to art a role that only philosophy or social science can adequately fulfill. The intuition is that we do not need works of art to offer a class analysis of modern society, since Marxism already does so:

> Such formulations provoke the question whether literature is not hereby assigned a function which could only be fulfilled in the medium of theory. The representation of the social totality requires a conceptual analysis, which can hardly be transposed into the medium of sensibility.
>
> (AD 12)

However, Marcuse's intuition is backed up by an argument. The medium of art is sensible imagery, whereas that of theory is conceptual thought. Hence, art has a medium that is not fit for conveying scientific truths about society and history. Marcuse makes this point obliquely, quoting a remark of Goldmann's from an exchange of his with Adorno. The remark concerns the difference between art and philosophy: "in art there is no death, only Phaedra dying" (AD 13). At issue here is not just the distinction between art and philosophy, the sensible and the conceptual, but also between the particular (Phaedra dying) and the universal (death). Hence, we can complete Marcuse's thought in the following way. Art's medium, the sensible image, relates us to concrete particulars: the specific people, places, and periods that are the subject-matter. Hence its conclusions about society and history are likely to be limited in scope and lacking in general applicability. Theory's medium, the abstract concept, allows for general statements that make up a science: laws, tendencies, and trends. At best, then, the type of art envisioned by the orthodox Marxist will be redundant, simply reiterating the claims of *Capital*. At worst, it will be inferior, falling below the rigor required by philosophy and social science.

Marcuse also objects that the focus on content rather than form will actually counteract rather than further the goal of revolutionary change. The more artists focus on politically relevant subject-matter, the more they neglect the imperative of giving form to this subject-matter. And if this is so, then they will neglect the opportunity to reshape the perceptual experience of their audience. They will leave the perceptual habits of their audience intact and unchallenged. This would be a dereliction of the artist's role. It is here, at the level of our habits of perception, that art can make its most decisive contribution to altering social conditions:

> The political potential of art lies only in its own aesthetic dimension. Its relation to praxis is inexorably indirect, mediated, and frustrating. The more immediately political the work of art, the more it reduces the power of estrangement and the radical, transcendent goals of change.
>
> (AD xii)

The admittedly somewhat counterintuitive implication of this line of argument is that focusing on class struggle is an unproductive way for an artist to promote it. This is so inasmuch as a work of art with this content may remain conservative at the (all-important) level of form: "The more immediately political the work of art, the more it reduces ... the radical, transcendent goals of change" (*AD* xii).

By the same token, turning away from politically charged subject-matter, when this is called for aesthetically, may be more conducive to what Marcuse calls "negation of the realistic-conformist mind." This is because it is part and parcel of the defamiliarization that form always involves vis-à-vis content:

> True, the aesthetic form removes art from the actuality of the class struggle—from actuality pure and simple. The aesthetic form constitutes the autonomy of art vis-à-vis "the given." However, this dissociation does not produce "false consciousness" or mere illusion but rather a counter consciousness: negation of the realistic-conformist mind.
>
> (*AD* 8)

Following others in the Frankfurt School, Marcuse therefore advocates recovering for Marxism much art that is bourgeois, apolitical, or even politically conservative—but formally experimental:

> The degree to which the distance and estrangement from praxis constitute the emancipatory value of art becomes particularly clear in those works of literature which seem to close themselves rigidly against such praxis. Walter Benjamin has traced this in the works of Poe, Baudelaire, Proust, and Valery.
>
> (*AD* 19)

Unexpectedly, Marcuse reclaims for Marxism a central idea of modernist aesthetics which might seem to sit uneasily with radical politics: the rejection of everyday modes of thought and speech in favor of alternative modes only available to those who stand outside convention. Significantly, Marcuse rejects these common modes of expression even where they are used to convey revolutionary sentiments. "Banalization" is counterproductive because it eliminates form and with it the possibility of challenging received habits of thought in the way only art can: "deliberately formless expression 'banalizes' inasmuch as it obliterates the opposition to the established universe of discourse an opposition which is crystallized in the aesthetic form" (AD 43).

One of Marcuse's more elusive ideas is that great art, though it has a political effect, only has it in an "indirect" way. In other words, it must have its effect on society via an additional factor, the reshaped perceptions of its audience. It cannot have its effect on society directly since, without this detour, established modes of perception go unchallenged. It is one thing when an environmentalist author produce poetry that awakens in people a sense of awe in the face of the natural world, and quite another when ecoterrorists blow up an oil pipeline. In a sense, it is understandable to want a direct influence on society, as defenders of the orthodox Marxist view of culture do. Yet Marcuse thinks this temptation should be resisted. For Marcuse, the received Marxist view rests on a fundamental misunderstanding of the nature of art, a conflation of the "objective" and the "subjective":

> This emancipation, and the ways toward it, transcend the realm of propaganda. They are not adequately translatable into the language of political and economic strategy. Art is a productive force qualitatively different from labor; its essentially subjective qualities assert themselves against the hard objectivity of the class struggle.
>
> (AD 37)

Admittedly, Marcuse does not spell out the difference between the "objective" factors and the "essentially subjective" ones. Here, I think it would be legitimate to question whether Marcuse's distinction is as absolute as he seems to think. Revolutionaries too attempt to win the hearts and minds of the public, in addition to seizing the means of production or smashing the state. One possibility is that this distinction is not so much between the mental and the psychical as between the superstructure and the base. I want to dwell on this possibility here.

Seen in this light, the disagreement between Marcuse and the orthodox Marxist would concern whether art, as part of the "superstructure," could ever lead to a revolutionary transformation of society. The schema—the base–superstructure dichotomy—

> implies a normative notion of the material base as the true reality and a political devaluation of nonmaterial forces particularly of the individual consciousness and subconscious and their political function. If historical materialism does not account for this role of subjectivity, it takes on the coloring of vulgar materialism.
>
> (*AD* 3)

At most, the argument runs, art can alter the ideology of society's members; for example, their worldview. Yet revolution requires a more fundamental change in the "base," the economic structure; for example, seizing the means of production from the capitalist class. In every truly revolutionary transformation, it is the class structure which changes first, then art, religion, and philosophy. Altered consciousness cannot, in and of itself, bring about revolution. The tail does not wag the dog.

In Marcuse's view, this position is too extreme, and nothing like it is warranted by Marxism's break with traditional (Cartesian) philosophy: "a devaluation of the entire realm of subjectivity takes place, a devaluation not only of the subject as ego cogito, the rational subject, but also of inwardness, emotions, and imagination" (*AD* 3). The Marxist rejection of Cartesian dualism does not entail that psychological factors are irrelevant to radical politics and revolutionary strategy. To the extent that orthodox Marxists have devalued or ignored human psychology, they have simply accepted the reification characteristic of the bourgeoisie: a class with an economic interest in the reduction of everything and everyone to a commodity that can be bought and sold: "Marxist theory succumbed to that very reification which it had exposed and combated in society as a whole. Subjectivity became an atom of objectivity; even in its rebellious form it was surrendered to a collective consciousness" (*AD* 3–4). Similarly, Marcuse repeatedly emphasizes the uncomfortable parallels between bourgeois ideology and orthodox Marxism's dismissal of inwardness, subjectivity, individuality, and so on: "this attitude is not too remote from the scorn of the capitalists for an unprofitable dimension of life" (*AD* 38). Here, Marxism is complicit with the thought and culture of the very economic system it seeks to overthrow.

To be sure, Marcuse is not so naïve as to believe that innovative works of art and the new modes of consciousness they encourage are sufficient for a revolutionary transformation of society as a whole. Beckett and Kafka are no match for the truncheons and tear gas. To maintain otherwise would be to follow Hegel in giving ideas, consciousness, or "spirit," an outsized role in history. Whatever Marcuse's disagreements with orthodox Marxists, he is not a vulgar idealist. Still, he is insisting on the necessity of these new modes of consciousness, and presumably of the works of art that inculcate them in people. As he writes, "Art cannot change the world, but it can contribute to changing the consciousness and drives of the men and women who could change the world" (*AD* 32). For Marcuse, the transformation in subjectivity that is required if society is to change requires a new sensibility that art can instill in people. This is so even if a new sensibility falls far short of the ultimate goals of revolutionary change:

> The possibility of an alliance between "the people" and art presupposes that the men and women administered by monopoly capitalism unlearn the language, concepts, and images of this administration, that they experience the dimension of qualitative change, that they reclaim their subjectivity, their inwardness.
>
> (*AD* 4)

For Marcuse, a transformed subjectivity is necessary not just for the revolutionary overthrow of capitalism but for the socialist society that will succeed it. This follows from Marcuse's reinterpretation of the socialist ideal along psychoanalytic lines. For Marcuse, "from each according to his abilities ..." means that Thanatos, the death drive, aggression, must be kept in check by Eros, life, and love. As he writes, "solidarity and community have their basis in the subordination of destructive and aggressive energy to the social emancipation of the life instincts" (*AD* 17). For Marcuse, the need for transformation is addressed to the individual-qua-individual, and not just qua member of her class. The received Marxist view attempts to bypass the psychological transformation stage, but in doing so it flies in the face of the fact that people are individuals in addition to members of classes. In this regard, it embraces a form of determinism incompatible with revolutionary action:

> The deterministic component of Marxist theory does not lie in its concept of the relationship between social existence and consciousness, but in the reductionistic concept of consciousness which brackets the particular content of individual consciousness and, with it, the subjective potential for revolution.
>
> (*AD* 4)

The proposal, implicit here, seems to be that an individual must come to grips with her particular life-experiences, thoughts, and feelings before she accepts her role in the class struggle and embraces the need for revolution.

According to Marcuse, the received Marxist view correctly observes that new modes of consciousness are not by themselves sufficient, but wrongly concludes from this that they are not necessary at all. It is almost as if a revolution could be brought about by automata with no inner lives at all, though obviously this is a caricature of the received view. More accurately, the received view acknowledges the role of human psychology in the revolution but denies that the most important motivation will be those artistic influences; dire need born of poverty may contribute, but a transformed aesthetic sensibility is less likely to do so. Marcuse, however, does not think empty stomachs are sufficient; he insists on "a transformation of consciousness":

> The necessity of the political struggle was from the beginning a presupposition of this essay. It is a truism that this struggle must be accompanied by a change of consciousness. But it must be recalled that this change is more than development of political consciousness—that it aims at a new "system of needs". Such a system would include a sensibility, imagination, and reason emancipated from the rule of exploitation.
>
> (*AD* 36)

The term "system of needs" is Hegel's name for the division of labor: the scheme of cooperation and interdependence whereby each of us can only satisfy our needs by working for others and helping them do the same. Under capitalism, the system of needs is organized via the market, but as Marcuse indicates, there may one day be "a new system of needs"—just as there have been others pre-dating capitalism. For Hegel, it is crucial that the system of needs does not simply work "behind the backs of individuals," but, rather, educates them in new ways of thinking. They become conscious of their inter-dependence, motivated by it, and so on—at least within the limits that the economic system allows.

By invoking Hegel, Marcuse is able to challenge the rigid dichotomy between a change in the base and the superstructure. Economies are not just flows of goods, services, and money, but also structures of mutual recognition. Under capitalism, individuals relate as buyers and sellers, largely indifferent to one another's particular identities and needs. Under communism, matters would be different. However, the crucial point is that our attitudes towards one another reflect the economic institutions in which we participate. For this reason, Marcuse envisions a change in society as brought about by people who have "unlearned" their social conditioning and passionately yearn for a new way of life. However, he is not naïve enough to think that this yearning is sufficient for revolution. It is no match for truncheons and tear gas either, at least not all by itself.

In responding to the received Marxist view, Marcuse insists that his view is consistent with orthodox historical materialism, but he further notes that the received Marxist view may not be. According to this received view, art must attempt to bring about revolution through its content. It must, essentially, serve as propaganda for the revolution. Yet such a position only makes sense if we think that art is a causal power in society that is on a par with economic structures and forces. This is precisely what the base-superstructure model cautions against when it deems art part of "social conscious-ness." Strange as it may sound, historical materialism, as Marcuse interprets it, lends support to the traditional idea of the autonomy of the aesthetic: specifically, the idea that art is independent from the production process—or, at least, *relatively* independent. Indeed, Marcuse goes further, arguing that it is precisely in virtue of its form that the work of art is able to be autonomous: "the aesthetic form removes art from the actuality of the class struggle-from actuality pure and simple. The aesthetic form constitutes the autonomy of art vis-à-vis 'the given'" (AD 8). As we saw earlier, it is content which links art to the social world. Form, then, provides a measure of critical distance from society. Once we appreciate this, we will reconcile ourselves to a conception of art as exerting an "indirect, frustrating and mediated" influence on people's psychologies at the level of its form. Yet the received Marxist view, in effect, treats art as if it were immediately effective in a way that is possible for the economic structure, or perhaps the legal and political institutions.

Marcuse also rejects the received Marxist view that great art can only be produced by members of an ascendant class (the proletariat) and never by those of a class in decline (the bourgeoisie.) His first line of attack on this idea stresses the universal significance of art: because of its concern with an unvarying human nature, art is intended for all human beings. Hence, it can be produced by all human beings:

> The universality of art cannot be grounded in the world and world outlook of a particular class, for art envisions a concrete universal, humanity (Menschlichkeit), which no particular class can incorporate, not even the proletariat, Marx's "universal class."
>
> (AD 16)

However, Marcuse also doubts that the working class is still a revolutionary class, capable of playing a role in the transformation of society as a whole. In the nineteenth century, the industrial proletariat is, indeed, a class that had nothing to lose but its chains. In the twentieth century, however, the lower classes have been "integrated." They have the opportunity to become white-collar workers with pensions and stock options. What is more, they have access to mass entertainment. If anything answers to the title of art for the masses, it is Hollywood and not Brecht. Under these conditions, Marcuse holds that a certain elitism is warranted, even if one's ultimate political goals are populist. If an artist wants to produce truly revolutionary art in a society where the population consumes the propaganda of the culture industry, then "this is a process which may require them to stand against the people, which may prevent them from speaking their language. In this sense 'elitism' today may well have a radical content" (*AD* 35). It may well be that only a small minority of society's members have the freedom from toil necessary to produce great art, which is formally innovative and challenges received habits of perception and thought. It is also, in all likelihood, art which is not produced for a great profit, a further reason why the artists may need some distance from the dictates of the market.

5. The 1960s counterculture

At times, however, Marcuse may seem to go too far in his insistence that cultural innovation can yield a revolutionary transformation of society at large, especially in his analysis of 1960s counterculture. Marcuse characterizes this movement as bringing about something that should be impossible, according to orthodox Marxism and historical materialism: the superstructure affecting the base: "The movement of the sixties tended toward a sweeping transformation of subjectivity and nature, of sensibility, imagination, and reason. It opened a new vista of things, an ingression of the superstructure into the base" (*AD* 33). Evidently, Marcuse thinks of the art and music of the 1960s as inspiring a cultural movement (in the superstructure) which threatens capitalism and imperialism (in the base). He describes this as a process in which originally "utopian" ideas from the aesthetic domain come to be realized in society, which is precisely the opposite of what orthodox historical materialism would predict:

> Even now in the established society, the indictment and the promise preserved in art lose their unreal and utopian character to the degree to which they inform the strategy of oppositional movements (as they did in the sixties). While they do so in damaged and broken forms, they nevertheless indicate the qualitative difference from previous periods. This qualitative difference appears today in the protest against the definition of life as labor, in the struggle against the entire capitalist and state-socialist organization of work (the assembly line, Taylor system, hierarchy), in the struggle to end patriarchy, to reconstruct the destroyed life environment, and to develop and nurture a new morality and a new sensibility.
>
> (*AD* 28)

In this evaluation of the 1960s counterculture as an instance of superstructure affecting the base, Marcuse may seem to have made a complete departure from anything reasonably called Marxist. A similar departure can be found in his apparent suggestion that a revolutionary overthrow of existing society could follow the lead of art and culture, rather than the other way around: "art does not stand under the law of revolutionary strategy. But perhaps the latter will one day incorporate some of the truth inherent in art" (*AD* 57). However, there are resources in Marcuse's account for a response.

At one point, Marcuse expresses his dissatisfaction with the rigidity of the superstructure–base schema, insisting that Marx and Engels' original formula was more "dialectical." Among Marxists, this term can be used to mean almost anything, but Marcuse seems to be advocating a more flexible version of the base–superstructure model. In particular, Marcuse seems to suggest that the designation of base as cause and superstructure as effect is much too crude, and that there is likely a reciprocal relationship between them. This could be true even if the base remains the ultimately more powerful factor. In the end, alternations in consciousness cannot by themselves change the class structure of society, and this is registered in the idea that the base has primacy over the superstructure. However, this does not mean that the superstructure cannot affect it in any way at all. Indeed, the original model seems to suppose that the superstructure, though it is the effect of the base, "reacts back" on the latter. If art, religion, and philosophy had no effect on the class structure whatsoever, then the former could not play its assigned role of stabilizing the latter. This does not mean that altered consciousness is sufficient for a revolution, but it does mean that it can, in certain rare instances, create serious disturbances in the established order.

Marcuse acknowledges that the 1960s counterculture failed in most of its aims, but his insistence that it represents "an ingression of the superstructure into the base" is meant to remind us that it was no mere culture sideshow to real politics either.[9] It posed a threat to the established order, not just in the lyrics of its protest songs, but in the streets: "the indictment and the promise preserved in art lose their unreal and utopian character to the degree to which they inform the strategy of oppositional movements' (*AD* 28). We should not forget this, even if the establishment was ultimately effective in neutralizing the threat. Historical materialism tells us that the economic, legal, and political structures are more powerful than art and culture—but this belief-system cannot be used to refute the idea that the latter may, for a time, prevail over the former. In contrast to the portrayal of him as a naïve enthusiast of the hippie movement, Marcuse's outlook, as interpreted here, more than accounts for the failure of many social movements, such as those of the 1960s (or even the socialist revolutions in central Europe whose failure was arguably one of the inciting incidents of critical theory). For Marcuse, a certain pessimism about even the most successful social movements follows from a correct view of the human condition in which Eros (love) is always menaced by Thanatos (death):

> Art declares its caveat to the thesis according to which the time has come to change the world. While art bears witness to the necessity of liberation, it also testifies to its limits. What has been done cannot be undone; what has passed cannot be recaptured.
> (68–69)

This pessimism extends to the future socialist society that Marcuse himself advocates, but in which certain problems of the human condition will inevitably remain.

Marcuse's case for aesthetic formalism, and against an aesthetics of content, turns on the idea that art's role is to challenge our habits of perception: not so much what we tend to perceive, but the way we perceive it. In this way, we will be able to achieve critical distance from our social world. This is a process Marcuse understands in terms of Freud's distinction between the reality principle and the pleasure principle. Great art, formally innovative art, stimulates aggressive and sexual instincts which are unable to find expression in social life. Marcuse's account also draws on Marx's critique of capitalism, insisting that the altered perceptions great art enables us to enjoy are "de-reifying" and enable us to relate to objects and people as more than commodities.

The received Marxist view is suspicious of formalism, and urges that art seek to promote socialism at the level of its content so that it becomes something more like propaganda. However, Marcuse argues that this is counterproductive, and that it will only lead to art's co-option by capitalism—something that has already taken place in the culture industry. At a deeper level, Marcuse's dissatisfaction with the received Marxist view lies in its overly rigid interpretation of the base-superstructure model of society, which it wrongly takes to mean people's individual psychologies are irrelevant from the perspective of the class struggle. For Marcuse, a clear counterexample to this is the 1960s, a period in which art and culture, as well as a transformed psychology, played an important role in encouraging people to resist global capitalism and American imperialism. Marcuse does not overestimate the role of art and culture, and acknowledges that they are never by themselves sufficient to bring about a revolutionary transformation of society. Yet contra the received Marxist view, Marcuse insists that art and culture are not insignificant either.

Summary

Marcuse is an aesthetic formalist, a figure who holds that the value of a work of art chiefly resides in its form rather than in its subject-matter. This position has precedent in classical German philosophy, especially in Kant's writings. Yet Marcuse attempts to develop a version of formalism that is consistent with critical theory, and therefore with Freud and Marx. For Marcuse, formally innovative art challenges the modes of perception to which human beings, living under late capitalism, are habituated. In so doing, it facilitates the revolutionary transformation of society. Marcuse's position appears to be inconsistent with orthodox Marxism, at least in the role Marcuse ascribes to the "superstructure" in effecting social transformation (for example, Marcuse regards the 1960s counterculture as an "ingression of the superstructure into the base"). Orthodox Marxist aesthetics risks crudely instrumentalizing art and transforming it into propaganda.

The role of Freudian psychoanalysis in Marcuse's account lies in the idea that formally innovative works can be aids to resisting a repressive society, one in which the expression of human beings' aggressive and sexual instincts is curtailed in the name of social harmony. The role of Freudian analysis in Marcuse's aesthetic theory distances it even further from orthodox Marxism, inasmuch as Freud provides Marcuse with a universalistic set of standards for works of art. For Marcuse, following Freud, there are historically invariant truths of the human condition expressed by great art. Given Marcuse's reputation as a naïve optimist, it is worth noting that he includes among these invariant truths the pessimistic expressed especially well in works of tragedy.

Notes

1 I thank Vid Simonti for this point.
2 I thank Vid Simonti for helping to clarify Greenberg's position for me in discussion.
3 Marcuse's differences with Brecht are discussed further in Bronner (1988: 113).
4 I therefore do not agree with Bronner when he says that, in Marcuse's ideal future society, "Thanatos, the death instinct, will be eliminated" (1988: 121).
5 This designation is somewhat anachronistic, though not (I think) incorrect. Kant was recruited for formalism by Bell and Greenberg, but was not known this way in his own time. Thanks to Vid Simonti, once more, for this point of clarification.
6 Marcuse himself discusses this idea ("purposiveness without purpose") in *Eros and Civilization*, 177.
7 For a similar view of art, see Peter Burger's *Theory of the Avant-Garde*. I thank Vid Simonti for the reference.
8 See Benjamin's essay, "The Author as Producer." I thank Vid Simonti for the reference.
9 I therefore think Bronner goes too far when he calls *The Aesthetic Dimension* "a work of defeat" (1988: 136).

Further Reading

Adorno, T., Benjamin, W., Bloch, E., Brecht, B., and Lukács, G. (2020) *Aesthetics and Politics*, London: Verso. [Useful for context concerning the pre-history of Marcuse's ideas. Anthology encompassing debates over realism and form in Marxist aesthetics, especially in the early Frankfurt School. Helpful afterword by Frederic Jameson.]

Bronner, S. (1988) "Between Art and Utopia: Reconsidering the Aesthetic Theory of Herbert Marcuse," in A. Feenberg, R. Pippin, and C. Webel (eds.), *Marcuse: Critical Theory and the Promise of Utopia*. London: Bergin & Garvey. [Critical overview of Marcuse's aesthetics from his dissertation on the romantic novel to *The Aesthetic Dimension*.]

Guyer, P. (2008) "Marcuse and Classical Aesthetics', *Revue International de Philosophie*, Vol. 4, No. 246, 349–65. [Overview of the mostly German tradition of aesthetics that Marcuse drew on in works like *Eros and Civilization* and *The Aesthetic Dimension*.]

Six

Human nature

This chapter considers Marcuse's conception of human nature and the role of this conception in his broader philosophical project. Here, as always, Marcuse arrives at his conclusions through sustained engagement with the history of ideas. In this chapter, then, we will focus on the legacy of Freudian psychoanalysis in Marcuse's thinking, primarily in *Eros and Civilization*. Our specific aim is to understand how Marcuse's radical politics employs the late Freud's model of human life, i.e., as a competition between two primal human instincts, aggression and sexuality. In the conclusion of the chapter, we will consider what Marcuse calls "a biological foundation for socialism" in the later work *An Essay on Liberation*. There, we find a later version of Marcuse's theory which retains the earlier conception of socialism as the victory of biological life over the forces that would mutilate and destroy it. This later version is much less beholden to the Freudian apparatus and may for that reason prove more convincing. The "marriage of Marx and Freud," as it is sometimes called, lay at the heart of critical theory, and was a rapprochement attempted by its members. A fuller account of Marcuse's place in this story would have to consider his debate with Fromm, a figure Marcuse would accuse (perhaps unfairly) of advocating conformism, joining forces with "ego-psychology" and betraying the subversive legacy of Freud's theory of the instincts.[1] However, I will focus exclusively on Marcuse here.

As we have already said, Freud provides Marcuse with a theory of human life as dominated by two great forces: Eros and Thanatos. Provisionally, we can understand these terms to refer to the sexual and aggressive instincts, but they will require more clarification.

DOI: 10.4324/9781003307075-6

Famously—or perhaps notoriously—Freud understands Eros quite broadly. It includes not only our interest in sexual pleasure, but also friendship and romantic love. Indeed, even "higher" cultural pursuits (art, science, etc.) draw on Eros. Thanatos is more controversial still, and even some Freudians prepared to accept the notion of Eros reject Thanatos. It too has a broad reach, describing not only aggression, but destructiveness in general. In just the same way that Eros can encompass both overt and subtle forms of physical pleasure-seeking, so too does Thanatos encompass the full spectrum of destructive activity, such as warfare, but also the human project of mastering nature, the use of tools and technology for this purpose, and even perhaps certain mental operations required by science ("analysis," because of its association with the activities cutting, splitting, and breaking down might be an example).

The Freudian apparatus becomes more unwieldy still when we realize that Eros and Thanatos are not only individual but socio-logical forces as well, and that there are difficult questions about how they relate. Occasionally, Marcuse describes the student-led, anti-war movement of the 1960s as a revolt of Eros against Thanatos. For Mar-cuse, Freud is a thinker for whom the individual and collective fate of humankind depends on the interplay of Eros and Thanatos.

As should already be evident, Marcuse does little to blunt the controversial force of Freud's ideas. Indeed, Marcuse chooses to draw on what is likely among the most contested phase of Freud's career, regarded with suspicion even by many orthodox Freudians: the late Freud's "metapsychological" doctrines. These include the rather pessimistic idea, no doubt inspired by Freud's experience of treating patients returning from World War I, of a distinct death drive in human nature. Henceforth, human existence will be under-stood as a struggle between Eros and Thanatos, rather than driven by the former alone. This is already considered a speculative part of Freud's theory, not easily verified. We have already said that it is not only a psychological doctrine but also a sociological one. Yet Freud extends the theory even further. At times, it seems more like a cosmological or metaphysical doctrine than a medical or scientific one. Freud sometimes refers to Eros and Thanatos as tendencies in all living matter, seeing them in "anabolic" and "catabolic" processes. Even Freud's early theories have their detractors and are criticized for being unnecessarily speculative; for example, going beyond anything directly implied by the firsthand observations made in his case studies. Yet the later Freud seems even more so, offering a theory of such obscure topics as the forces underlying all life and matter (1920: 49–50).

As if Marcuse's reliance on the late Freud's theory of Eros and Thanatos were not enough, there are even more controversial Freudian doctrines which Marcuse adapts. These include Freud's prehistory of the human race, as put forth in works like *Moses and Monotheism* and *Totem and Taboo*. Central to the late Freud's prehistory is the idea of primitive humanity as presided over by a tyrannical father-figure, who monopolized sexual pleasure for himself. This father-figure was eventually deposed by his sons—murdered by them, in fact. Yet the guilt over this crime would haunt humanity through the ages. Freud found echoes of this event in the Old and New Testaments of the Bible. Needless to say, this account too has struck readers as being among the more speculative and less scholarly in Freud's oeuvre.

Given Marcuse's basic sympathy with Freudian theory in its entirety, one might expect him to recommend the adoption of Freudian psychoanalysis wholesale. However, this is not so, as Marcuse discerns a conflict between orthodox psychoanalysis and critical theory.

As is well known, Marcuse is no mere disciple of Freud, but a rebellious pupil. Marcuse is intent on reclaiming psychoanalysis for radical politics; in particular, the revolutionary overthrow of capitalism and its replacement by socialism. Though a critic of modern society, Marcuse is a political optimist in at least the following sense. He believes human beings could live happily and sanely in a future socialist society. Indeed, Marcuse further contends that the problems Freud views as inherent to human life are only problems of capitalist society, and could therefore be resolved through a transition to socialism.

This sets Marcuse at odds with the pessimistic vision of social life offered in Freud's *Civilization and its Discontents*. There, Freud describes society as a necessary bulwark against unruly human impulses, aggressive and sexual instincts whose full expression is incompatible with the basic requirements of social order. Yet Freud also sees the constraints of civilized life as a source of psychological suffering and neurosis. Social order, then, can only be purchased at the cost of human happiness and psychic health. Yet order is necessary and we challenge it at our peril. To do so is to invite chaos: in the family—incest; and in society—the war of all against all. Though he recommends piecemeal reforms, like the easing of repressive social mores, Freud does not think that any society will be able to avoid this unhappy fate.

By contrast, Marcuse tries to show that a happier life within society is possible, and to do so on the basis of the very Freudian doctrines that seem to render happiness and civilization incompatible. For Marcuse, a future socialist society would be able to reconcile the need for order and the requirements of human happiness.

This chapter explores his proposal for how to do so and asks whether it is plausible. The main objection to Marcuse's vision in *Eros and Civilization* is that it is unrealistically utopian or fantastical. Even a liberated reader could be forgiven for finding it excessively fixated on the role of sex and sexuality in a future socialist society (though it ought to be borne in mind that Eros is much a broader notion than sexuality). As we will see, Marcuse describes the non-repressive society as one whose members leave behind "genitality," re-eroticize their bodies, and rediscover the "polymorphous perversity" of infancy. Certainly, Marcuse's association with the student left has not helped the reception of *Eros and Civilization*, though the latter was first published in 1955. In spite of this, it can be tempting see in it little more than an erudite defense of "free love."

Yet it is not sex per se, but Eros (in Freud's expansive sense of the term) which Marcuse treats as the agent of human liberation. From friendship, romance, and sex to familial loyalty, patriotism, artistic creativity, and child's play, love in all its diverse forms has dominion over the human psyche. Marcuse's *Eros and Civilization* stands as one of the most complex and sophisticated attempts to explore the implications of this fact for radical politics. As I hope to show, distinguishing between sexuality in the narrow sense and Eros reveals Marcuse's analysis to have a counterintuitive implication. For him, it is the repressive society, rather than the non-repressive one, which is fixated on sexuality, narrowly defined. By contrast, it is the non-repressive society which would be less invested in sexuality, because it would have other outlets for erotic instincts.

Yet even the more modest idea of a non-repressive, erotic civilization is not without its problems. Is Marcuse then expressing the naïve idea that love conquers all, or a Marxist-Lennonist credo which states that "love is all you need"? In my view, this would be a fateful misunderstanding, since Marcuse shares with the late Freud the idea of another primal force in human life which is permanently waiting in the wings to undermine the achievements of Eros: Thanatos, or the death drive. There is nothing naïve in Marcuse's version of the Freudian idea that Eros and Thanatos vie for control of the psyche, and Marcuse goes beyond Freud in exploring the consequences of their interplay for the critique of capitalism and imperialism, the path to their revolutionary overthrow, and the prospects for socialism.

1. Freud and philosophy

To begin with, it is important to note that Marcuse proposes we con-sider Freud from a *philosophical* point of view, though what this means is not entirely clear:[2]

> The purpose of this essay is to contribute to the philosophy of psychoanalysis—not to psychoanalysis itself. It moves exclu-sively in the field of theory, and it keeps outside the technical discipline which psychoanalysis has become. Freud developed a theory of man, a "psycho-logy" in the strict sense. With this theory, Freud placed himself in the great tradition of philosophy and under philosophical criteria. Our concern is not with a corrected or improved interpretation of Freudian concepts but with their philosophical and sociological implications. Freud conscientiously distinguished his philosophy from his science; the Neo-Freudians have denied most of the former. On thera-peutic grounds, such a denial may be perfectly justified. How-ever, no therapeutic argument should hamper the development of a theoretical construction which aims, not at curing indi-vidual sickness, but at diagnosing the general disorder.
>
> (EC 7)

In emphasizing the continuities between Freud and philosophy, Mar-cuse insists that Freud is offering a logic of the soul, a "psycho-logy." By this, Marcuse presumably does not mean that Freud is a Carte-sian dualist, rather than a physicalist. He simply means that Freud is providing a model of the mind which must be understood as a successor to those in the philosophical tradition. In particular, Marcuse regards the Freudian model of the mind as a naturalistic version of Kant's. Indeed, Marcuse will at various points compare the ego under the reality principle to Kantian reason, and the superego to Kant's conscience, under the dictates of the Categorical Imperative:[3]

> Under the reality principle, the human being develops the function of reason: it learns to "test" the reality, to distinguish between good and bad, true and false, useful and harmful. Man acquires the faculties of attention, memory, and judgment. He becomes a conscious, thinking subject, geared to a rationality which is imposed upon him from outside.
>
> (EC 14–15)

Marcuse further emphasizes the distance of this Freudian conception from anything that is justifiable on purely scientific grounds ("Freud conscientiously distinguished his philosophy from his science"). To this extent, then, there may be some truth to the charge that the late Freud's metapsychology is speculative. It certainly does not seem as if the Eros–Thanatos model (or the idea of the primal horde) is forced upon us by the observed facts of human nature (and human prehistory). Further, Marcuse notes that these doctrines cannot be substantiated on purely therapeutic grounds. They are to be assessed in terms of their ability to clarify the deepest truth of the human situation, not in terms of their ability to heal the sick.

Marcuse is well aware that there are Freudians who insist on retaining only what is empirically verifiable and medically useful in Freud's theory: the neo-Freudians, or ego-psychologists. However, he rejects this approach, at least for the purposes of his project in Eros and Civilization. For Marcuse, the neo-Freudians' abandonment of the late Freud is not just questionable from a scholarly point of view, but in terms of its psychological motivations; in short, he suspects it is an attempt to repress the most scandalous truths about human beings and give psychoanalysis mainstream appeal:

> As psychoanalysis has become socially and scientifically respectable, it has freed itself from compromising speculations.

Compromising they were, indeed, in more than one sense: not only did they transcend the realm of clinical observation and therapeutic usefulness, but also they interpreted man in terms far more offensive to social taboos than Freud's earlier "pansexualism"—terms that revealed the explosive basis of civilization. The subsequent discussion will try to apply the tabooed insights of psychoanalysis (tabooed even in psychoanalysis itself) to an interpretation of the basic trends of civilization.

(EC 7)

Finally, Marcuse notes the way in which psychoanalysis is inseparable from social theory. For Freud, the psyche is not self-standing, but, rather, a product of social relations; in particular, the ego is formed when the id confronts social prohibitions, and the super-ego when it internalizes parental authority figures as compensation for the dissolution of the oedipal complex. This doctrine Marcuse regards as philosophical, inasmuch as it does not take the psyche and its illnesses at face value but examines how they reflect social totality ("diagnosing the general disorder"). Marcuse does not himself make the reference, but the City–Soul analogy in Plato's *Republic* would be a classical philosophical instance of seeing the condition of the individual psyche as related to that of the social whole. Marcuse believes that the late Freud is a philosopher in this sense, somebody who considers the larger sociological context in which psychology's subject-matter is formed. This would presumably contrast with a more empiricist approach that would stop short at the facts about the psyche, rather than inquiring into the way these facts are generated by social relations.

2. Eros and Thanatos

For Marcuse, Freud's concept of Eros is best defined in terms of what he called "the pleasure principle." The latter is simply that within the human mind which seeks pleasure, regardless of the cost. The pleasure principle is connected with sexual desire, which Freud believed even infants experience. Infants are "polymorphously perverse," experiencing sexual (or proto-sexual?) gratification on all surfaces of the body (EC 49, 201–02). Yet what the pleasure principle involves should not be equated with the sexual desire for others that mature adults feel, either when they simply lust after others or when they love them (if we distinguish the two). Originally, the pleasure principle is simply desire for one's own pleasure. In this sense, it is narcissistic. Indeed, "primary narcissism" is Freud's name for the self-enclosed, almost solipsistic form of pleasure-seeking characteristic of infants (EC 168). At this stage, the pleasure principle disregards others entirely except insofar as they are the bringers of warmth, milk, nourishment, and so on. So extreme is its lack of interest in others that when nourishment is lacking, it will choose to gratify itself in fantasy. The infant, as primary narcissist, pays no heed to other minds.

Not only other human beings, then, but even the external world itself is of little significance from the perspective of the pleasure principle. Regard for others and for the real world are both later acquisitions. The pleasure principle also should not be confused with the desire for self-preservation. This is a later development, one which often requires us to forsake pleasure. Yet the pleasure principle is single-minded in pursuit of its goal, and therefore heedless of self-preservation (EC 30). It urges us to seek enjoyment, even if this means the loss of our very lives. Self-preservation not only succeeds, but subordinates, our early interest in pleasure for pleasure's sake. What is more, the pleasure principle is ignorant of the end of procreation as well (EC 40). The interest we take in procreation comes at a later stage, and it too requires the subordination of pleasure seeking to the end of perpetuating the species. For Freud, the so-called "perversions," most of which involve non-procreative sexual activity for the sake of one's own gratification, are of interest because they point towards a more primitive interest in pleasure totally unconnected with the interest we take in perpetuating the race (EC 49). Ultimately, Freud reverses the received Victorian conception of normality and perversion. Conceptually and genetically prior to "normal" procreative sexuality is the so-called "perversion" of pleasure for pleasure's sake.

The pleasure principle is not only the first motivation human beings have in their lives, as infants, but, in a sense, the energy-source for all others—though, as we will see, Freud's monism concerning Eros is later overturned by the introduction of a distinct death drive in human nature. As is well known, Freud regarded the pleasure principle as highly malleable. It could be denied immediate satisfaction and granted only a delayed variety, or satisfied using substitutes; for example, in fantasy, in play, in friendship, in socially sanctioned forms of loving relationships like marriage, and even, finally, in higher cultural pursuits like art and science deemed more socially acceptable than the gratification of bodily desire. All of these are instances of repression, the denial of immediate gratification. Yet they also all involve sublimation, the seeking of this gratification along a less direct, more circuitous route. Because it is pleasure, rather than procreation, which is sought, these substitutes are at least moderately effective. In a sense, the pleasure principle can never be denied completely, and will in the end find satisfaction in some way. There is a type of conservation principle at work in Freud's model of the mind, not unlike those in physics. In Freudian psychology, this principle dictates that the desire we have as infants may undergo various changes, but is never truly eliminated or destroyed.

Yet while the model that is taking shape is monistic, subsuming self-preservation and procreation under Eros, this changes in the late Freud with the discovery of Thanatos. Freud discovers Thanatos, not as a principle entirely separate from Eros, but as a component of it: specifically, in the aggressive dimension of sexuality itself, a phenomenon attested to for Freud by sadism and masochism.[4] Far from being an aberration, aggression, directed at oneself or at another, turns out to be an ingredient in all sexual relationships, and this points towards another principle of mental functioning than Eros alone.

Yet Thanatos is meant to explain not only our aggression towards other human beings, but also a more primitive interest we have in simple destruction; for example, destroying inanimate objects and nonhuman organisms. Much like Eros, Thanatos is originally self-directed. Just as narcissism is prior to love of the other, masochism is prior to sadism. Indeed, Freud sees in human beings, and perhaps in all living creatures, a desire to control the circumstances of their deaths and die in their own way (EC 26). Shocking as it is, this conclusion is based on the simple thought that we only ever evade death temporarily, and that we know this. At some level, then, we conceive of our efforts to live another day as undertaken for the purpose of dying another way.

As if this elaboration on the death drive were not speculative enough, Freud sees beneath this a further desire on the part of human beings, and perhaps all living things, to return to the inert condition of inorganic matter. As ever, Freud seeks the normal in the pathological. Freud thinks he sees signs of this in the "repetition compulsions" characteristic of obsessional neuroses, like the "Fort! Da!" game or the "shell-shock" of soldiers returning from World War I (1920: 15). It is as if living beings, and especially conscious ones, seek a peaceful return to the inert, quiescent condition of inorganic matter when life and its vicissitudes become overwhelming. The death drive or Thanatos Freud thinks of as obeying the Nirvana principle: the cessation of tension, slackening and peace (EC 25). It is significant to note that Thanatos has always remained much more controversial than Eros and has seemed to many to be dispensable. Yet Marcuse clearly thinks it must be retained.

Having considered these two principles of mental life, we must now ask how they relate. Perhaps surprisingly, Freud contends that the death drive has a constructive role to play in normal, healthy development.[5] Explaining the relationship between Eros and Thanatos, however, will require us to introduce the later Freud's tripartite model of the mind as made up of id, ego, and super-ego. The id, originally governed by the pleasure principle, must learn to inhibit its aims in the face of restrictions imposed upon it by society and nature. In other words, it must learn to respect the reality principle, which allows as much gratification as is consistent with self-preservation. Hence, a part of the id splits off and becomes the ego, which is directed outward towards reality. The ego subjects the (rest of) the id to its dictates, and the pleasure principle becomes subordinate to the reality principle. Here, there is a role for Thanatos. In the first place, the ego must be aggressive towards the id in order to control it. In the second, destructiveness and aggression towards reality (and towards others) can be a means of obtaining gratification that is denied. The human ability to remake the natural world, through tools or technology, presupposes this interest in destruction. The third mental function to emerge is the super-ego, and the details of its genesis are complex. The super-ego is the conscience, an internalized parental or other authority figure, which brings the ego and id in line with the demands of social morality. Its genesis takes place during the dissolution of the oedipal complex, when the child, learning that it cannot have uninterrupted access to a parental love object, internalizes this object as compensation. Less important than how the super-ego arises is that here again there is a role for Thanatos. The super-ego too must be aggressive in its efforts to curb the ego and id. Of course, it is possible for people to develop overly strict super-egos, whose aggressiveness is excessive. When this occurs, the result is what Freud calls melancholia and what we would call aggression. Still, the pathological is not as far from the normal as we might suppose. Self-regulation involves aggression turned inward towards oneself.

The picture that emerges is one in which Thanatos is subordinate to Eros, helping the latter achieve its aims through an indirect route. This is not only consequential for the individual but for the species. The subordination of Thanatos to Eros is responsible for civilization itself, the human being's mastery of nature and of his fellow human beings:

> Still, the entire progress of civilization is rendered possible by the transformation and utilization of the death instinct or its derivatives. The diversion of primary destructiveness from the ego to the external world feeds technological progress, and the use of the death instinct for the formation of the superego achieves the punitive submission of the pleasure ego to the reality principle and assures civilized morality. In this transformation, the death instinct is brought into the service of Eros; the aggressive impulses provide energy for the continuous alteration, mastery, and exploitation of nature to the advantage of mankind. In attacking, splitting, changing, pulverizing things and animals (and, periodically, also men), man extends his dominion over the world and advances to ever richer stages of civilization. But civilization preserves throughout the mark of its deadly component.
>
> (EC 51–52)

However, as Marcuse notes, Freud seems to have been haunted by the possibility that Thanatos is ultimately fundamental. Freud notes that even when we pursue pleasure, we seem to aim at a release from tension. This aim seems equivalent to the death drive's longing for a return to the condition of inert matter. This leads Freud to a model in which it is Thanatos that is victorious, so that all Eros can do is take various detours to the final aim: death. Marcuse thinks that Freud never completely resolved the issue of whether Eros or Thanatos is supreme. At one point, Marcuse offers a reason for thinking Eros is more fundamental. If the death drive aims at relief from tension, then is this not implicitly a form of pleasure-seeking (the pleasure of relief)? In another place, Marcuse suggests that the predominance of the death drive over the life-instincts is an artifact of history, and the association between Thanatos and capitalism is a common trope in his more polemical writings.

However, it is clear Marcuse is less interested in the question of which force is in fact more fundamental than he is in that of which ought to be. This is not simply a normative question for Marcuse, but one of social engineering. How could society be ordered in such a way that the proper balance of the love and death drives is achieved?

3. Surplus repression: a Marxist critique of Freud

The point of departure for Marcuse's critique of Freud concerns a possible ambiguity in the latter's theory of civilization. Why, exactly, does the pleasure principle need to be subordinate to the reality principle, and how much sacrifice exactly is necessary? Marcuse thinks Freud never adequately answered this question, and that he simply assumed there was a fixed and unchanging amount of repression imposed on people by their natural and social environment. It is not difficult to see why this might be the case. In every society, there is some minimum necessary amount of work that must be done if people are to meet their basic needs for food, clothing, and shelter. Similarly, it seems that certain limits on sexual activity are inevitable and would have to be imposed in every society; for example, the prohibition on incest.

Pace Freud, however, Marcuse argues that the level of resistance from nature and society to the pleasure principle is not fixed and unchanging. Marcuse, following Marx, views humanity as engaged in a historically ongoing project of mastering nature, in the course of which the productive forces (tools, technology, etc.) are always improving. Similarly, Marx insists that each epoch in the history of humankind's struggle against nature involves a different class structure, and therefore a different set of social obstacles to individual self-realization. It varies depending on which historical mode of production is in question:

> The various modes of domination (of man and nature) result in various historical forms of the reality principle. For example, a society in which all members normally work for a living requires other modes of repression than a society in which labor is the exclusive province of one specific group. Similarly, repression will be different in scope and degree according to whether social production is oriented on individual consumption or on profit; whether a market economy prevails or a planned economy; whether private or collective property.
>
> (EC 37–38)

One way to understand Marcuse's argument for the claim that the reality principle will vary from society to society would be to see this argument as institutionalist in the following sense. The reality principle is impotent by itself. It must make use of a whole ensemble of institutions, practices, relationships, tools, techniques, laws, and so on ("every form of the reality principle must be embodied in a system of societal institutions and relations, laws and values which transmit and enforce the required 'modification' of the instincts") (EC 37). Yet all of these will index it to a particular society, which will demand a particular level of repression. Marcuse describes this social world as the "body" of the reality principle, and the implication seems to be that without its body it could not act. Occasionally, as we have seen, Marcuse uses Kantian language to describe the ego and super-ego as reason. Here he channels Hegel in describing social institutions like the family, civil society and state as "objective mind," or, in psychoanalytic terms, as "the embodiment of the reality principle."

Marcuse is most interested in the form the reality principle assumes under capitalism, rather than under previous modes of production (feudalism, slavery, etc.). Under capitalism, our technological mastery over nature is extremely advanced, but few of society's members are able to fully enjoy the fruits of this system. The class structure, in which most are exploited laborers, forecloses an equitable distribution of resources, and, perhaps worse still, consigns most people to lives of toil. Yet in a future socialist society, technological mastery of nature could be used for the benefit of all mankind. It would not just be used for the sake of a class of owners of the means of production who live off the labor of others. Marcuse accuses Freud of neglecting this possibility because of "the assumption that scarcity is as permanent as domination—an assumption that seems to beg the question" (EC 134).

Marcuse's Marxist-inspired amendment to Freud's theory requires a new set of psychoanalytic concepts. Instead of "the reality principle," we should now speak of "the performance principle" (EC 35). As we saw, the reality principle describes the need to subordinate pleasure to the demands of the real world. Redescribing the reality principle as the performance principle reflects the insight that what the so-called "real world" demands of us will vary depending on the stage we have reached in the history of production. Each mode of production, slavery, feudalism, capitalism, or socialism, demands the performance of a different type—and, more importantly, a different amount—of labor. Each reflects a different degree of control over nature. This then allows us to pose the question of whether the performance a given system demands of us is genuinely required of us by our surroundings. Is what is being asked of us the minimum that would be necessary to feed, clothe, and house ourselves, as well as reproduce society and its relations? Marcuse is clear that there will be a certain amount of repression necessary in any society, and that Freud was correct to this extent. Yet it may be that the performances demanded of us under capitalism serve not basic human needs, but rather the hegemony of the ruling class.

Under capitalism, workers are exploited, and Marcuse derives from this Marxist category another a psychoanalytic one for his reformed Freudian theory: surplus repression. For Marx, exploitation is defined as a process through which capitalists extract surplus labor (or surplus value) from workers: labor (or value) over and above what is required to meet the cost of reproducing their own labor power, i.e., their wages. From 9am to 12pm, I may produce for my employer just the value that he must pay me as a wage at the end of the day. If I only worked for these three hours, my employer would not earn a profit. Yet from 12 to 5, I produce for him surplus value, value over and above what he will pay to me as a wage. This surplus value will become his profit, which he will then reinvest at the end of the cycle. How, then, do we get from surplus value (labor) to the notion of surplus repression? Via the following premise. Marcuse notes that for Marx, as well as for Freud, labor requires the repression of desire. When I am working, I am not enjoying, and vice versa (except in those rare and happy moments when the two just happen to coincide, perhaps). Freud, especially, possesses a rationale for the claim that work is typically experienced as unpleasant. For him, there is no original work instinct, meaning that work requires the inhibition and redirection of other more primal instincts (EC 82–83).

The idea that work is necessarily—or predominantly—unpleasurable may seem to be an arbitrary and unwarranted assumption. In a sense, Marcuse would agree that this pessimistic conception of work ought to be challenged. He looks forward to a future socialist society in which, as he puts it, work will be play (EC 170). Yet for Marcuse, this is not the case under capitalism. Work will only be play in a classless society. It is not a standing possibility for us here and now. Nor has it been in previous class societies. If this assumption is granted, it follows that, just as capitalism demands surplus labor of workers, so too will it correspondingly demand surplus repression of them. For Marx, the great crime of capitalism is exploitation, the extraction of surplus value. Seen through a Freudian lens, this crime amounts to the imposition of excessive and unnecessary repression. Again, Marcuse concedes that there is some minimum level of repression that will be required in any society. Yet he thinks present-day society goes well beyond this.

What is more, Marcuse accuses Freud of undue pessimism about the prospects of a happy life for human beings in society. Freud holds that there is a level of repression that is necessary in any society if basic order is to be maintained. Yet, because he lacks Marx's categories of exploitation and surplus labor, he fails to see that the level of it in present-day society is excessive: surplus repression. In fairness, Freud may have thought some reduction of repression was possible under present social conditions; for example, through a modest relaxation of sexual repression. Yet Marcuse's point is that a significantly greater reduction is possible only if we go beyond present social conditions. The repressive society must be deposed through revolution.

More discouraging still is Freud's conviction, not simply that repression is necessary, but that it can only increase as civilization grows. As the bonds among people become more extensive, so too does the need to repress anti-social behavior:

> Reinforcing the sense of guilt: Since culture obeys an inner erotic impulse which bids it bind mankind into a closely knit mass, it can achieve this aim only by means of its vigilance in fomenting an ever-increasing sense of guilt.
>
> (EC 80–81)

For Freud, this trend will continue until our guilt is so great as to be intolerable. There is another more subtle reason why repression is likely to increase. When Eros is sublimated, its power to resist Thanatos decreases. Yet the power of Thanatos is always increasing, due to the need for greater control over the human being.

An obvious objection to this line of argument is that both Eros and Thanatos are repressed for the sake of civilization, and that both should be comparably restricted. Hence, we should expect to see the world become more peaceful. Yet while both Eros and Thanatos are sublimated, Eros is more so. Unrefined, crude aggression is socially tolerated, even encouraged:

> It seems that socially useful destructiveness is less sublimated than socially useful libido. To be sure, the diversion of destructiveness from the ego to the external world secured the growth of civilization. However, extroverted destruction remains destruction: its objects are in most cases actually and violently assailed, deprived of their form, and reconstructed only after partial destruction; units are forcibly divided, and the component parts forcibly rearranged. Nature is literally "violated." Only in certain categories of sublimated aggressiveness (as in surgical practice) does such violation directly strengthen the life of its object. Destructiveness, in extent and intent, seems to be more directly satisfied in civilization than the libido.
>
> (EC 86)

Freud saw in World War I an example of the increasing destructiveness of modern society, and the idea that Thanatos remains tolerated in a way Eros does not seems to have been his explanation. As Marcuse critically observes, there do not seem to be resources in Freud's account for arguing that the ever-increasing guilt felt by human beings is irrational. The increase in the guilt we feel is appropriate to ever greater demands that large and complex societies place upon us.

Marcuse must show, contra Freud, that a non-repressive society is a genuine possibility for us, and that the result would not be mere chaos. Marcuse looks forward to a future socialist society in which as much labor as possible is automated, and its products are distributed according to human need. In this way, surplus labor, and therefore surplus repression, would be reduced to a minimum:

> the surplus repression necessitated by the interests of domination would not be imposed upon the instincts. This quality would reflect the prevalent satisfaction of the basic human needs (most primitive at the first, vastly extended and refined at the second stage), sexual as well as social: food, housing, clothing, leisure.

> (EC 152)

Ideally, there would be no more labor or repression than was necessary for the collective to meet its members' needs, possibly due to automation: "Under the 'ideal' conditions of mature industrial civilization, alienation would be completed by general automatization of labor, reduction of labor time to a minimum, and exchangeability of functions" (EC 152). More concretely, the future society would be one in which the length of the working day is reduced to the minimum necessary with the remainder left over for leisure: "the reduction of the working day to a point where the mere quantum of labor time no longer arrests human development is the first prerequisite for freedom" (EC 152). Yet the aspiration to shorten the working day to its socially necessary minimum does not even begin to capture Marcuse's hopes for this future society, as we will now see.

For Marcuse, the change brought about by this society is not merely quantitative, but qualitative as well. Opportunities for leisure are not simply more plentiful but also more satisfying. This is because the absence of meaningless toil strengthens our various capacities for pleasure:

> The available resources make for a qualitative change in the human needs. Rationalization and mechanization of labor tend to reduce the quantum of instinctual energy channeled into toil (alienated labor), thus freeing energy for the attainment of objectives set by the free play of individual faculties.
>
> (EC 93–94)

To understand Marcuse's rationale for the claim that the change would not only be quantitative but qualitative, we need to recall Freud's idea of "polymorphous perversity."[6] At least as it figures in Marcuse's project, this is the idea that the infant is capable of experiencing pleasure on the entire surface of its body and is only later forced to repress this ability. The result of this repression is the limitation of sexual pleasure to the genitals, and to certain prescribed forms of activity. For Freud, the traces of polymorphous perversity persist, and can be found in the perversions. Yet maturity requires that it be given up in favor of a more constrained form of sexual activity. Marcuse's addition to this narrative lies in his idea that, with the reduction in time necessary for work, the space for pleasure will grow. He means this in a fairly literal sense. On his view, we will rediscover our capacities for pleasure in the other areas of the body:

> No longer used as a fulltime instrument of labor, the body would be re-sexualized. The regression involved in this spread of the libido would first manifest itself in a reactivation of all erotogenic zones and, consequently, in a resurgence of pregenital polymorphous sexuality and in a decline of genital supremacy.
>
> (EC 201–02)

Here, we should bear in mind the broad connotations of Freud's notion of Eros. Marcuse's claim is not so much that sexual activity will be unfettered, but that Eros (life instinct) will. The consequences, then, are not simply more sexual activity, but more of all of those activities which are erotic in Freud's broad sense of the term: friendship, romantic love, creativity, play, and so on. In this connection, it is noteworthy that Marcuse frequently describes the hippie movement as attempting to reclaim the body as an instrument of pleasure, rather than labor. Yet he never explicitly refers to the idea of free love, though it could plausibly be seen as a consequence of his view. More important to him is the idea that life should be taken up by creative pursuits, loving relationships, and not toil for the military–industrial complex. By shifting the emphasis in Marcuse's account of a future, non-repressive society from sex in the narrow sense to Eros in the broader sense, we can respond to some common objections Marcuse's theory faces.

Admittedly, it is at this point that Marcuse's theory appears at its most utopian and unrealistic, and Marcuse does address objections from this direction. The first objection is that he is in effect proposing a vision of socialism in which the populace become, as Marcuse puts it, "sex maniacs." In response, Marcuse concedes that the socialist society he envisions would be less sexually repressive in some respects, but denies that it would be characterized by an absence of all restraint.[7] Marcuse even speculates at one point that the flowing of erotic energy into other channels, such as work, would lead to less interest in sex (narrowly defined), not more. This redirection of erotic instincts would give them a non-sexual outlet: "In contrast, the free development of transformed libido within transformed institutions, while eroticizing previously tabooed zones, time, and relations, *would minimize the manifestations of mere sexuality by integrating them into a far larger order, including the order of work*" (EC 202, my emphasis). So far as I know, Marcuse's idea that a non-repressive society would be less sex-obsessed has not been noted in the literature, but it is a promising one we will consider at length below. Still, Marcuse does own one implication of his argument, which is that monogamy and the nuclear family would lose their compulsory status: "This change in the value and scope of libidinal relations would lead to a disintegration of the institutions in which the private interpersonal relations have been organized, particularly the monogamic and patriarchal family" (EC 201). Although Marcuse does not envision a future in which all prohibitions are lifted, he does seem to look forward to the lifting of those that maintain the nuclear family.

Yet there is a lingering suspicion that the future Marcuse envisions is less a political utopia than a perverted fantasy.[8] Admittedly, this accusation of perversion may seem moralistic or puritanical, but even Marcuse would likely grant that there are certain sexual behaviors that are incompatible with even the most tolerant social order. In response, Marcuse turns the tables on his opponent. He argues that it is actually the repressive order of the present which provokes "perverted" outbursts of extreme sexual license. It is the bottling up of sexuality in present-day society which leads to eruptions of perversity, and a more tolerant future society would not necessarily be subject to them.[9] Marcuse reminds us that we live in a society in which repression and perversion are two sides of the same coin. He refers to

> the hideous forms so well known in the history of civilization; in the sadistic and masochistic orgies of desperate masses, of "society elites," of starved bands of mercenaries, of prison and concentration-camp guards. Such release of sexuality provides a periodically necessary outlet for unbearable frustration; it strengthens rather than weakens the roots of instinctual constraint; consequently, it has been used time and again as a prop for suppressive regimes.
>
> (EC 202)

Hence, Marcuse concludes that this objection rests on a questionable assumption. This is the assumption that the normal sexuality in a future non-repressive society would be identical to the pathological forms of it present in our own: "the free development of transformed libido beyond the institutions of the performance principle differs essentially from the release of constrained sexuality within the dominion of these institutions." Marcuse therefore recommends that the category of perversion be broken down into those incompatible with any stable society, and those incompatible with "the performance principle" (capitalism):

> The term perversions covers sexual phenomena of essentially different origin. The same taboo is placed on instinctual manifestations incompatible with civilization and on those incompatible with repressive civilization, especially with monogamic genital supremacy.
>
> (EC 202)

Just as Marcuse insists on distinguishing between necessary repression and surplus, so too does he distinguish between those perversions which would have to be proscribed in any society and those which are only proscribed under capitalism.

A final objection is that the future society Marcuse envisions would be, in some pejorative sense, regressive, and that the lifting of prohibitions would reverse the process of maturation that all individuals and societies must undergo. In response, Marcuse proposes that there is much of value in childhood, as well as in daydreams and fantasies, which could be recovered through such a process of regression. At times, Marcuse describes this healthy form of regression as a recovery of the child's capacity for imagination and fantasy, both of which are suppressed in adult life by the performance principle.[10] If repression under capitalism is excessive, then the ideal of mature adulthood that prevails in this society is likely to be over-demanding:

> Not all component parts and stages of the instinct that have been suppressed have suffered this fate because they prevented the evolution of man and mankind. The purity, regularity, cleanliness, and reproduction required by the performance principle are not naturally those of any mature civilization. And the reactivation of prehistoric and childhood wishes and attitudes is not necessarily regression; it may well be the opposite—proximity to a happiness that has always been the repressed promise of a better future.
>
> (EC 203)

At the social level, he is similarly skeptical that all of the advances of modern society are worth preserving, and this leads him to welcome any form of regression that would mean a reduction in militarism, consumerism, and so on. At one point, Marcuse concedes that the standard of living in a future socialist society would, in a sense, be reduced: there would be fewer luxuries, consumer goods, and less military technology available. Yet this would be compensated for by freedom from toil, and Marcuse clearly thinks the trade-off is worth it. An interest in childhood, if regressive in some sense, turns out to have progressive implications.

A critic might object that Marcuse's ideal future society is unrealistic, not so much because of its relaxed restrictions on Eros, but because of those on Thanatos. Here, the threat feared by the critic is not so much incest or perversion, but, rather, the war-of-all-against-all. Freud clearly thought aggression and violence were significant problems, likely to present themselves in any civilization.

In response, Marcuse reiterates that some minimal level of repression is necessary for social order but insists that capitalism is far too repressive. Marcuse does not think a future socialist society will be free of any use of coercive force or violence, since no society can avoid this entirely:

> Once again, the distinction between repression and surplus repression must be recalled. If a child feels the "need" to cross the street any time at its will, repression of this "need" is not repressive of human potentialities. It may be the opposite.
>
> (EC 224)

No society, socialist or otherwise, can forgo the repression of the whims that might lead a child to cross the street in heavy traffic. Yet Marcuse is not naïve enough to think that this is all the coercion a future socialist would require. As he emphasizes, any complex human endeavor will require coordination, a division of tasks, and ultimately authority. To the extent that these must be enforced, violence will be required. If nothing else, there is the authority of the expert, and this too may be inseparable from the use of coercive force:

> mature civilization depends for its functioning on a multitude of co-ordinated arrangements. These arrangements in turn must carry recognized and recognizable authority. Hierarchical relationships are not unfree per se; civilization relies to a great extent on rational authority, based on knowledge and necessity, and aiming at the protection and preservation of life. Such is the authority of the engineer, of the traffic policeman, of the airplane pilot in flight.
>
> (EC 224)

To this extent, some forms of authority found under capitalism will also be found under socialism: traffic policemen, pilots, and engineers are not unique to capitalist society. Finally, there is Marcuse's contention that even some level of alienated labor will remain necessary, a claim that is somewhat unexpected given his utopian projection in other contexts of a future socialist society in which "work has become play":

> All the technological progress, the conquest of nature, the rationalization of man and society have not eliminated and cannot eliminate the necessity of alienated labor, the necessity of working mechanically, unpleasurably, in a manner that does not represent individual self-realization.
>
> (EC 222)

Seen in this light, Marcuse's vision is not so much of a society without coercive force (or even forced labor) but one in which this force is employed in a rational way. This is a society in which the use of coercive force is minimized to as great an extent as possible.

In spite of all this, it may still seem as if Marcuse is surprisingly unconcerned with the violence and aggression which he and Freud agree are inherent in human nature, and which are given to eruptions that threaten social order. One obvious reason Marcuse is not concerned about aggression in a future socialist society is that he believes it is modern capitalism which is the far greater instigator of unnecessary violence. As we have seen, Marcuse follows Marx in regarding capitalism as a system that depends upon the promise of limitless growth, ever-expanding profit and production. However, Marcuse also clearly accepts Lenin's point that, eventually, this rapacious appetite for profit will lead to war and imperialism (Marcuse, as a critic of Soviet communism, would not credit the point to Lenin, but their analyses are similar enough). Marcuse sometimes captures this connection between capitalism and imperialism through the phrase "productive destruction." This is meant to remind us that the relentless search for profit will require destruction, chiefly in the form of war. Marcuse therefore joins a long line of socialist thinkers for whom the elimination of the profit motive will mean the elimination of the main source of violent conflict.

In a new preface to *Eros and Civilization*, written in 1966, Marcuse makes clear that he shares the student left's view of imperialism as a product of capitalism. In particular, he regards the United States as an imperial power, albeit one which uses its military might to allow capital to go anywhere it wants and do anything it needs to across the globe: Central and South America, Iran and Vietnam. For Marcuse, then, socialism would remove one of the major incentives to war in the modern world: the relentless drive for profit that prevails under capitalism.

Although it is only intermittent in his account, Marcuse's idea that socialism will end Thanatos's reign has an environmentalist component. Capitalist profit-seeking also drives another form of destruction, namely, the destruction of the natural environment. The ecological critique of capitalism is well-known, but Marcuse goes beyond it by explaining its instinctual roots in the appetite for destruction that is part of Thanatos.

4. Evaluation

Perhaps the most significant reservation anyone should have about Marcuse's Freudian-inspired account of human nature concerns its core claim that Eros and Thanatos are the two driving forces of human nature. This claim might seem totalizing, as if every facet of the psyche could be subsumed under one or the other force.[11] Responding to this objection requires us to concede that this chapter has oversimplified Marcuse's account somewhat. Marcuse does not simply present us with the mature Freud's view that Eros and Thanatos are the main drivers of human behavior, but also with the various stages along the way that led Freud to this conclusion. In particular, Marcuse shows how Freud came to think of instincts like self-preservation and sexual reproduction as capable of being subsumed under a more general category. The sense of Freud's trajectory that of a thinker who came to see common-sense distinctions between human motivations as increasingly arbitrary (EC 23).

The reason this matters is that the full story of Freud's arrival at his mature standpoint might convey the empirical, scientific basis for his final model better than I have been able to do here. This is a limitation of the present chapter, and also of Marcuse's account. While he does outline the reasoning that led Freud to an increasingly simple model of human instinctual life, he does not present the empirical evidence on which this reasoning was based. It seems to me that sifting through this empirical evidence would be an important prerequisite to accepting Marcuse's Freud-inspired conception of human life as dominated by the two great forces of Eros and Thanatos. The hope is that one would find convincing evidence for why more pluralistic models are insufficient, and why the diversity of human motivations needs to be subsumed under just two.

Another likely source of concern has to do with the role of sexual repression in Marcuse's discussion. It would be fair to wonder if Marcuse's ideal of a non-repressive society can still speak to us today in the twenty-first century, when, in much of the West at least, an unprecedented level of sexual permissiveness prevails. Interestingly, Marcuse noted this trend in his own time, but did not appear to think it especially promising from the point of view of the cause of human liberation (EC xiii). Paradoxically, Marcuse suggests, a certain permissiveness can co-exist with repression:

> This extension of controls to formerly free regions of consciousness and leisure permits a relaxation of sexual taboos (previously more important because the over-all controls were less effective). Today compared with the Puritan and Victorian periods, sexual freedom has unquestionably increased (although a reaction against the 1920s is clearly noticeable). At the same time, however, the sexual relations themselves have become much more closely assimilated with social relations; sexual liberty is harmonized with profitable conformity. The fundamental antagonism between sex and social utility—itself the reflex of the conflict between pleasure principle and reality principle—is blurred by the progressive encroachment of the reality principal on the pleasure principle.
>
> (EC 94)

Marcuse offers a few reasons—in fact little more than suggestions—for thinking that the repressive society could be sexually permissive.

The first is that other forms of social control, beyond sexual repression, may have intensified to such a degree that they compensate for looser sexual mores. The second is that repression could be lifted in a way that is conducive to the interests of the ruling class; for example, when advertisers take advantage of relaxing standards of sexual morality to sell products. Yet what is perhaps Marcuse's most convincing reason is not alluded to here and must be found in a previous passage. The non-repressive society Marcuse envisions is not exactly one in which sex is less repressed, but one in which Eros is. Marcuse thinks it is characteristic of modern, capitalist society to confine our erotic lives to sex and sexual reproduction. The infant's "polymorphous perversity," the eroticization of its entire body, gives way to the restricted erotic life of the mature, productive member of society (Marcuse calls this "genitality").

5. Conclusion: the fate of the doctrine

Although there are resources in Marcuse's account for responding to some of the more common criticisms of his doctrine in Eros and Civilization, it is likely that most will be repelled by Marcuse's reliance on the late Freud's speculation concerning the forces underlying all life and matter. Hence, it is worth considering certain later iterations which do not rely extensively on the late Freudian doctrine, though they undeniably echo some of its main themes. As we will see, these sources indicate two lines of departure from the earlier theory: first, in the direction of a more commonsensical account of the phenomena; and second, in the direction of a more naturalistic, biology-based account.

A place to begin is the preface to a later edition of Eros and Civilization, where Marcuse relates his work in the mid-1950s to the aims of the peace movement of the 1960s:

> Revolt against the false fathers, teachers, and heroes—solidarity with the wretched of the earth: is there any "organic" connection between the two facets of the protest? There seems to be an all but instinctual solidarity. The revolt at home against home seems largely impulsive, its targets hard to define: nausea caused by "the way of life," revolt as a matter of physical and mental hygiene.

The body against "the machine"—not against the mechanism constructed to make life safer and milder, to attenuate the cruelty of nature, but against the machine which has taken over the mechanism: the political machine, the corporate machine, the cultural and educational machine which has welded blessing and curse into one rational whole. The whole has become too big, its cohesion too strong, its functioning too efficient—does the power of the negative concentrate in still partly unconquered, primitive, elemental forces? The body against the machine: men, women, and children fighting, with the most primitive tools, the most brutal and destructive machine of all times and keeping it in check—does guerilla warfare define the revolution of our time?

(EC xvi–xvii)

While Marcuse seems to have retained some Freudian tropes, such as a conception of political rebellion as a form of parricide, the model he presents in the later work seems much more flexible. Marcuse continues to believe that it is ultimately our human instincts that serve rebellion against the established order, but he now embraces a more straightforward conception of how this will take place. It is not so much Eros which inspires the revolt against capitalism, but, rather, this system's infringement on basic human needs for sanity, health, and bodily autonomy. While Marcuse continues to describe the capitalist-imperialist machine as driven by death, he means something far more concrete than Thanatos. He is referring to the way the military might of the West be used against peoples seeking their autonomy from the reign of capital.

This subsequent model of revolt achieves its most developed form in *An Essay on Liberation*, where Marcuse speaks of a "biological foundation for socialism" (EL 7). Here too, we have the same broad affinities with the earlier Freudian model, but also a greater concreteness and perhaps even a shift. Marcuse is more straightforward in describing the role of instinctual life under capitalism: false needs stimulated by advertising, and aggressiveness inspired by nationalism, patriotism, and militarism. Marcuse stresses the ways in which our very instinctive lives can be reshaped by capitalism, referring to them as "second nature" (EL 11). Once we are habituated to this system, our responses become automatic, unreflective, and therefore more likely to escape scrutiny. It is not so much the Freudian psyche, but rather the body which is Marcuse's focus now. Marcuse therefore insists on the need for a reform of human instinctual life if socialism is to replace capitalism, and in this respect departs from the orthodox Marxist idea that revolution always concerns control of the productive forces, rather than the vicissitudes of human psychology.

Ultimately, it seems clear that Marcuse regards the later theory as continuous with the earlier. This is evidenced in passages where the "biological foundation for socialism" seems to be equated with Eros in Freud's sense of the term:

> Prior to all ethical behavior in accordance with specific social standards, prior to all ideological expression, morality is a "disposition" of the organism, perhaps rooted in the erotic drive to counter aggressiveness, to create and preserve "ever greater unities" of life.
>
> (EL 10)

The quoted phrase is Freud's, but there are significant changes from the earlier doctrine. Here, it is noteworthy that Marcuse presents the theory of Eros as a conjecture, rather than a firmly established truth. Not only the metaphysical character of the earlier doctrine, but also its dogmatism seem to have been reduced.

Summary

Marcuse's debt to Freud is considerable. He respects not only the latter's therapeutic method and scientific discoveries but also his model of the psyche as governed by two forces, Eros and Thanatos. Marcuse objects to Freud's cultural conservatism, attempting to supplement Freudian psychoanalysis with Marx's historical materialism. The latter allows us to see that the amount of necessary repression in a society is not fixed, but varies in accordance with the mode of production. Capitalism leads to a more repressive society than necessary, and a future socialist society will curtail repression to its socially necessary minimum. Though this appears to bring with it the risk of a relapse into barbarism, Marcuse denies this implication.

He argues that it is the repressive society which produces outbursts of perversity, and that a future socialist society will differ. It will not necessarily be characterized by more or different sexual behavior, but by the eroticization of areas of life that under capitalism are non-erotic; for example, work. In later writing, Marcuse appears to experiment with two alternatives to the Freudian model: one more commonsensical, and another more naturalistic. Yet from the insistence on capitalism's excessive demands on our instinctual lives to the conviction that human nature rebels against this system, there are clear continuities with the earlier Freudian model.

Notes

1 See J. Rickert's "The Fromm–Marcuse Debate Revisited" (1986). Rickert presents compelling evidence that each figure's criticisms of the other rested on misunderstandings and distortions.
2 One interesting facet of Marcuse's philosophical Freudianism is the idea that psychoanalysis has an ontological dimension. This Heideggerian dimension of Marcuse's theory of Eros has been explored by Habermas (1968: 10–11) cited in Feenberg (2023: Ch. 4 n. 28). It is more recently taken up and discussed by Feenberg (2023: Ch. 4: 87, "Being"). I will leave it to the side here.
3 This type of translation of Kant's faculty psychology into Freudian terms has been undertaken in our own time by Longuenesse (2017).
4 "From the very first we recognized the presence of a sadistic component in the sexual instinct" (1920: 53).
5 This paragraph summarizes some of the main themes in Freud's essay *The Ego and the Id* (1923).
6 I here follow Whitebook (2004: 87).
7 This criticism is related to the one treated by Feenberg (2023: 83) when he discusses those critics of Marcuse who view his ideal of a non-repressive society as nothing more than "orgasmic mush."
8 Does Marcuse intend to eliminate all repression? This question is taken up by O'Connor (2019: 317–18).
9 Here I differ slightly from Whitebook (2004: 76). As he glosses Marcuse's claim, it is that practices which *appear* perverse in our repressive society will no longer *appear* so under socialism. Doubtless this is true of certain practices; for example, homosexuality.
   However, I am arguing for a claim concerning fact, rather than appearance. I base this claim on Marcuse's allusions "sadistic and masochistic orgies of desperate masses … of starved masses… of prison and concentration camp guards" (EC 203). These appear to be genuinely perverted behaviors, and responsibility

for them is laid at the door of the repressive society. Hence it seems clear that some genuine perversions, especially those that are sadistic, might dissipate under socialism.

10 Here, I follow Feenberg, who puts the point well: Marcuse "is repeating in the domain of personality structures the dialectical pattern of development of Marx's philosophy of history. There is no return to infancy but rather a recapitulation of certain positive aspects of the early stage of development at the level of civilized adult personality" (2023: 83–84):

11 Hyman (1988: 155) makes this criticism.

Further reading

Feenberg, A. (2023) *Towards a Ruthless Critique of Everything Existing*, London: Verso. [Ch. 4 "The Politics of Eros" offers a philosophically sophisticated discussion of Marcuse's debt to Freudian psychoanalysis, and branches out into topics in *Eros and Civilization* not touched upon here; for example, aesthetics and ontology.]

Hyman, E. J. (1988) "Eros and Freedom: The Critical Psychology of Herbert Marcuse," in A. Feenberg, R. Pippin and C. Webel (eds.), *Marcuse: Critical Theory and the Promise of Utopia*, London: Bergin & Garvey. [Helpful discussion of *Eros and Civilization*, especially of guilt, the death drive, and aggression. Criticizes Marcuse for relying on the late Freud's dual-drive theory.]

O'Connor, B. (2014) "Play, Idleness and the Problem of Necessity in Schiller and Marcuse," *British Journal for the History of Philosophy*, Vol. 22, No. 6: 1095–1117. [Philosophically sophisticated account of Marcuse's recovery from Schiller of a model of freedom as play.]

O'Connor, B. (2018) "Marcuse on the Problem of Repression," in P. Gordon, E. Hammer, and A. Honneth (eds.), *Routledge Companion to Critical Theory*, London: Routledge, 311–23. [Reconstruction focused especially on "surplus repression."]

Rickert, J. (1986) "The Marcuse–Fromm Debate Revisited," *Theory and Society*, Vol. 15, No. 3: 351–400.

Whitebook, J. (2006) "The Marriage of Marx and Freud" in F. Rush (ed.), *Cambridge Companion to Critical Theory*, Cambridge: Cambridge University Press. [Overview of the argument of *Eros and Civilization* focused on the idea of an "immanent critique of Freud" that brings to light a historical and economic dimension of repression.]

Seven

Politics and society

Although the overarching aim of this volume is to present Marcuse's thought as philosophical—indeed, as having deep continuities with the history of philosophy—this chapter constitutes something of an exception. In attempting to understand Marcuse's fundamental political orientation, we will not find him approaching issues of politics in the way that many political philosophers have done, and still do today, especially in recent Anglophone (analytic) political philosophy.

In particular, we will not find Marcuse attempting to answer a familiar set of abstract questions that arise in modern, and even more so, contemporary Anglophone, political philosophy: what is the proper distribution of resources in society? What is the value of equality, and how is it best realized? Should democracy be defended instrumentally or non-instrumentally? In terms of which: growth, equality, or freedom? When and under what conditions is political authority justified? And so on.

At first, it seems that the reason for this divergence lies in Marcuse's membership in a rival tradition of thought. Marcuse is a socialist, whereas these are questions that have preoccupied figures in the liberal tradition, understood as the dominant tradition in Anglophone political theory and including left-egalitarians, libertarians, and others.

Yet it would be understating things to conclude that Marcuse is simply interested in exploring a different set of questions. More fundamentally, Marcuse is not interested in the usual methods of contemporary Anglophone political philosophy at all. Even socialists in this tradition have tended to pose and attempt to answer abstract

DOI: 10.4324/9781003307075-7

questions, using thought-experiments and counterexamples. Yet Marcuse is not an "analytic Marxist," and one will not find defenses of socialism in his writings like those made by G. A. Cohen; for example, Cohen's thought-experiment of a camping trip (2009). This thought-experiment is intended to elicit the intuition that "from each according to his abilities ..." is an appropriate ground-rule for many small-scale ventures, e.g., camping trips. Cohen asks, why not extrapolate from this small-scale venture to a large-scale one? Whatever the merits of this approach, one will not find similar arguments for socialism in Marcuse's writings.

Perhaps the main difference between Marcuse and socialists in contemporary Anglophone philosophy concerns the level at which their analysis operates. While Marcuse reflects on questions from a socialist perspective, he does not attempt to defend the most basic premises of his socialist outlook against objections from those who do not share it or who occupy radically opposed positions (libertarians, free-market capitalists, even liberal egalitarians).

This raises the concern that Marcuse is a dogmatist, not in that his Marxism is doctrinaire but in that it is so often presupposed, rather than argued for—let alone argued for from first principles. My point is not that Marcuse's writings are devoid of questioning, dialogue, and debate. On the contrary. It is simply that it is rarely the fundamental premises of socialism that are in question. Whereas analytical Marxists and others may be tempted to argue for the principle "from each according to his abilities ...," and indeed to do so in such a way that if successful they would win over their bitterest opponents, Marcuse does not take this approach. What, then, does his alternative approach consist of, and can it avoid the pitfall of "preaching to the converted"?

I want to propose that Marcuse's unique approach reflects the historical materialist belief that political *philosophies* represent rather superficial aspects of *political life*. A historical materialist ought to focus instead on political movements as they have arisen in history, as well as the regimes they have created (where these movements have succeeded). Hence, Marcuse's interest is not primarily in liberal doctrines, as formulated by political philosophers in the latter half of the twentieth century. It is, rather, in liberalism as a movement that gave rise to the American and French Revolutions and resulted in the liberal democracies that many of us inhabit today. To the extent Marcuse engages with liberal philosophical voices, they tend to be those who were more than academic theorists, those present during an important phase in the rise of liberalism. These are figures who were politically engaged in the societies in which they found themselves, influenced by and influential on practical life; for example, Mill and Tocqueville.

As with liberalism, so with fascism—also communism, and the new left. Marcuse is as interested in the philosophical spokespeople for these movements as he is in their institutions, their social configurations, their historical pasts, and possible futures. Heidegger and Schmitt are discussed alongside dictatorships, state planning, and militarism; Marx and Engels alongside the totalitarian systems which claimed their legacy (falsely, in Marcuse's view).

In his book *Philosophy and Real Politics* (2008), Raymond Geuss urges that we abandon the allegedly timeless truths captured in the thought-experiments of Rawls, Nozick et al., and attend to the concrete realities of contemporary political life. Geuss's inspirations here are Weber, who was the first to insist on a value-free social science and famously defined the state as an agency that has a monopoly on the use of coercive force in a territory; and Lenin, who said that the chief question of politics was "who does what to whom?" Once we leave behind ideal theory and its task of constructing a perfectly just society, we can interrogate the existing one: its institutional arrangements, its regimes of power, its structures of caste, class, and privilege, its ideological means of legitimating itself to its members, and so on. Marcuse would agree that philosophy ought to be engaged with real politics, rather than ideal theory (though Marcuse's work remains highly theoretical in other respects).

In this chapter, I examine Marcuse's political outlook, mindful that he does not practice political philosophy in a now current and historically influential manner. I am interested in Marcuse's effort to situate himself in a new world order defined by the battle lines between liberal capitalism, communism, and, to a lesser extent, fascism. Including fascism might seem curious, given its defeat by the Allies. Yet as we will soon see, Marcuse maintains that there are disturbing continuities between the victors and the vanquished, the U.S. and U.S.S.R. on one hand, and Nazi Germany on the other.

For Marcuse, the U.S. is more like its foes than it would like to recognize:

> By virtue of the way it has organized its technological base, contemporary industrial society tends to be totalitarian. For "totalitarian" is not only a terroristic political coordination of society, but also a non-terroristic economic-technical coordination which operates through the manipulation of needs by vested interests.
>
> (ODM 5)

The key for understanding these commonalities between modern America, the U.S.S.R., and even fascist regimes lies in the Frankfurt School ideas of state and monopoly capitalism. These are names the critical theorists gave to a new, highly centralized form of capitalism that had replaced the laissez-faire form of a previous era.[1]

Others in the critical theory tradition claimed there were unsettling parallels between liberal democracy, communism, and fascism, and suggested that each of these systems either was or could easily become totalitarian. This bleak perspective seems to epitomize the totalizing pessimism of post-war critical theory and raise the concern that it is insufficiently appreciative of the Enlightenment project and liberal modernity. This was the criticism leveled by Habermas at Adorno and Horkheimer, who seemed to undercut their own critique of modernity's pathologies by suggesting that reason and science themselves were implicated. As I will argue in this chapter, Marcuse's analysis is best interpreted as claiming, not that liberal capitalism and its foes are identical and that there is no basis for preferring one over the other, but rather that liberal capitalism exhibits disturbing continuities with communism and fascism.[2] What is more, Marcuse intends to warn us that there are totalitarian tendencies in all three systems, which, if left unchecked, could make liberal capitalism more closely resemble its foes.

As we have said, Marcuse is not the only mid-century intellectual who noticed disturbing parallels between the Soviet Union, the United States, and the Nazis; and his stance may seem less extreme when we recall that even liberal commentators took this view. George Orwell did so as well in 1984, commonly misread as concerned only with the Soviet Union. For Orwell, the threat of totalitarianism existed in the West as well. Hence, Marcuse's analysis of the connections between these three systems might be seen as a socialist counterpart to Orwell's liberal one. In the closing section, we will revisit the question of the relationship between liberal anti-totalitarianism, epitomized by a figure like Orwell, and the socialist anti-totalitarianism of the Frankfurt School.

1. Fascism and liberal capitalism

Marcuse's perspective on fascism is materialist, in that he encourages us to examine its institutional structure, rather than its official ideology.[3] Marcuse makes the case for this approach by noting that the ideological debate is something of a muddle. At the level of ideology, fascism presents itself as radically opposed to liberalism (N 4). Yet the contrast typically remains at the level of values and ideals as if the contest were merely one of opposed "Weltanschauungen." Hence, the contest between fascism and liberalism, at least as the former group presents it, appears to be one of freedom versus authority; courage versus cowardice; hierarchy versus equality; nationalism versus cosmopolitanism; reverse these two! discussion versus decision, and so on.

Yet in his piece "State and Individual Under National Socialism," Marcuse argues that this ideological clash between fascism and liberalism masks underlying institutional continuities between the two:

> We can already discern the reason why the total authoritarian state diverts its struggle against liberalism into a struggle of "Weltanschauungen," why it bypasses the social structure basic to liberalism: it is itself largely in accord with this basic structure.
> (N 6)

When we examine fascism more closely, in terms of its institutions, we will find surprising continuities between it and liberalism (CPHK 1: 69). In particular, both have at their core the highly concentrated and regulated form of capitalism the Frankfurt School call monopoly or state capitalism (in fact, there are differences, but they do not matter for our purposes here).[4] Fascism disguises these continuities by adopting a critique of capitalism that focuses on its more superficial elements. Fascists are well aware that liberal democracies are accompanied by capitalist economies, and criticize aspects of the latter. Yet as Marcuse points out, it is nearly always the capitalism of an earlier phase of history, one involving large numbers of individual producers competing with another, and not the small number of massive firms that dominate the economy under monopoly capitalism. Hence the fascist criticizes the venal "merchant," who moves from place to place and is loyal to no nation—but not the captain of industry (N 7). For Marcuse, then, fascism has held onto monopoly capitalism, and is in this respect identical with liberalism.

As indicated, monopoly capitalism and state capitalism are not equivalent, but they are closely related and often coincide. Monopoly capitalism, a highly concentrated form of capitalism, requires massive state intervention in the economy. In other words, monopoly capitalism quickly becomes state capitalism. In a former phase of capitalism, the state was meant to avoid intervening in the economy as far as possible. The unregulated behavior of large numbers of individuals of buyers and sellers would ensure social order. It would ensure a harmony of interests between buyers and sellers and a form of growth that benefited all. The right to private property marked a zone of privacy in which the state should not interfere.

Yet in the age of monopoly capitalism, this equilibrium can no longer be counted upon, and the state must intervene in the economy in decisive ways. Hence there is cooperation between the heads of major firms and members of the government. This ensures forms of regulation that may seem benign, such as stabilizing the economy during crises, providing for the unemployed, ensuring cooperation between labor and capital, and so on. However, it also brings with it the risk that state power will be completely subordinate to the interests of a small number of unaccountable economic oligarchs. Wars might be fought simply because they are good for business, and government is not in a position to refuse its patrons in the capitalist class. Indeed, Marcuse understands big business as partly responsible for the Nazis' military conquest of neighboring countries. While the Nazis may have had ideological motives, their wars of aggression were encouraged by the business community, or at least tolerated.

For Marcuse, then, both liberal democracies and fascist states are authoritarian in at least one sense: capital's reign is for the most part unchecked. In fascism, of course, the fiction is adopted that the people is one, united by race, nationality, history, or destiny. The official story is that there are neither workers nor owners, but simply Germans. To some limited extent, Marcuse concedes, the gulf between these classes closes, making fascism at least somewhat successful in taming class antagonisms. For the most part, however, the insistence on common identity is an ideological diversion that serves the preservation of the status quo and allows class-based domination and oppression to continue.

Ironically, then, the very developments which were meant to lead to socialism appear realized in fascism; for example, the overcoming of the distinction between state and society, the subordination of production to the interests of society as a whole. Of course, the appearance is deceptive, and the parallel is weak. It was Marx who first defined communism as a system in which Hegel's distinction between state and civil society is overcome.[5] Under capitalism, a superficial equality and freedom in the political domain are meant to compensate us for the inequality and unfreedom we suffer in the economy. As in religion, we are split, living our celestial and terrestrial lives. Marx clearly thinks the bargain is not worth it and looks forward to a system in which the "universality" of the state is realized in the economy, a world in which the general will governs not only politics but production. It is easy to see that fascism is nothing more than a grim parody of this socialist ideal. Whereas under socialism, the state would control the economy, and it would finally be subject to democratic control, fascism operates differently. Marcuse sees the fascist state as having adopted a servile posture towards business. Similarly, it is not the interests of society as a whole which are decisive here, even if that is what is claimed. It is rather those of big business, and perhaps also its abettors in the Nazi Party and the military. Yet the fact that fascism resembles socialism in these superficial respects is important to Marcuse and the Frankfurt School. It allows them to argue that fascism enjoys its renown because it offers a substitute for socialism, albeit a poor one. In this way, fascism appears less as an alternative to capitalism than as a desperate means of preserving the latter when it is in jeopardy (threatened by crises, class-antagonisms, and revolutions, as it was during the Weimar era).

Is Marcuse claiming that there are no meaningful differences between fascism and liberal capitalism? Or that the two systems are morally equivalent? This seems implausible, and exaggerated, even by Marcuse's own ultra-leftist standards. Even if one accepts the Marxist idea that capitalist countries uphold human rights in a tendentious way, intended to serve capital, there seems to be no comparison between this and the egregious human-rights abuses of the Nazis. Marcuse's position that fascism is a form of monopoly capitalism, like the U.S., stems from an early essay of his. Certainly, the full extent of the Nazis' crimes was not clear at that time, though Marcuse, as a refugee himself, knew how grave the situation was. Monopoly capitalism aside, one is thankful that liberal democracies do not share other features of the Nazi government which Marcuse discusses at length: the identification of law with the arbitrary will of an unelected leader; the irrationalist ideology of absolute submission to the state and total sacrifice in war; biological racism as the foundation for state policy; eugenics; a form of Lebensphilosophie in which the will of the stronger is celebrated and "might makes right"; elimination of the rule of law and its replacement by sets of privileges; and, of course, an extremely aggressive policy of military expansion, as well as the mobilization of all facets of society for the sake of war. The threat of all of these is real in liberal democracies, which have their own experience with demagogues, militarism, racism, and foreign wars. Yet there hardly seems to be an equivalence.

Fortunately, Marcuse does not appear to maintain that liberal democracy and fascism are equivalent, but rather takes a more modest position. It is that because the two share a monopoly-capitalist economy, liberal democracy may be in danger of degenerating into fascism. The aim of Marcuse's analysis is not to assert a moral equivalence between Nazi Germany and the U.S., and his position is compatible with regarding the former as far worse. Indeed, he contributed to the war effort on the side of the Allies. Still, this does not blunt Marcuse's critique. This critique would be that the U.S., like Nazi Germany, finds itself in a phase of capitalist development when the division between state and civil society has been eroded, and authoritarianism is a standing possibility. This is because a small number of firms are capable of instrumentalizing the government, the police, and the military for their aims.

Clearly, Marcuse took the example of fascism to be instructive for the U.S. In the anti-war movement, as well as his opposition to the C.I.A's activities in Latin America, Marcuse was undoubtedly taking a line he had taken decades earlier with the rise of the Nazis. He was objecting to a form of imperial expansion undertaken by the state and the military primarily for the sake of their abettors in business. During the civil rights movement, Marcuse was extremely disturbed by the presence of racist, xenophobic, and ultra-nationalist groups in the U.S. This is not just because of the lawlessness and violence of these groups, but because they embodied tendencies which, if left unchecked, could lead democracy to devolve into fascism.

If anything, Marcuse's warning that liberal democracies risk degenerating into authoritarian states is even more prescient today. Throughout the postwar period, Marcuse would interpret current events in terms of this dynamic. An interesting example can be found in Marcuse's essay "Watergate: When Law and Morality Stand in the Way" (CPHM 2: 187–93). Marcuse regarded Watergate as just one notable instance of the ways in which liberalism and monopoly capitalism prove irreconcilable. In particular, Watergate is an example of how the liberal ideal of the rule of law is increasingly imperiled by the strong executive of the modern state, himself the supreme functionary of monopoly capitalism. Marcuse describes Watergate as "not an aberration but the extreme political form of the normal state of affairs" (CPHM 2: 187).

Yet while Marcuse does not equate liberal democracy and fascism, his analysis is more pessimistic than it might at first appear. He not only thinks liberal democracies could degenerate into fascist regimes, but that there are powerful forces which make this more than a slim possibility. In order to understand why, we need to consider "reason," the main philosophical category in terms of which the European Enlightenment defended liberal institutions like the market (N 9–12).

When it first comes on the scene in the early-modern period, free-market capitalism is rational in two senses:

First, the individuals behave rationally, meaning instrumentally. They are self-interested and pursue only their own advantage. They are efficient, in that they aim to take the least costly means to their ends. Crucially, they are permitted to do so, having been freed from the total social control of them and their lives by state, church, and family that is characteristic of feudalism. What is more, it is assumed that, once freed from traditional constraints, they will behave instrumentally (rationally). Often, this assumption is questioned by critics of rational choice theory and free-market economics. These critics point to findings from behavioral economics, which show that rational decision-making is undermined by a large number of biases, distortions, and self-deceptions. However, it is not here that Marcuse concentrates his attacks. His objection is not that the rational, self-interested utility-maximizer of rational choice theory is a fiction and that theories reliant on him are idealizing. It is rather that the protagonist of free-market economics has been deprived of the institutional sphere in which such a person could flourish, and become subject to insidious new forms of social control. Ultimately, then, there is common ground between Marcuse and bourgeois defenders of the market, who praise the market for encouraging self-reliance. It is just that Marcuse does not confuse monopoly capitalism with the free market in its heroic, early phase.

Second, and perhaps more importantly, the market, as an institution, can be evaluated as rational when considered as a whole (totality), and not just at the level of its members. The social whole is rational because it achieves goods like growth, stability, and order. It does so through the unregulated, self-interested behavior of its members, which turns out to be surprisingly conducive to the common good (as if it were guided by an "invisible hand" or by Hegel's "cunning of reason").

To understand why liberal democracies have a tendency to become fascist, we need to grasp the role of the irrational in fascism; in other words, the presence of factors which are not open to rational debate and discussion. These include the tendencies of organic life itself (according to the prevailing Lebensphilosophie); phenomena such as health, strength, and cleanliness; the will of the leader; the nation and people ("blood and soil"); the pathology presented by the outgroup (Jews, communists, homosexuals, gypsies); and so on. Crucially, in all of these cases, reasons come to an end, and all one can do is submit. Indeed, this is an important aspect of the strategy fascist regimes employ. If they appealed instead to self-interest, they would be revealed to be largely useless in promoting their people's welfare. Hence, an ideology of unthinking obedience, blind faith, and unconditional service helps reconcile people to a system that is not completely in accord with their interests.

Reformulated, then, Marcuse's question is how liberal democracy, an allegedly rational system, could degenerate into something irrational. Marcuse's answer is that, sooner or later, liberal democracy, though it continues to allow for the pursuit of individual self-interest, ceases to promote the good of the whole. In other words, it is rational in the first sense, but not the second. This lapse coincides with the transition from free-market capitalism to monopoly capitalism. Increasingly, the system serves the interests of a small number of captains of industry, and only accidentally or not at all the mass of people. How, then, do liberal democracies address these failures? How, in particular, do they avoid the seemingly inevitable conclusion that a transition to socialism is necessary? Here, Marcuse sees an opening for appeals to the irrational; for example, the nationalistic invocation of the *Volk*:

> Universalism must divert both consciousness and action from the only possible way to realize the "whole" and from the only possible form of that whole into another, less dangerous direction: it substitutes the "primal given" of the folk, of folkhood.
>
> (N 15).

Another even more blatant example would be the fascist idea that poverty produced by the market is somehow natural, perhaps because it is in accord with the tendency in nature for the strong to prey on the weak. Hence Marcuse refers to the fascist tactic of

> naturalizing the economy as such to the naturalization of the monopoly capitalist economy as such and of the mass poverty it brings about; all of these phenomena are sanctioned as "natural."
>
> (N 18)

As monopoly capitalism ceases to serve most people's interests, we should see politicians appeal to factors like race, nation, the military, charismatic authority, and so on.

Where empty rhetoric fails, they will offer more tangible benefits. For example, those arising from an expanded military, party apparatus, illegal foreign wars, the secret police, and government bureaucracy. A new far-right regime might even manage unemployment by handing out positions in these areas. The way is paved for fascism, though the irony is that fascism is no true solution to liberal capitalism's problems. Fascism is a vain attempt at "bringing to heel" instincts that rebel against the falling standard of living" (N 20).

For Marcuse, then, there is not only a path from liberal democracy to fascism but powerful historical forces encouraging society to take that path; in particular, Marcuse appeals to the intense need liberal-capitalist societies will feel to cover up monopoly capitalism's irrationality by giving the mass of people something else to cling to in their desperation. Yet the consolations that the right offers, such as a certain sense of purpose or belonging, are poor substitutes for the welfare, equality and freedom that a socialist alternative to capitalism would provide. Similarly uncompelling are the material rewards fascism provides. For most people, they will amount to little more than the opportunity to sacrifice their lives in war for the sake of powerful, entrenched social interests.

Having reviewed Marcuse's analysis of how liberal democracies may degenerate into fascist regimes, we can revisit the question of the relationship between liberalism and fascism. As we saw, a concern Marcuse's account raises is that he somehow equates the two. Importantly, Marcuse is very clear about an enormous discrepancy between fascism and liberalism: the former does away with the rule of law and the autonomy of the judiciary. Yet here too Marcuse's analysis of why this occurs suggests that liberal democracies are also at risk. The rule of law and the independence of the judiciary serve to protect individuals from the army and police, big business, and the state. Hence, we can understand how capitalist countries in which the latter segments of society grow powerful might be tempted by a different judicial system.

While it is common to think of the fascist regimes of Europe as ones in which the state, or leader, was all-powerful, Marcuse is skeptical of this analysis. Of course, Hitler and his party promulgated a view of themselves as all-powerful, and this was an important plank in Nazi ideology. Yet the truth is more complex, as Marcuse explains:

> Ideologically, he is the embodiment of the German race, its infallible will and knowledge, and the seat of supreme sovereignty. In

reality, however, he is the agency through which the diverging interests of the three ruling hierarchies are coordinated and asserted as national interests. He mediates between the competing forces; he is the locus of final compromise rather than sovereignty. His decision might be autonomous, particularly in minor matters, but it is still not free, not his own, but that of others. For it originates from and is bound to the philosophy and policy of the governing imperialist groups which he has served from the very beginning.

(CPHM 1: 76)

Rather than see him as all-powerful, Marcuse sees in Hitler a figure who must respond to pressure from three groups: big business, the military, and the party itself. Hitler was entrusted with finding compromises between these groups, but this is not the same as being all-powerful.

The question of Hitler's role in the Nazi state is understandably fraught, not just because of the complexities of the historical issues but because of the ethical implications. On one hand, Marcuse's analysis, which minimizes Hitler's power, may seem to exonerate a man who to many is the very personification of evil. Yet if one accepts the idea that Hitler was all-powerful, one risks the opposite error: excusing Hitler's enablers. Anybody who has studied the Nuremberg trials and Eichmann's knows that Nazi war criminals often defended themselves by reminding their accusers that, in the Nazi regime, the Führer's word was incontestable and had the force of law. Yet Marcuse's position is clearly that other segments of society retained influence, and that responsibility cannot be laid at the door of Hitler alone. What is more, these are segments of society that were powerful even before the Nazi rise to power. Hence, Marcuse tells us that the Nazis cannot be considered a revolutionary party. The large German firms that preceded them prospered under their reign—and even after.

Yet if the Nazis do not represent a revolution, they equally well cannot be said to constitute a restoration (CPHM 1: 69–70). Marcuse recognizes that the previous Reich did not continue under the Nazis. To a great extent, the Nazis modernized the German state. They made the army more meritocratic in its selection principles. They abolished arbitrary privileges and hierarchies which were holdovers from feudalism. Marcuse's conviction that the Nazis were no mere restoration is crucial. This allows him to argue that fascism represents a standing threat, even in liberal-capitalist countries. Though right-wing and deeply illiberal, fascism is also in a sense modern: it avoids the inefficiencies and arbitrariness of earlier forms of government. That is why, for Marcuse, it is legitimate to worry that modern America will become fascist, but not that it will reinstitute the Wilhelmine Reich.

Marcuse often denies that fascism is totalitarian, though his point is the rather subtle one that fascism does not involve a "Leviathan" state that controls the whole of society. Just as often, it is big business which employs the state—really, the army, and the party—for its ends. The official position of Hitler and of the Nazis was that the state is nothing, and the movement everything; the state, a mere means, and cultural renewal, the end. Of course, the Nazis themselves made this point to emphasize the populist character of their movement, but Marcuse regards their argument as leading to a different conclusion. It is that the powerful elements of the economy remained so under the Nazis. If these segments of society served the Nazis, then it is also true that the Nazis served them. In this light, it is ironic that the Nazis are considered advocates of state supremacy. As Marcuse writes, "the National Socialist state has been casting away the last remnants of independence from the predominant social groups—it is becoming the executive organ of the imperialist economic interests" (CPHM 1: 72).

Ultimately, then, fascism is characterized less by state supremacy than by the erosion of any division between state and society: fascism "tends to abolish any separation between state and society" (CPHM 1: 70). What is more, this process is intended to shore up the power of the already dominant economic groups "by transferring the political functions to the social groups actually in power" (CPHM 1: 70). Finally, the state serves these groups with its imperialistic conquests. Once we see that this is the case, liberal capitalism appears more similar to fascism than it might have initially seemed. Under monopoly capitalism, economy (civil society) and state are no longer distinct. They are, instead, integrated. Individuals are thoroughly subordinate to the large firms. Smaller ones are outcompeted. The large firms, in turn, obtain the backing of the state, its bureaucracy, its police, its educational system, and its military.

A concern one might have about Marcuse's analysis of the Third Reich is that it at least partially exonerates Hitler and the Nazis and places blame instead on the capitalist system. Yet Marcuse need not deny that Hitler and the Nazis were ruthless, power-hungry murderers bent on war and genocide. Nor need he deny that they held considerable power in Germany. Marcuse's point is merely that their rise to power was facilitated by segments of the economy and of society that stood to gain from their program. Ultimately then, Marcuse is questioning whether Hitler and the Nazis held as much of an iron grip on German society as they claimed. It is occasionally said by those wishing to deny that Hitler alone was responsible for the Nazi atrocities that he was elected, and enjoyed popular support. Marcuse is making a Marxist version of this point, reminding us of the role of the business community in Hitler's rise.

Marcuse may have found confirmation of his theory of the commonalities between liberal capitalism and fascism during his time in the O.S.S. There, Marcuse helped design the program of denazification. Yet as he would recall years later in an interview with Habermas, many of the most prominent Nazis in society were permitted to retain their positions of influence:

> HABERMAS: Are you of the impression that what you did then was of any consequence?
> MARCUSE: On the contrary. Those whom we had listed first as "economic war criminals" were very quickly back in the decisive positions of responsibility in the German economy. It would be very easy to name names here.
> (Marcuse 1978/CPHM 1: 22)

Not only would the new liberal democratic West Germany tolerate their presence: it was doing so with the approval of the Allies. The Americans were, in the meantime, actively recruiting former Nazis to participate in the Cold War against Soviet Russia, offering amnesty in exchange for service. In the 1960s, the student movement in Germany would be galvanized by the realization that so many former Nazis had retained their positions of power in government and business. How could this have happened? Marcuse's analysis suggests one answer. Different as they might be, fascism and liberalism exhibit a common vulnerability: neither is able or willing to stand up to monopoly capital.

2. Liberal capitalism and Soviet communism

Given his claim that liberal democracy and fascism share an underlying basis in monopoly capitalism, one might expect Marcuse to embrace what appeared to many to be the only remaining alternative: Soviet communism. It was a central tenet of much mid-century communist thinking that fascism was only a more extreme manifestation of tendencies already latent in liberal capitalism. Yet there is more to the story, and Marcuse, like others in the Frankfurt School, never held that commonalities between liberal capitalism and fascism in any way implied the superiority of the Soviet Union. For Marcuse, as for others in this tradition, the commonalities between fascism and liberal democracy extended to the Soviet Union as well. Often, Marcuse's diagnosis appears to be based on the thought that the Soviet Union possessed something not unlike the state or monopoly capitalism found in the U.S. and Nazi Germany. The caveat is that Marcuse would not go so far as to describe the Soviet Union as capitalist.

At the base of all three societies is an extremely concentrated form of heavy industry. The productive forces do not differ significantly between the three societies. Is this consistent with the historical materialist belief that it is ultimately these forces that dictate the nature of a society? It would appear to be. The Soviet leadership adhered to a Marxist precept that technology itself is neutral, and only its application renders it capitalist or socialist:

> Marx stressed the essentially "neutral" character of technology: although the windmill may give you a feudal society, and the steam-mill an industrial capitalist society, the latter may just as well give you another form of industrial society.
>
> (SC 184)

However, this response only goes so far for Marcuse. Marcuse does not share the Soviet-Marxist idea that technology is neutral. As in the U.S., a centralized form of industry leads to an erosion of the division between civil society and state. The economy's goals are adopted by the state, the police, and the military. As in the United States, so in the Soviet Union these economic goals are pursued not just through coercion at home but through military conquest abroad. Indeed, Marcuse even notes commonalities in the superstructure, extending well beyond the base. The morality of both cultures is essentially repressive and oriented towards the need for constant work and sacrifice.

A natural objection is that the Soviet Union, even if it resembled the monopolistic and state-run capitalism of liberal democracies and fascist regimes, differed because it was communist, not capitalist. Yet as Marcuse emphasizes, the centralization of industry in the Soviet Union had nothing to do with the socialist ideal of public ownership of the means of production. It was only an expedient adopted to accelerate technological progress as fast as possible:

> nationalization is but a technological political device for increasing the productivity of labor, for accelerating the development of the productive forces and for their control from above (central planning)—a change in the mode of domination, streamlining of domination, rather than prerequisite for its abolition.
>
> (SC 82)

The use of nationalization for the sake of maximizing productivity undermines the Soviet Union's claim to be a radical alternative to the West.

Much as he does in his analysis of fascism, Marcuse regards the U.S.S.R. as the type of society that Western liberal democracies can degenerate into if they are not vigilant. At his most pessimistic, Marcuse predicts convergence between the U.S. and Soviet systems in the postwar period, and speaks as if the defeat of the Nazis has done little more than eliminate one type of fascism:

> the basic institutions of large-scale mechanized industry and the explosive growth of the productivity of labor commanded by it will bring about political and cultural institutions irrevocably different from those of the liberalist period—a historical tendency which is likely to supersede some of the present most conspicuous differences between the Western and the Soviet system.
>
> (SC 4)

Though Marcuse's prediction that the U.S. and Soviet Union would converge may seem excessively bleak, at least in hindsight, it is based on a sound materialist principle. This is the principle that two societies which share a mode of production cannot diverge too significantly in their political, cultural, and other institutions. In both systems, the imperative of never-ending growth will overpower the rights and freedoms of the individual, whether these are defended in liberal or socialist terms. Even so, Marcuse was well aware that the convergence had yet to take place. He notes crucial differences between the U.S. and Soviet systems, especially in their legal and political "superstructure." "As against this common technical-economic denominator stands the very different institutional structure—private enterprise here, nationalized enterprise there" (SC 6). Still, Marcuse insists that both share the same set of productive forces in their "base," and fears that this will be decisive for the future of both societies.

Though Marcuse agrees with the common criticism that the U.S.S.R. was a totalitarian society, he makes this criticism from a socialist, rather than a liberal, perspective: in particular, he uses a definition of totalitarianism that can only be understood against the backdrop of Marx's "historical materialism." Marcuse begins by invoking the historical materialist thesis that societies can be understood as composed of a superstructure and a base. The former compromises ideology, morality, religion, law, and politics; the latter, the economy (in particular, the forces and relations of production). Though elements of the superstructure exist to serve the base, they retain a certain autonomy. Occasionally, there may arise contradictions between the former and the latter. In the end, the base prevails, but the superstructure, as partially autonomous, functions as a reservoir of ideas for those interested in criticizing society. Christianity, for example, though its dominant function is to serve capitalism, contains countervailing ideas and practices that may be seized upon by communists in their efforts to subvert the status quo. Yet in the Soviet Union the superstructure was ruthlessly and thoroughly instrumentalized to serve the base, and in a much cruder way than tends to happen naturally. Hence it lost all its autonomy and "antagonistic" potential, and simply became another adjunct to production:

> The functional differences between base and superstructure therefore tend to be obliterated: the latter is methodically

and systematically assimilated with the base by depriving the superstructure of those functions which are transcendent and antagonistic to the base. This process, which establishes new foundations for social control, alters the very substance of ideology. The tension between idea and reality, between culture and civilization, between intellectual and material culture—a tension which was one of the driving forces behind Western civilization—is not solved but methodically reduced.

(SC 124)

Marcuse is particularly withering on the subject of Soviet art and culture, which he regards as so crudely propagandistic that they represent a regression to the most primitive phase of art: magic. Ultimately, then, Soviet society was totalitarian in a way that even industrial capitalism was not; in particular, base was collapsed into superstructure, and a single form of power prevailed throughout.

One might object that this is no betrayal of Marxism but, rather, nothing other than what Marx himself predicted would happen in a genuine socialist society. The historical materialist model is only meant to apply to pre-communist modes of production, those in which human beings have not yet achieved control over the productive forces. With the transition to communism, necessity gives way to freedom, and the productive forces are used to provide for human need, rather than the greed of a particular class. However, there is a crucial difference between this socialist ideal and the U.S.S.R. The latter society remained enslaved to the productive forces, since everything in it was subordinate to the goal of developing them. As a backward, feudal society, Russia lacked the productive capacity to produce social wealth which an industrial capitalist society would have. All by itself, this would be reason enough to prioritize technological progress. Yet Russia also had to compete with the capitalist world, economically, militarily, and culturally. This constitutes a further reason why it was dissuaded from using what productive power it had for the betterment of its average members.

Another reason likely to be emphasized by liberal-capitalist critics of socialism is graft and corruption. Marcuse's view of the Soviet Union differs, however. Corruption is not a point of emphasis. If the Russian state did not improve the lot of its people, then this is less because its leaders were greedy and more because of the historical and economic constraints the regime was under. In its emphasis on structural forces over individual agency, this is a largely Marxist analysis of a Marxist regime. Indeed, one might worry that Marcuse essentially accepts the self-justification of the Soviet leadership. What room remains for critique in his allegedly critical account?

Marcuse clarifies just how far his agreement extends with the Soviet Union and where it leaves off in a passage from the unpublished "33 Theses." There, Marcuse expresses an ambivalent perspective. On the one hand, the leaders of the Soviet Union were correct in their observation that a changed world situation necessitated a new approach to the realization of socialism: socialist revolutions in Europe had failed; the Western proletariat was no longer a revolutionary class in a revolutionary situation; world revolution was no longer likely, and so on and so forth: "The two-phase-theory gained historical justification in the Soviet Union's struggle against the surrounding capitalist world, and in the necessity to 'construct socialism in one country.' It justifies the non-existence of socialism in this situation" (CPHM 1: 224). Yet Marcuse's sympathy with the Soviet position extends no further than this. As he goes on to observe, the specific approach to realizing socialism adopted by the Soviet Union is absurd, not just in that it reproduced the worst aspects of monopoly capitalism and imperialism but in that it exacerbated them. He elaborates:

> By accepting capitalist rationality, it plays out the weapons of the old society against the new one: capitalism has better technology and greater wealth (technological); this foundation allows capitalism to let people live better. Socialist society can imitate and outdo this only if it forgoes the costly experiment of abolishing domination and imitates and outdoes the capitalist development of production and the productivity of labor, i.e. the subordination of wage labor to the production apparatus. The transition to socialism becomes rebus sic stantibus pointless.
>
> (CPHM 1: 224)

Perversely, hyper-industrialization was the means which the Soviet Union took to achieve the end of socialism. Technically, this is coherent, even if it has a ring of paradox about it. One may induce illness for the sake of health, fight a war for the sake of peace, work for the sake leisure, and so on. However, Marcuse doubts that the chosen means will conduce the end in this case.

In the same unpublished manuscript, Marcuse presents his alternative proposal for socialists in Russia. Socialists must not be satisfied with anything less than the workers' ownership of the means of production and must reject all of the official excuses for postponing this development. As Marcuse notes, this may mean accepting some measure of anarchy in the initial transition: "the will to abolish domination and exploitation appears as the will to anarchy" (CPHM 1: 226). The true revolution requires accepting economic stagnation. Yet it is clear Marcuse believes the Soviet leadership overestimated the technological prerequisites for socialism. Marcuse's use of the term "anarchy" is significant, in that it suggests that socialism in the modern world may profit from engagement with another leftist tradition that has often opposed it. This is a surprising concession. Marcuse is conceding that twentieth-century Marxism, especially in the East, required a dose of something Marxists have typically denounced as utopian: the anarchist's rejection of authority, hierarchy, and government in any form. Admittedly, this is very speculative, since Marcuse never, so far as I know, expressed any support for anarchism.

As we have noted, Marcuse was not alone in his belief that fascism, liberalism, and communism were—or risked becoming—totalitarian. Because of this, however, it is crucial to be clear about the differences between his thesis and those of others. One version of this pessimistic thesis is based on Weber's analysis of modern society in terms of the process he calls "rationalization."[6] This is the process whereby all facets of social life are subject to routinization, calculability, and control. Instrumental reason crowds out other modes of reasoning, those based on values, traditions, or an interest in self-disclosure. What is more, rationalization manifests itself in bureaucracy, a form of government that is the opposite of charisma. Whereas in charisma, authority is vested in individuals, under bureaucracy it is vested in impersonal norms, carried out by faceless masses of functionaries. To certain Weberians, it is bureaucracy which constitutes the totalitarian core of all modern societies, be they communist, fascist, or liberal.

Yet although he never explicitly addresses it, Marcuse would reject this analysis. Marcuse notes that the Soviet Union is a thoroughly bureaucratized state, but he does not regard bureaucracy as the ultimate cause of unfreedom. Bureaucracy is secondary to the economy. Bureaucracy is a mode of government adopted for the sake of maximizing productive output.[7] Hence, Marcuse does not agree that bureaucracy would bedevil even a genuine socialist society, in which workers controlled the means of production. Such a society would not heed the imperative, common to liberal capitalism and Soviet communism, of unlimited growth.

3. Speech, toleration, and the liberal tradition

Since Marcuse criticizes liberalism for its totalitarian tendencies, it is worth directly considering his views on liberal democracy. For this purpose, I propose to turn to Marcuse's essay "Repressive Tolerance." I choose this essay, rather than One-Dimensional Man and other writings, because I would like to focus on liberal ideals like toleration. Many readers will be familiar with the Marxist critique of liberalism as hypocritically embracing free-market capitalism, even where this system contradicts liberal ideals like freedom and equality. They will also be familiar with the Frankfurt School thesis, taken up in One-Dimensional Man, that modern capitalism, in contrast to the earlier, laissez-faire variety, poses a new and unprecedented threat to human freedom, happiness, and perhaps even survival. My aim here is to focus more narrowly on liberal ideals and traditions themselves, in order to understand Marcuse's critique of them.

While it is sometimes assumed that the essay is exclusively concerned with the question of the nature and limits of free speech, this is a misreading. For while the term "toleration" encompasses the willingness to allow rival groups to express their points of view, Marcuse uses it in a more capacious way. For Marcuse, toleration refers to the peaceful coexistence of rival individuals and groups within the bounds of law and public morality. Hence, toleration is not simply a matter of allowing controversial speakers on campus, but also of not going to war with rival Protestant sects. Clearly, the issue of toleration is central to the liberal tradition, which grows out of the wars of religion. Yet Marcuse approaches toleration in a new light when he asks whether progressives have reason to tolerate militarism, police brutality, advertising, mass media, consumer-culture, racism, and so on. Here, he means to include not just the messages spread by these groups, but also their actions in society.

Marcuse will insist that there is no reason for progressives to tolerate these regressive tendencies in society, whether they are legal or not. He will base this on his belief in objective truth in moral matters, and the need for those who are on the side of justice and the good life to not shrink from what is required to make these ideals a reality. Marcuse appears to endorse extra-legal means of resistance, even violence, and he distinguishes between regressive violence, which has no justification, and progressive violence that revolutionizes society and moves history forward.

In his insistence that progressives have no reason to tolerate the status quo, Marcuse appears to set himself at odds with the liberal tradition. Toleration is often considered the main virtue of liberal democracy, a system in which competing ways of life, religious creeds, and belief systems can peacefully coexist. Within certain limits, they are tolerated by the state, which attempts to remain neutral between them, and not favor one over the others. Similarly, they are encouraged to tolerate one another, and are not permitted to use force in order to suppress one another. Often, the toleration found in liberal democracies is described as an innovation that enables them to put an end to the interminable wars of religion that spilled so much blood in early-modern Europe. Only by eliminating official state religion and tolerating rival groups do societies achieve peace and prosperity. In private life, individuals and communities are left free to pursue their conceptions of the good life, so long as they respect the laws that safeguard the framework in which everybody coexists; for example, the laws protecting basic rights to physical security, private property, and freedom of speech and association. The claim is not that the state is indiscriminately tolerant, since there is much that it will forbid. Yet it is as tolerant as can reasonably be expected under present historical conditions, when societies are pluralistic and individuals and groups must agree on some shared framework for interaction.

Marcuse's critique of this case for liberalism is announced in the title of his essay "Repressive Tolerance." His claim is that the ideal of toleration, intended to emancipate, may, in fact, repress. This is particularly so under modern conditions. Even if there was a time when toleration freed religious and political minorities from the oppression of the state or of the majority, this time is long past. Today, toleration serves a repressive function because it masks domination and oppression. In modern society, there are extreme inequalities of wealth, power, and privilege, and those on the losing end of them are nearly powerless. By being encouraged to tolerate those who defend the status quo—or advocate an acceleration of current rightward trends—the oppressed are effectively deprived of any means of resisting. Hence Marcuse insists that

> The toleration of the systematic moronization of children and adults alike by publicity and propaganda, the release of destructiveness in aggressive driving, the recruitment for and training of special forces, the impotent and benevolent tolerance toward outright deception in merchandising, waste, and planned obsolescence are not distortions and aberrations, they are the essence of a system which fosters tolerance as a means for perpetuating the struggle for existence and suppressing the alternatives.
>
> (CPT 83)

To Marcuse, then, the ideal of toleration is a ruse. It asks that all of society's members and groups respect one another's right to exist, but ignores the domination and oppression that forms the backdrop of this coexistence. As an example of this, Marcuse considers the prevalence of far-right ideology in American society. He cites groups like the K.K.K. The demand to tolerate such groups is excessive and would only further weaken the already precarious position of minority groups.

Yet fringe groups, minorities (religious, ethnic, ideological), and dissenting individuals, do not form Marcuse's primary target, even if this has been the historical focus of discussions of toleration in the liberal tradition. For Marcuse, this focus obscures a crucial facet of the problem, namely the way in which we are so often called upon to tolerate the status quo, or social whole. As he writes:

> I propose a shift in the focus of the discussion: it will be concerned not only, and not primarily, with tolerance toward radical extremes, minorities, subversives, etc., but rather with

tolerance toward majorities, toward official and public opinion, toward the established protectors of freedom.

(RT 91–92)

Once we undertake this shift in the framing of the issue of toleration, Marcuse thinks, we will see that the ideal of tolerance has a repressive, pacifying function, serving to reconcile people to an unjust social order.

In response, a defender of liberal democracy might argue that Marcuse has failed to understand the ideal of tolerance and what it entails. Tolerance in liberal democracies does require that we respect one another's basic rights to free speech, security, and private property. It does not require that we acquiesce to anything that is done to us by others. It may be that far-right groups like the Ku Klux Klan have the right to voice their views, but this does not mean that members of minority groups must stoically accept harassment, intimidation, or violence. They can reasonably expect the state to protect their basic rights, where extremist groups threaten to infringe upon them. What is more, they may even be justified in exercising the right to self-defense, where state intervention is not possible. In short, the ideal of a toleration society has clearly defined limits. The burdens it imposes on society's members, though weighty, are not unreasonable. We may have to endure speech that is offensive, but we can take some solace in the fact that physical assault, murder, etc., are not tolerated.

Essentially this response upholds behavior, speech, etc., which is consistent with law and order, but condemns any of their manifestations beyond these limits. Yet as a leftist critic of liberal democracy, Marcuse regards the prevailing order as itself violent. For him, violence is not the exclusive prerogative of groups like the Klan. Violence is just as much the favored means of the police, the military, and the courts. This violence is visited not just on the truly malevolent, but on anyone who resists the military–industrial complex. Striking workers and the peace movement are likely to be beset with violence too. More subtle forms of coercion are exercised by the media, advertising, and public relations. These too impinge upon freedom, in particular the freedom of thought and conscience. A critic might object to calling these phenomena violent or coercive.

After all, they occur within the bounds of the law, and are legitimate, whereas extra-legal violence and coercion are not. Yet it is clear Marcuse does not invest this distinction with as much weight as his liberal-democratic opponents do. For him, then, there is illegitimate violence and coercion exercised by nothing over and above than the normal, day-to-day operation of society's major institutions.

For Marcuse, then, intolerance towards the prevailing social order is justified, even where it is inconsistent with law and order. If there is a difference between the peace movement and the K.K.K., it will not be the case that one operates within the bounds of decent society and the other does not. It will be that one is progressive, and the other regressive. One has truth, justice, and freedom on its side, the other only ignorance, injustice, and oppression. This may seem like a fatal weakness in Marcuse's position. Every group believes itself to be morally in the right. Hence, law and order function as a common standard against which we judge differing groups, each of which believes itself to be right. Yet Marcuse appears to think that, in the modern world, we cannot avoid taking our stand on what we believe is right and being willing to accept the costs.

Indeed, Marcuse sometimes observes that partisanship was not beneath the group which gave birth to ideals of toleration, the bourgeoisie of the eighteenth century.[8] They too held themselves to be in the right and did not tolerate their rivals in the medieval church, the aristocracy, and the monarchy. Instead, they swept their rivals away, often violently. Far from discrediting the bourgeoisie, this is for Marcuse a point in their favor. They liberated Europe from religious superstition and political ignorance. Thus, their ideal of toleration cannot be taken at face value. It is not a banner under which all individuals and groups could or should rally. It is instead the rallying cry of a particular class, which could, at a certain phase in its development, speak for the interests of humanity as a whole, but which has long ceased to do so. For Marcuse, the military–industrial complex must now suffer the same fate as the *ancien régime*, and the struggle against the former calls for no more moderation than the struggle against the latter did.

Just as there can be repressive tolerance, so too is there the possibility of emancipatory intolerance.

At least under present historical conditions, tolerance can only ever be justified instrumentally, and not as an end in itself (confusingly,

Marcuse does say in an early part of the essay "Toleration is an end in itself," but then goes on to qualify this claim, observing that it does not apply under present social conditions) (CPT 82). It is justified insofar as it advances other more important progressive ideals and is not justified where it does not. In this qualified sense, Marcuse's position is illiberal. He does not accept formal constraints on the pursuit of substantive ideals, values, and goals. He is unapologetic in his insistence on a conception of the good life for individuals and societies. In this respect, he more closely resembles one of the warring Protestant sects than he does the secular, modern liberal. Whereas the former are willing to fight and die for a conception of the good, the latter prefers the peace that comes when we agree to be neutral between any such conceptions. Yet for Marcuse this neutrality is simply a mask for class-based domination and oppression.

As I have said, an important nuance in Marcuse's position is his belief that tolerance *would* be an end in itself, if society were to progress to a point where freedom and equality existed (CPT 82). As he makes clear, human beings desire peaceful coexistence with one another for its own sake. However, Marcuse thinks we have not yet reached this stage. To pretend that we have is lunacy.

In the essay, Marcuse discusses John Stuart Mill, the political theorist whose case for tolerance has become canonical for liberal democracies (RT 86). Like Marcuse, Mill regards toleration as, in some sense, secondary. For Mill, it is a useful means to discover the truth but is not an end in itself. Nor is toleration something we resort to because we have come to believe there is no absolute truth, or, at any rate, no way for us to know it. However, Marcuse objects to a tendency in Mill for which socialists often criticize liberals: their belief that in the modern, Western world, the preconditions for a just social order are in place.

As Marcuse correctly observes, even Mill acknowledges that tolerance would be of limited usefulness if one were dealing with those who are not yet mature persons; in particular, those who cannot reason and think for themselves. This group might be thought to include the very young, the criminally violent, and the severely mentally ill. More problematically, it might be thought to include the people Mill calls "uncivilized." By this, he means those in traditional societies where practices of enlightened discussion have not yet taken root. Mill takes his society to have reached the point where toleration is possible, at least in most circumstances. Marcuse, however, denies that this is true of late capitalist societies, and maintains that progressives are in the exceptional circumstances Mill describes: specifically, circumstances where toleration is of limited usefulness because of the intransigence of one's opponent. It is not so much uncooperative individuals whom progressives confront today, but rather an entire system. This system is not only hostile to progressive goals, but possessed of powerful means of suppressing alternative perspectives before they are even voiced.

To Marcuse, Mill's case for tolerance presupposes background conditions of relative parity between the participants. Only through fair competition do the best ideas have a chance to prevail. If the deck is stacked in favor of the powers that be, then the resultant competition is a sham whose outcome is predetermined. Discussion will serve no other purpose than to create the illusion of fair competition, the appearance that every point of view receives its due and therefore that the one which prevails ought to do so. Marcuse thinks that this illusion prevails in late capitalist societies. In these societies, socialist and anti-war views are often heard but are almost guaranteed in advance to be ineffective. Marcuse finds a vivid instance of sham toleration in modern media. On television, "impartial" discussions of current events on news programs are interspersed with programming that glorifies the status quo: advertising of consumer products, and ideologically manipulative entertainment. The prevailing society always emerges from these free and frank discussions unscathed.

Here, it would be fair to respond that Marcuse is setting the bar for impartiality impossibly high. On his view, the fairness of a televised debate over some isolated question of policy is compromised from the outset, because "the system" as a whole is never seriously questioned. To this, the response might be that Marcuse is confused. Impartiality demands that we not take sides in the debate in question, not that we not take sides on any other issue; for example, capitalism versus socialism. The broader issue of how society is organized may not be up for discussion, but this does not preclude us from a free and fair exchange of ideas on narrower questions. Even Marcuse acknowledges at one point that no society can be asked to impartially consider the question of its own right to exist.

Perhaps Marcuse's mistrust of much political discourse reflects his totalizing approach to politics (indeed Marcuse does invoke the Hegelian-Marxist notion of totality at a crucial point in the essay) (RT 83). Primarily important for Marcuse is the question of how society as a whole ought to be organized. Other controversies are secondary, in that they are either pre-decided by the nature of the system in question or else are superficial. For Marcuse, then, the most vital questions of politics do not allow us to proceed piecemeal, but, instead, ask us to take in the entire social totality at a single glance.

But surely it is not pointless to debate gay marriage, as so many activists and commentators have done in recent decades. The result was its legalization, and this is a powerful reminder that isolated instances of progress are possible even against the backdrop of repression.

As we have seen, Marcuse thinks the game of public discourse is rigged, at least under late capitalism. In Marcuse's terminology, this questionable form of toleration is "abstract" or "pure," presumably because its neutrality is superficial. As he writes, "I call this non-partisan tolerance 'abstract' or 'pure' inasmuch as it refrains from taking sides—but in doing so it actually protects the already established machinery of discrimination" (RT 85). How, exactly, is the game rigged, though? Without a clear answer, Marcuse will seem like those conspiracy theorists who are only capable of vague allusions to an omnipresent power that quashes all dissent. One answer has already been alluded to and is found in Marcuse's discussion of the media. Like other left-wing critics of mass media, Marcuse insists that it is a threat to democracy. Though it appears to promote an exchange of rival viewpoints, it in fact takes the side of the power structure in countless ways, some subtle and others less so. Dependent on advertisers, the media is in thrall to corporate interests and, through them, to America's military objectives.

A second answer, though merely implicit, arises in Marcuse's discussion of toleration in education (RT 113–14). Marcuse claims that there exists in the pedagogy of postwar America various schools of thought that insist on the merits of a permissive approach to childrearing, relatively free of repression. This approach is meant to result in a "self-actualized" child and is defended on Freudian grounds, specifically with reference to the idea that repression, at least where it is excessive, leads to neurosis. Yet as Marcuse points out, even Freud recognizes the need for a minimum amount of oppression if the child is to grow up into an autonomous adult capable of integration into society. To be sure, Marcuse is not interested in promoting an ideal of maturity as submission to the demands of civilization. Yet he does share with Freud an ideal of maturity as autonomy, self-discipline, and the capacity to dictate the course of one's own life rather than be buffeted by the chaotic forces of the id (or the arbitrary and excessive demands of the super-ego). Accordingly, Marcuse is concerned that permissive parenting, though it may free children from the heteronomy of the parents, will not lead to autonomy. It will simply lead to another form of heteronomy which we might call "social heteronomy."[9]

Not only nature but also society threatens children with unfreedom. Under late capitalism, the spontaneous inclinations of the child are likely to be influenced by society, which has made unprecedented inroads into the family. Modern media, advertising, the education and medical systems, the social welfare services, political parties, and so on—all of these factors will influence children's inclinations. Far from allowing a child's individuality to flourish, permissive parenting is likely to deliver the child over into the hands of social forces that encourage conformism. For Marcuse, a more repressive parental regime is required to produce an autonomous individual, capable of deciding for him or herself how to live. In its absence, the result will be what Marcuse's Frankfurt School colleagues Adorno and Horkheimer call the liquidation of the autonomous individual. This figure is a hard-won historical achievement, a product of bourgeois culture in its effort to emancipate itself from servility, superstition, and feudalism.

A final answer lies in Marcuse's Orwell-inspired conviction that the very language we use biases us in favor of the political status quo (RT 86–87). In Orwell's 1984 the authoritarian regime promotes its rule with slogans like the following memorable one: "Freedom is slavery, war is peace, ignorance is strength." The party's control over the populace is so complete that it has even succeeded in overriding logic; in particular, the law of non-contradiction, which forbids us from declaring a thing to be its exact opposite. It is worth remembering that Orwell wrote *Nineteen Eighty-Four* as a warning to liberal democracies, one Marcuse intends to heed.

Marcuse believes he witnessed a similar corruption of logic and language occurring in the political cultures of Western liberal democracies. In America, war is peace in the sense that the culture has already decided in advance that these terms are not antithetical but complementary: "For example, thesis: we work for peace; antithesis: we prepare for war (or even: we wage war); unification of opposites: preparing for war is working for peace" (CPT 96). Here, Marcuse is referring to the idea that the only realistic way to pursue peace is through readiness for war: bases in foreign countries, espionage and clandestine services, investment in military research, and so on. Marcuse's suggestion seems to be that certain beliefs are so entrenched in our society that they come to affect the very meanings of the terms we use.

It would be legitimate to wonder if Marcuse's concerns on this score are excessive. Can anyone seriously maintain that it is not possible to be against war in modern America, because the very terms of the discussion have been defined in advance as making this incoherent? Clearly, Marcuse and others succeeded in questioning the war in Vietnam. Perhaps Marcuse is best understood as identifying an obstacle to dissent, but not an insurmountable one.

In the example Marcuse puts forward, it appears as if not just a belief, but a pattern of them—an inference, or argument—has come to be incorporated into the meaning of a word. Marcuse's position here resembles the inferentialism of Robert Brandom (1994), which maintains that the meaning of a word is determined first by the propositions in which it figures, but ultimately by the inferences in which those propositions figure. Marcuse finds resources for the critique of ideology in this doctrine in the philosophy of language. Beliefs and arguments will be shielded from scrutiny as long as those who challenge them seem to lack command over even the basic vocabulary on which they must rely.

Does Marcuse then think that liberal democracies are as repressive as more overtly totalitarian societies, like Nazi Germany or the U.S.S.R? The answer seems to be no. As Marcuse writes:

> With all its limitations and distortions, democratic tolerance is under all circumstances more humane than an institutionalized intolerance which sacrifices the rights and liberties of the living generations for the sake of future generations.
>
> (CPT 99)

However, he goes on to qualify his point, urging us to not conclude on this basis that there can be no improving upon liberal democracies. In Marcuse's view, a future socialist society would break with both the sham toleration of liberal democracies and the open repression of communist dictatorships:

> The only authentic alternative and negation of dictatorship (with respect to this question) would be a society in which "the people" have become autonomous individuals, freed from the repressive requirements of a struggle for existence in the interest of domination, and as such human beings choosing their government and determining their life.
>
> (CPT 105)

Though critical of liberalism, Marcuse affirms democracy, insisting on facing new forms of totalitarianism with an insistence that the people control the power that is exercised over them.

4. Towards a socialist alternative

In this chapter, I have considered Marcuse's conviction that liberal capitalism, fascism, and communism exhibit commonalities that render each of them totalitarian. In light of this, it would be natural for a reader to wonder what alternative Marcuse proposes. Here, a fourth system suggests itself: social democracy, a system that attempts to combine the efficiency of markets with a commitment to equality, usually expressed in a social welfare state. Marcuse notes that this system has arisen in postwar Britain and Western Europe, but he regards it as insufficient. He believes that the wealthy and powerful will always contrive ways to overcome the bulwarks this system erects against inequality and class-based domination and oppression. As in his criticism of Soviet communism, Marcuse is unwavering in his commitment to the socialist ideal of a society in which there is democratic control of the economy.

How, though, does Marcuse think socialists ought to achieve the transition to a future socialist society? Here, he admits that his position is unorthodox in (at least) two respects:

First, Marcuse sees potential in the middle classes in the United States and Western Europe, as well as students and members of minority groups. He does not place faith in the working classes, believing that they have been largely integrated into monopoly capitalism. Their loyalty has been purchased with improved working conditions, cheap consumer goods, the offshoring of burdensome work, patriotism and militarism, consumer culture, and so on. One of the main inducements to comply with late capitalism is a culture of permissiveness marked by weakening taboos against sexual gratification ("repressive desublimation").

Second, Marcuse believes alterations in consciousness and sensibility can lead to revolution, something orthodox Marxists would not have deemed possible. Marcuse sees in the "hippie" culture of the 1960s a new outlook on life that deemphasizes work and focuses instead on creativity, community, and sustainable forms of living. According to orthodox Marxism, the role of new outlooks in any proletarian revolution should be minor at best. These outlooks belong to the superstructure, the domain of social life that includes ideology, religion, morality, and other forms of "social consciousness." According to orthodox Marxism, superstructural phenomena like these are epiphenomenal (causally inert). Causal efficacy is possessed exclusively by "the base," made up of the productive forces and relations of production (class relationships). Some orthodox Marxists hold the more moderate view that the superstructure, though not epiphenomenal, does exert a weaker causal role than the base—and that where the two conflict, the base tends to prevail. Even on this more moderate view, however, Marcuse's position would count as unorthodox, because of the importance it ascribes to superstructural factors. Marcuse's departure from orthodox Marxism becomes particularly pronounced in his aesthetics, where he insists on the role of formally innovative art in changing people's perception and thereby inspiring social change.

While the task of evaluating Marcuse's outlook on the geopolitics of his moment goes beyond the scope of this chapter, I do want to consider one possible shortcoming of this account. In emphasizing the commonalities between liberalism, communism, and fascism, Marcuse may risk falsely equating the three. In particular, he may risk ignoring the genuine moral progress achieved by liberal societies, even if this progress has been insufficient. In this connection, it is worth noting that Marcuse often displays an awareness that the United States is not literally a fascist country, even if it exhibits tendencies in this direction:

> This is not a fascist regime by any means. The courts still uphold the freedom of the press; "underground" papers are still being sold openly, and the media leave room for continual and strong criticism of the government and its policies. To be sure, freedom of expression hardly exists for the blacks, and is effectively limited even for the whites. But civil rights are still there, and their existence is not disproved by the (correct) argument that the system can still "afford" this kind of protest. Decisive is rather whether the present phase of the (preventive) counter-revolution (its democratic-constitutional phase) does not prepare the soil for a subsequent fascist phase.
>
> (CR 76)

In the end, it seems to me, Marcuse's critique of liberal democracy is best approached as a warning of things to come, rather than an account of where things stand. More accurately, Marcuse's claim is that there is a standing threat to genuinely progressive achievements of liberal democracy, as long as they coexist with monopoly capitalism. This does not make liberal democracy identical to fascism or communism. However, it does mean the former could degenerate into the latter. What is more, Marcuse thought this threat would only become more acute in future years.

Summary

Marcuse does not approach political philosophy in the way that contemporary Anglophone political philosophers do, e.g., through thought-experiments designed to capture a transhistorical ideal of justice. He is, in Raymond Geuss's terms, a philosopher of real politics. This means his thinking about society and politics is focused on the contemporary geopolitical situation. Marcuse describes a world in which liberal capitalism and communism, having defeated fascism on the battlefield, risk degenerating into it. All three systems are, or tend to become, totalitarian, due to their underlying "mode of production." This mode of production is what Pollock called "monopoly" or "state" capitalism, something of a misnomer in the case of the Soviet Union, but not entirely inapt. This system is characterized by the erosion of any division between "civil society" (the economy) and "the state" as well as an imperialist stance towards other nations. Marcuse's critique of liberal capitalism is expanded upon in his essay on toleration. The lesson of this essay is that the progressive ideals of liberalism, in its heroic early phase, take on a regressive, conservative function in its degenerate late phase. Marcuse's critique of liberalism may appear to assert a false moral equivalence between liberalism and fascism or Soviet communism. Yet even those who defend liberal capitalism should pay attention to Marcuse's warning. He has a compelling sociological case for the idea that this system at least is at risk of becoming totalitarian.

Notes

1 Hence by "liberal capitalism" I mean the twentieth-century variety, not the earlier laissez-faire one. However, it would be a serious mistake to think that Marcuse is not a critic of capitalism per se, but only of an advanced form of it: monopoly or state capitalism. I thank Arash Abazari for pressing me for clarification on this point.

2 In preparing this chapter, I have benefited from Kellner (1984), especially the chapters on the Frankfurt School critique of fascism (Ch. 4) and of Soviet communism (Ch. 7). For background on the Frankfurt School idea of state or monopoly capitalism, I am indebted to Postone (2006).

3 See Kellner (1984: 112–15) who criticizes as reductive this materialist tendency in Marcuse and the Frankfurt School's analysis of fascism; Kellner believes that the culture and ideology of fascism are more important than these Frankfurt School authors allow.

4 For a discussion, see Pollock (1978).

5 The *locus classicus* of this critique is Marx's "On the Jewish Question" (1978: 26–53). For a helpful overview of the Hegelian position on state and civil society, see Pelczynski (1984: 1–14).

6 For an introduction to the rationalization thesis, see Weber's pair of lectures "Science as Vocation" and "Politics as Vocation." Both can be found in the Gerth and Mills anthology *From Max Weber* (2009).

7 Kellner also discusses the role of bureaucracy in Marcuse's analysis of the Soviet Union.

8 This is how I interpret Marcuse's remark from the introduction: "In other words, today tolerance appears again as what it was in its origins, at the beginning of

the modern period—a partisan goal, a subversive liberating notion and practice" (RT 81).

9 I owe this term to the work of Tuomo Tiisala.

Further reading

Kellner, D. (1984) *Marcuse and the Crisis of Marxism*, London: Macmillan. [Comprehensive overview of Marcuse's life and thought, focused on his relationship to Marxism. Includes an extensive treatment of Marcuse's view on fascism (Ch. 4) and Soviet communism (Ch.7).]

Leiter, B. (2017) "Justifying Academic Freedom: Mill and Marcuse Revisited," SSRN, June 3. http://dx.doi.org/10.2139/ssrn.2943774/. [Uses Marcuse and Mill to defend academic freedom in research and teaching. Particularly helpful on the idea of academic freedom as an instrumental value.]

Neumann, F. (2009) *Behemoth: The Structure and Practice of National Socialism* 1933–44, Chicago: Ivan R. Dee. [Landmark study by a member of the institute. Many parallels with Marcuse's analysis.]

Pollock, F. (1978) [1941] "State Capitalism: Its Possibilities and Limitations," in A. Arato, and E. Gebhart (eds.), *The Essential Frankfurt School Reader*, New York: Urizen Books, 71–95. [Classic statement of the Frankfurt School idea of state capitalism, and the erosion of the distinction between civil society and state.]

Eight
Marcuse today

In this final chapter, I conclude by considering what Marcuse might still have to teach us today. I restrict my focus to possible lessons for our current philosophical culture; in particular, the twenty-first-century Anglophone philosophical culture in which I work and with which I am most familiar. Before proceeding, however, I want to distinguish my approach to considering Marcuse's contemporary relevance from two alternative, but equally legitimate perspectives.

Since Marcuse was a politically engaged intellectual, it might seem more fitting to consider Marcuse's relevance to contemporary political life. His prescience is obvious, at least to me. For those to whom it is not obvious, the following points may be illustrative. In the first place, one might simply point to the massive revival of interest in a socialist alternative to capitalism among those on the left in Britain and North America. This revival has been marked by the intergenerational alliance between youth and old age exhibited in the case of Marcuse. Just as the 1960s saw Marcuse, an elderly émigré, join forces with militant youth activists like Abbie Hoffman and Angela Davis, so too does our moment witness an alliance between figures like Corbyn and Sanders—themselves relics of the 1960s counterculture—and Alexandria Ocasio-Cortez, "The Squad," and Greta Thunberg.[1]

Our historical moment is not unlike the one in which Marcuse's life and thought began to unfold. We are living in the wake of a financial crisis worse than any since the Great Depression of the 1930s. To this parallel between Marcuse's circumstances and our own, one might add others: the resurgence of the far right, not only in Europe but also in

DOI: 10.4324/9781003307075-8

the U.S.; the form of fascism this movement promotes, even in liberal democracies; state or monopoly capitalism and its threat to the autonomous individual; the cooption and destruction of the traditional working classes; the awesome and ever-growing power of science and technology over all facets of life, something potentially liberating but under current conditions used to dominate and oppress; foreign wars whose rationale often appears to be a pretext for imperial conquest; a culture of aggression, machismo, and violence, promoted in part by the easy availability of advanced gadgets of all kinds (Marcuse refers to car culture frequently, but the present affords many more examples); finally, and more optimistically, the promise of social movements among those who find the prevailing regime intolerable, namely students, members of minority groups, and artists.

A fuller discussion of Marcuse's political relevance than this one would go into each of these points in detail and with a more critical agenda. It would be important to ask whether Marcuse's diagnosis genuinely fits late capitalism, or merely seems to do so. Do we, for instance, live under the reign of state or monopoly capitalism? Or rather under the reign of a more dynamic, flexible variety synonymous with the "start-up" culture of Silicon Valley and the tech industry? Do Trump, Orban, and other far-right politicians and parties pose a threat like that of fascist leaders in the 1930s? Or do they instead demand a new set of concepts and categories adapted to the realities of the twenty-first century?

Yet in appraising Marcuse's legacy, I will fall back to the more abstract, philosophical plane on which this book has unfolded. I prefer to adopt an approach more in line with the overriding aim of this book, which seeks to contribute to the effort to revive interest in Marcuse as a serious philosopher.

Even in this connection, I will proceed selectively, focusing on Marcuse's relevance to contemporary Anglophone philosophy. Others are more qualified than I am to speak to Marcuse's position in European intellectual life.

Certainly, it seems clear that Marcuse's militancy differentiates him sharply from recent critical theorists; for example Habermas, who embraced a liberal, Enlightenment program, that few in earlier generations of critical theory would have adopted; and Honneth, Habermas's successor, who takes this moderating tendency further, urging that critical theory defend the modern market economy through a reactualization of Hegel's project of reconciliation. Both Habermas and Honneth insist that their positions are not intended to be uncritical towards the status quo. On the contrary, they argue that a critique of the present remains possible, and that a return to the Enlightenment or to Hegel will facilitate this critique. Such a critique would be immanent, one that convicts modern Western societies of failing to uphold the very ideal in terms of which they often justify themselves ("reason"). When one abandons this ideal, one is left at an impasse. This is sometimes said to be the situation of first-generation critical theory, whose totalizing and pessimistic critique of Enlightenment modernity seems to undercut its own normative premises.

Since it is not my aim in this chapter to compare Marcuse's thought to subsequent critical theory, I will restrict myself to just one remark. It is that Marcuse's project constitutes something of a happy medium between the projects of Habermas and Honneth, on one hand, and those of Adorno and Horkheimer, on the other (though the Horkheimer of the 1930s was closer to Marcuse). Marcuse appeals to a robust conception of reason and grounds his critique of modern society in weighty normative premises, e.g., a conception of human nature. However, he retains much of the core Marxist critique of modernity, the epoch of bourgeois revolutions. These revolutions were undertaken in the name of humanity as a whole, but often predominantly served the interests of a specific class. A truly "universal" society will need to await a further revolution, one that overthrows capitalism and replaces it with socialism. This unshakable conviction separates Marcuse from later critical theorists, even if these figures are willing to criticize modern society in different terms.[2] Marcuse's life and thought serve as a reminder that we can reject as false the choice between Adorno and Horkheimer and Habermas. Unlike these figures, Marcuse succeeds in uniting the aspiration to radical critique, on one hand, and to rationalism, on the other.

1. "Analytic critical theory"

In recent decades, there has been a remarkable shift in Anglophone philosophical culture, one which should be of interest to adherents of critical theory. This is a shift towards philosophical engagement with real-world social and political problems, and from a more radical political perspective than has been common in departments of Anglophone philosophy. This movement has sometimes been called analytic critical theory, in order to distinguish it from the continental variety founded in Frankfurt.[3] Its leading figures include prominent analytic philosophers, like Jason Stanley, Sally Haslanger, Tommy Shelbie, Kate Manne, and others.[4] It retains not only analytic philosophy's methodological commitment to clarity and rigor, but also some of its substantive doctrines and insights. Unlikely as it may seem, insights from analytical philosophy of language, metaphysics, philosophy of science, and philosophy of mind are often put to new and surprising uses. Here, one might think of debates about the meaning of social construction, especially in the areas of feminism and philosophy of race. It is, then, "core" analytic philosophy, and not just moral or political philosophy, which is recruited into the service of the new analytical critical theory. Indeed, traditional approaches in moral and political philosophy of the analytic tradition are often seen as impediments to analytic critical theory and its effort to address real-world social problems.

Often singled out for criticism is the Rawlsian methodology, which seeks an ideal theory.[5] An ideal theory, in Rawls's terms, assumes a certain level of compliance on the part of the population, and goes on to ask what a perfectly just society would be like if this level of cooperation could be assumed (Rawls 1999: 8). Non-ideal theory would concern itself with the existing, unjust societies we inhabit, rather than looking beyond them to some ideal future one. There is some debate over whether analytical critical theorists correctly understand Rawls' contrast. Nevertheless, it is clear that they mostly reject the project of ideal theory as he conceived of it and are interested instead in addressing social problems in actually existing, imperfect societies. In other words, they are partisans of non-ideal theory.

Unlike analytic critical theory, Marcuse's project likely cuts across the dichotomy between ideal and non-ideal theory.[6] On one hand, Marcuse is a utopian thinker, who is relatively confident in his ability to conceive an ideal future society. To be sure, he offers no blueprint, and he is well aware that the ideal socialist society will only be achieved if those seeking to bring it about are open to experimentation. To this extent, Marcuse observes Marx's prohibitions against attempting to offer too determinate an account of the future socialist society that revolution will help bring about. Still, Marcuse does insist on fairly specific conditions that this future society will need to meet: democratic control of the means of production; the end of profit-maximization without restraint, and its consequences (waste, destruction, imperialism, and war); reduction of repression and exploitation to their minimum socially necessary level; and so on.

Predominantly, analytical critical theory has focused on the problems of racism and misogyny, whereas Marcuse was predominantly interested in capitalism. A natural question to ask then is how analytical critical theorists who focus often (but not always) on race and gender might engage with their continental forebears, focused often (but not always) on class.

In approaching this question, it is worth noting the often sharp disagreements between Marxists, on one hand, and feminists and anti-racists, on the other. Marxists often accuse their opponents on the left of practicing "neo-liberal identity politics." This refers to the program of seeking expanded rights for minority groups without attention to the ways in which this process further shores up the capitalist system. For example, consider a capitalism in which women and members of minority groups occupy more positions on corporate boards. This system would be preferable, according to neoliberal identity politics. Yet it would, according to Marxists, only serve to perpetuate the class-based domination and oppression of capitalism by making it appear color- and gender blind. Indeed, it might serve to strengthen capitalism, rather than simply being compatible with it. Libertarian defenders of the free market have long noted the connection between liberal ideals of toleration and markets (here we might remember the idea, famous from Friedman's *Capitalism and Freedom*, that discrimination is bad for business).

For their part, feminists and anti-racists often accuse Marxists of "class reductionism." This is the error of assuming that economic justice will resolve all social problems, especially those afflicting women and members of ethnic minority groups. On this view, the effect of class reductionism is to unfairly minimize the suffering of women and minorities. They might argue that reparations will only serve to make poor Blacks members of the propertied classes, thereby converting them into a different type of oppressor. A critic of class reductionism might argue that this minimizes the legitimate interest Blacks have in being compensated for the labor that was forcibly extracted from their ancestors under slavery.

Marcuse always viewed liberalism as a radical tradition. Insufficiently radical perhaps, but radical nonetheless. The eighteenth-century revolutions were genuinely progressive and achieved some measure of freedom and equality. In retrospect, they were insufficient. They only allowed for formal freedom and equality that was consistent with a class society; for example, they allowed for equality before the law but stopped short of promoting economic equality. Still, Marcuse would not necessarily be in favor of the idea that progressives should be uncompromising and accept nothing less than communism. Indeed, his thought speaks to the ever-present possibility of regression in liberal-capitalist societies, their tendency to degenerate into something worse than simply hypocritical. Formal freedom and equality of women and minorities may be consistent with capitalism, but its rollback to premodern levels might be a symptom of something worse: not liberal capitalism, but fascism. Ultimately, though, it is difficult to determine definitively what Marcuse would make of the resurgent identitarian left.

Yet if Marcuse was not a class reductionist, might he nevertheless have insisted that class and economic life have primacy over race, gender, and identity? This would be a reasonable conclusion to draw from the centrality of capitalism to Marcuse's analysis of modern society, and the relative dearth of intellectual attention shown to race and gender in his writings. However, it is worth reminding ourselves once more that Marcuse's Marxism was unorthodox in various respects, especially in the role it accorded to Freud's psychology and theory of the instincts. Given the connection to family life, childrearing, and sexual reproduction, there is room in Marcuse's view for the feminist thought that Marx's theory of social reproduction in the workplace must be supplemented by a theory of social reproduction as it takes place in the home.[7]

Like Marcuse, the analytical critical theorist Jason Stanley has made fascism in America a central concern. However, there are crucial differences between the two. The first is that Stanley's focus is "fascist politics," and his main source is the *rhetoric* of the far right, whereas Marcuse's approach is consistently institutionalist. It is from political speeches, journalism, and public discourse that Stanley distills his theory of "how fascism works." These sources contain recurrent tendencies Stanley regards as characteristic of fascist thought in different times and places; for example, its anti-intellectualism, its defense of traditional gender roles and sexual morality, its embrace of militarism, its appeals to rural life and values against the corrupt mores of cities, and so on.

By contrast, Marcuse's analysis of fascism is focused on its institutional structure, in particular its status as a form of state or monopoly capitalism. Simona Aimar (2019) has criticized Stanley for focusing predominantly on rhetoric, rather than on power.[8] Marcuse might criticize Stanley along similar lines, or at least insist that his analysis would need to be supplemented by a theory of fascist government. As we have seen, Marcuse, like Stanley, faces the criticism that his analysis of America is alarmist, insofar as it implies America is (crypto-)fascist. Yet Marcuse has the resources to argue that liberal-capitalist institutions have fascist tendencies, even as he might insist that these tendencies have yet to be fully realized. Stanley could make a corresponding point, but it would not be based on the same institutional analysis.

While I have explored potential points of agreement between Marcuse and the analytic critical theorists, it is important to be clear about the disagreements that would likely arise. Much analytic critical theory is "idealist" in the sense that "materialists" (Marxists) have always severely criticized. By this, I mean that much analytic critical theory is more focused on abstract phenomena, like thought or language, than it is on concrete, material phenomena, like violence, power, and property. As examples of this tendency, we might cite Miranda Fricker's (2007) account of epistemic injustice, a wrong people suffer in their capacity as knowers when they belong to oppressive societies; the idea, developed for example by Basu and Schroeder (2018), of "doxastic wronging," a way of wronging others via our beliefs, as well as the same three authors' work in the philosophy of language on hate speech and other oppressive forms of discourse. Without denying that these forms of oppression from the epistemological and linguistic domain are both genuine and profoundly disturbing, a materialist like Marcuse might question whether these forms of oppression ought to be the central focus of critical social theory. For a materialist, language, consciousness, and thought are always secondary to class, power, and the control over resources. When we ignore this, we succumb to bourgeois ideology, whose main tactic is to distract people from the most fundamental facts of political life by encouraging them to focus on more superficial phenomena. We succumb to this ideology when we are more concerned with representation of women and minority groups on network television than we are with lack of access to healthcare, education, and even food among massive parts of the population. An understandable line of response might question the opposition between "ideal" and "material" factors drawn by Marxists. Even granting that social philosophy should focus on the concrete manifestations of oppression, many phenomena, e.g., speech acts which are both linguistic and behavioral, straddle the ideal/material divide.

It is worth noting that analogues of the Marxist or materialist perspective exist in recent Anglophone social philosophy, even if the exact doctrine does not. I interpret Kate Manne's analysis of misogyny as materialist, at least in the following sense. For Manne, sexism is the ideology of the patriarchy, but misogyny is its enforcement mechanism (2018: 20, Ch. 3). To be a misogynist is less a matter of holding sexist beliefs or attitudes than it is of participating in a system of subordination by policing women. It is possible to be a misogynist even if one does not consciously feel visceral hatred towards women. All that is required is that one's actions facilitate the subordination of women. In addition to being persuasive on its own terms, this analysis of misogyny strikes me as completely in line with the anti-idealist perspective of much Frankfurt School critical theory.

Yet in spite of these sporadic points of contact and concord, it would be a mistake to ignore the possibility of genuine clashes between Frankfurt School critical theory and new currents of social thought in analytical philosophy. Prima facie, there seems to be a clash between the feminist idea that society is fundamentally governed by patriarchy and the Marxist idea that it is instead fundamentally governed by capital. However, this incompatibility has begun to be queried by Marxist feminists like Vanessa Wills and others. Wills

(2018) proposes that we treat as false the choice between insisting on the primacy of class, on one hand, and that of race or gender, on the other.

While Marcuse's position serves as a Marxist counterweight to much non-Marxist theorizing in contemporary philosophy, matters are more complex than this, since Marcuse is by no means orthodox. We have noted repeatedly that Marcuse, though loyal to Marx's legacy, rejects overly rigid versions of the base–superstructure model; in particular, Marcuse is willing to allow that the domain of social consciousness (morality, ideology, art, religion, and so on) can react on that of social being (the economy). Hence it seems to me that Marcuse would not join in the vulgar Marxist rejection of any form of cultural or ideological politics as little more than a distraction.

Why, exactly, does Marcuse take this generous stance towards other social movements? One possible reason for this can be brought out indirectly via an earlier Marxist doctrine which might seem to have little to do with philosophy: Lenin's idea of "the weakest link." Lenin thought that socialist revolutions had a higher chance of success in Russia, because it was the weakest link in the international capitalist (imperialist) system: backward, agrarian, feudal, etc. This was precisely the opposite of Marx's view that socialist revolutions would first take place in advanced capitalist countries like England, "the demiurge of the bourgeois cosmos." Marx had not reckoned with the powerful obstacles to revolution thrown up by the ruling classes of the wealthiest capitalist nations.

Marcuse is critical of Lenin and of the Russian Revolution for attempting to institute socialism in an agrarian society. However, his own view of the student left seems broadly indebted to Lenin in at least the following qualified sense. Marcuse finds revolutionary potential in peripheral areas of the capitalist system, among members of minority groups, students, artists, and others. Marcuse was an ecumenical activist, who welcomed all sincere efforts to contribute to human liberation, from the civil-rights and women's movements to the ecological struggle. If one wanted to support this ecumenicism with a doctrine nearer at hand to Marcuse's thought than Lenin's theory of "the weakest link," one might invoke the category of totality. In a society whose parts are all connected to one another and to the whole, each liberation movement at least has the potential to strengthen the others. At the same time, this optimism about a united left opposition may no longer be appropriate. Whereas in Marcuse's time it could be taken for granted that different segments of the left were committed to economic justice and the critique of capitalism, this is no longer true today. Neoliberal identity politics is much more of a threat today than it was in Marcuse's time.

A final observation: Marcuse's profound investment in psychoanalytic thought appears to have no parallel among the analytic critical theorists. In leftist thought and practice, psychoanalysis has often served as an antidote to pathologies of traditional religion and morality that persist in secular societies. Unfortunately, some of these pathologies are present on the left today, within the academy and outside. One sees them in a moralistic fixation upon the individual; upon individual *choices*; upon the individual's inner life (or soul), where precursors of these choices are found; upon the need for public confession; and perhaps also in an understanding of prejudice as sin-like, an undetectable but dangerous contaminant diffused throughout the social body. To this secularized puritanism, always a standing threat in capitalist societies that draw their sustenance from the Protestant ethic, we might counterpose the psychoanalytical view of human beings; in particular, a view of human beings as in the grip of irrational, unconscious forces, ones which are as much social as individual and therefore out of the control of any particular person. These forces do not excuse, but can help to diagnose and explain, the darker dimensions of human behavior. In addition to promoting a materialist, rather than idealist, approach, Marcuse's correctives to contemporary leftist thought and practice might include this psychoanalytic rejection of moralistic politics, and the secularized religious impulse that lies behind it.

Summary

Marcuse's thought has often been eclipsed by his legacy as a public figure and activist, even in the tradition of the Frankfurt School critical theory that he helped create. This chapter considers Marcuse's relationship to present-day analytical philosophy, particularly the movement of analytic critical theory. Often, this movement exhibits a "Hegelian-idealist" tendency that Marcuse, as a Marxist, would reject: in particular, through its focus on thought and speech considered in abstraction from institutions. However, this tendency is not uniform, and it is balanced out by other "materialist" tendencies Marcuse would likely find more congenial. Marcuse would have abhorred neoliberal identity politics, but would also likely avoid class reductionism. He favored a united left opposition, focused not on moralizing but on ameliorating real material suffering wherever it arises.

Notes

1 As Tom Whyman points out to me, Marcuse was central to the writings of the late Mark Fisher, arguably the most important theorist of the Corbyn moment. See Fisher (2018).

2 Since Marcuse, following Hegel, regards philosophy as historically situated, it is also worth noting new tendencies on the horizon. Some of the most recent generation of critical theorists in Germany, like Daniel Loick and Eva von Redecker, have embraced a more militant, activist stance reminiscent of the early institute (indeed, Loick [2017] explicitly calls for a re-actualization of Marcuse's idea of a radical politics organized around the exigencies of organic life). If they do so, they will likely find an ally in Marcuse, who arguably remained more faithful to the first-generation program of interdisciplinary, Marxist social theory than did others in the Frankfurt School. Still, I will eschew any further comparisons with recent critical theory, preferring to focus on Marcuse's possible relevance in the philosophical culture of the Anglophone world.

3 See Stanley (2015: xv), who describes his project as treating questions from continental philosophy with the methods of the analytical tradition. See also Haslanger (2012: 22–30) who situates her work in the tradition of critical theory, though, of course, it also draws on the analytic tradition.

4 Some of the earliest and most important entries in this literature are Stanley (2015, 2018), Haslanger (2012), Langton (2009), and Manne (2018).

5 Critics include Williams (2005), Geuss (2001), and Larmore (1990).

6 In this respect, it may resemble Hegel's project as interpreted in Moyar (2021: 3–7).

7 See, inter alia, Fraser (2016).

8 See also Shaw (2020).

Further reading

Fraser, N. (2016) "Contradictions of Capital and Care," *New Left Review*, No. 100: 99–117. [An example of the type of Marxist-feminist theorizing that I believe harmonizes with Marcuse's Freudian–Marxist position.]

Fisher, M. (2018) "Acid Communism (Unfinished Introduction)," in D. Ambrose (ed.), *K-Punk: The Collected and Unpublished Writings of Mark Fisher from 2004–2016*, London: Repeater Books. [An influential recent appropriation of Marcuse by a U.K. cultural and critical theorist.]

Glossary

critical theory: typically refers to the Frankfurt School, an eclectic group of Marxist sociologists, philosophers, and others committed to interdisciplinary, emancipatory theoretical work. Yet the term is also used by Marcuse as a synonym for Marxism, at least in his early essay "Philosophy and Critical Theory." There, critical theory's twin commitments are said to be a concern for human happiness and a focus on the material (economic) circumstances of human life.

Eros: a force underlying the pleasure principle, and only contingently directed at various socially prescribed aims; for example, sexual reproduction. Seen as a cosmological principle, its tendency is constructive and towards the production of ever greater unities. Contrasted with Thanatos, the death drive. Marcuse looks to Eros as the psychological force that will bind together a future communist society.

essence: the nature of a thing, and therefore the source of standards about its proper function or health and flourishing. Stressed by the "two-dimensional" philosophy of the ancient world, by Hegel, and, in a different way, by critical theorists who insisted on the dehumanizing tendencies of capitalism.

form: Usually contrasted with content, i.e., the work of art's subject-matter. Form is the way or manner in which this subject-matter is presented, especially the style in which it is presented. Marcuse's aesthetic theory is formalist in that it regards form as the place where the unique value of a work resides; in particular, it is at the level of form that we find the boldest challenges to our received habits of perception. Modernism is understood by Marcuse as experimentation with form. Considerations of form also explain why work that is overtly political, or political in its subject-matter, fails to achieve its effect. Such work often remains conservative when considered at the level of its form.

idealism: a school of thought Marcuse designates (in at least one place) as the very inverse of positivism. Distinguished by its emphasis on negation, and its rejection of the idea of facts that are passively registered by us using our sense-organs. To the idealist, the facts are constituted, whether by a subject or by the social labor process.

negation: the denial or rejection of a proposition; or even, in a more ontological register, the destruction of things. Marcuse regards negation as a pre-condition for rational thought, insofar as it is critical of its surroundings. He praises philosophical schools that accord negation a central place, e.g., Hegelianism. Positivism is criticized for its insufficient respect for negation, and for negative facts.

one-dimensional thought: ideologies that discourage critics of society from seeking a second dimension along which it could be evaluated and criticized; for example, a dimension made up of the possibilities for a good human life that are thwarted by modern capitalism. Positivists are paradigmatic one-dimensional thinkers, but so are other figures in the analytical tradition: behaviorists; ordinary language philosophers; Quine and Wittgenstein. Marcuse's branding of analytical philosophers as one-dimensional may be somewhat uncharitable.

operationalism: Marcuse's term for a school in philosophy of science that encourages us to focus on the dispositional properties of entities, rather than their intrinsic ones. Also associated with behaviorism and with the tendency of modern thought to "dissolve matter into relations." Operationalism is a form of one-dimensional thought for Marcuse.

phenomenology: a philosophical movement that included Marcuse's teachers Edmund Husserl and Martin Heidegger. Marcuse was particularly interested in the latter's idea of "being-in-the-world," a non-dualistic alternative to the traditional Cartesian dichotomy between consciousness and nature. Heidegger's phenomenology, in particular, promised to restore to philosophy an emphasis on the sociohistorical and practical dimension of human existence.

positivism: for Marcuse, a deeply reactionary school of thought whose insistence that science focus exclusively on positive facts eliminates important resources for social critique; for example, normative principles, essences or natures, possibilities, and negative facts. Marcuse is particularly critical of the influence of positivism on social science.

potential: Aristotle's idea of the capacities that are natural to a thing of a certain kind, but which may not always be actively exercised or fully realized by it (they may be malfunctioning, or simply dormant). Marcuse views the idea of potential as an important resource for critical theory, and argues that modern society thwarts human potentialities.

repressive desublimation: a process whereby social prohibitions against sexual or aggressive behavior are eased to reconcile people with the status quo. Marcuse views late capitalism as engaged in repressive desublimation through the culture industry, the military and police, and other socially accepted outlets for the id. This process also explains the dissolution of the ego in modern society, and the decline of autonomy.

repressive toleration: using the value of tolerance as a pretext to cede control of discourse to the wealthiest and most powerful actors, e.g., the media, the military–industrial complex, and large multinational corporations. For Marcuse, as for Mill, toleration is not an end in itself but a means to something more important. If indiscriminate toleration does not serve this more important end then it should be abandoned. Liberal capitalists fetishize toleration, making it into an end in itself.

sense-certainty: the first and most basic standpoint considered in Hegel's *Phenomenology of Spirit*. Hegel accuses it of being self-undermining, because its efforts to know concrete particulars given to the senses require abstract universals contributed by thought. Hegel's critique of sense-certainty is seen by Marcuse as a forerunner of the Frankfurt School's critique of positivism.

superstructure: The area of society composed of art, religion, and morality, and also perhaps the legal and political institutions.

Distinguished from the base, which includes the economy—
in particular, the relations of production (class structure) and
forces of production. Traditional Marxist aesthetics relegates
art to the superstructure, and in this way renders it a (mostly)
impotent force in social change. Marcuse rejects this categoriza-
tion of art, insisting that it can have a more important role in
social upheaval.

surplus repression: an amended version of Freud's category of
repression. For Freud, civilized life requires us to repress certain
aggressive and sexual desires. Marcuse, drawing on Marx, amends
Freud's idea insisting that different amounts of repression are
required by different modes of production; for example, capitalism might require more repression of most people than communism. Surplus repression, then, is the extra repression required
by a certain mode of production, i.e., the amount beyond the
minimum necessary for people to function as responsible adults.
Marcuse did not think all repression could be eliminated.

state capitalism: first theorized by Marcuse's colleague Pollock, and
a mainstay of Marcuse's analyses of liberal capitalism, Soviet
communism, and fascism. Meant to designate a new phase in
capitalist development wherein a small number of firms control
the market and are able to rely on the state to do their bidding.
Even Soviet communism shares certain traits in common with
state capitalism, e.g., highly concentrated industry, state intervention in the economy, and imperialistic tendencies.

Thanatos: The death drive, first considered a component of Eros
by Freud but later regarded as a separate instinct. Reflected
in the sado-masochistic component of human sexuality, in
repetition-compulsion, and in pathologies Freud noticed in
his patients returning from World War I. Its tendency is to split,
break down or destroy. It is found in intellectual, scientific, and
technological accomplishments as well. It reflects not so much
a longing for death as for the organism to be able to die in
its own way. Even more fundamentally, the death drive is born
of a desire for the security of the inorganic, and anxiety over
the vicissitudes of organic life. Marcuse sees Thanatos at the
basis of many social pathologies, e.g., militarism, fascism, and
imperialism.

universal: a general concept connoting not just how particular things are but how they ideally would be; for example, justice, goodness, human. Closely connected with the nature or essence of a thing. Examples of universals include Plato's forms, Aristotle's substantial forms, and Hegel's "concrete universals." Universals are also, in Hegel especially, connected with the social whole, and with ideals of social harmony. Though construed in different ways in different philosophers' writings, the universal always functions as an important resource for social critique. Positivism is criticized by Marcuse for neglecting universals. Marcuse insists that universals have an important role to play, not only in ancient philosophy and German idealism but in historical materialist theory as well ("From each according to his abilities ..." is a universalizing principle).

Bibliography

Works by Marcuse

Here I provide bibliographic information for works by Marcuse cited in this volume, including the volumes of his collected papers recently published by Routledge. The chronology is jumbled, since I am often citing reprints. Readers interested in following these works in chronological order should consult the chronology at the beginning of the volume.

Readers hoping to deepen their understanding of Marcuse could begin with the texts listed here. However, this is not intended to be a comprehensive bibliography, and much is omitted; in particular, the original sources of the newly anthologized papers. Readers interested in a fuller accounting of Marcuse's work might consult the bibliography in Kellner's *Herbert Marcuse and the Crisis of Marxism* (1984), as well as the bibliographic information for individual papers given in the collected papers volumes.

Suhrkamp Verlag has been publishing a collected edition of Marcuse's works, but it is mainly useful for the reprinting it contains of Marcuse's dissertation on German literature.

(1955) [1941] *Reason and Revolution: Hegel and the Rise of Social Theory*, 2nd edn with supplementary chapter, London: Routledge, Kegan & Paul.

(1965) with Barrington Moore Jr. and Robert Paul Wolff, *A Critique of Pure Toleration*, Boston: Beacon Press.

(1966) [1955] *Eros and Civilization: A Philosophical Inquiry into Freud*, 2nd edn, Boston: Beacon Press.

(1978) *The Aesthetic Dimension*, Boston: Beacon Press. Originally published in German under the title *Die Permanenz der Kunst:Wider eine bestimmte Marxistische Aesthetik*, Munich: Carl Hanser Verlag, 1977. English version translated and revised by Herbert Marcuse and Sophie Sherover.

(1987) *Hegel's Ontology and the Theory of Historicity*, trans. Seyla Benhabib, Cambridge, MA: MIT Press.

(1991) [1964] *One-Dimensional Man: A Study in the Ideology of Advanced Industrial Society*, 2nd edn, London: Routledge.

(2005) *Marxist Writings*, ed. J. Abromeit and L. Wolin, Lincoln, NE: University of Nebraska Press.

(2013) with F. Neumann and O. Kirchheimer, *Secret Reports on Nazi Germany:The Frankfurt School Contribution to the War Effort*, ed. R. Loudani with a foreword by R. Geuss, Princeton: Princeton University Press.

(1998–2014) *The Collected Papers of Herbert Marcuse*, 5 vols., ed. D. Kellner, Abingdon/New York: Routledge.

Works about Marcuse

Abromeit, J. (2010) "Left Heideggerianism or Phenomenological Marxism? Reconsidering Herbert Marcuse's Critical Theory of Technology," *Constellations*, Vol. 17, No. 1: 87–106.

Abromeit, J. and Cobb, W. M. (2004) *Herbert Marcuse: Critical Reactions*, New York: Routledge.

Alford, F. (1985) *Science and the Revenge of Nature: Habermas & Marcuse*, Tampa/Gainesville: University Press of Florida.

Anderson, K. B. (1993) "On Hegel and the Rise of Social Theory: A Critical Appreciation of *Reason and Revolution* 50 Years Later," *Sociological Theory*, Vol. 11, No. 3: 243–67.

Bernstein, R. (1986) *Philosophical Profiles*, Philadelphia: University of Pennsylvania Press.

Bronner, S. (1988) "Between Art and Utopia: Reconsidering the Aesthetic Theory of Herbert Marcuse," in A. Feenberg, R. Pippin, and C. Webel (eds.), *Marcuse: Critical Theory and the Promise of Utopia*, London: Bergin & Garvey, 107–43.

Cobb, W. M. (2004) "Diatribes and Distortions: Marcuse's Academic Reception, in J. Abromeit and W. M. Cobb (eds.), *Marcuse: A Critical Reader*, Abingdon/New York: Routledge, 163–87.

Davis, A. (2004) "Marcuse's Legacies," in J. Abromeit and W. M. Cobb (eds.), *Herbert Marcuse: A Critical Reader*, Abingdon/New York: Routledge.

Feenberg, A. (2005) *Marcuse and Heidegger: The Catastrophe and Redemption of History*, New York: Routledge.

Feenberg, A. (2023) *Towards a Ruthless Critique of Everything Existing: Nature and Revolution in Marcuse's Philosophy of Praxis*, London: Verso.

Feenberg, A., Pippin, R., and Webel, C. (eds.) (1988) *Marcuse: Critical Theory and the Promise of Utopia*, London: Bergin & Garvey.

Fokos, B. (2007) "The Bourgeois Marxist," *San Diego Reader*, August 23, https://www.sandiegoreader.com/news/2007/aug/23/bourgeois-marxist/.

Ganesha, S. (2004) "Marcuse, Habermas and the Critique of Technology," in J. Abromeit and W. M. Cobb (eds.), *Herbert Marcuse: A Critical Reader*, New York: Routledge, 188–208.

Guyer, P. (2004) "Marcuse and Classical Aesthetics," *Revue International de Philosophie*, 349–65.

Honneth, A. (2003) "Herbert Marcuse und die Frankfurter Schule," *Leviathan: Zeitschrift fur Sozialwissenschaft*, Vol. 31, No. 4: 496–504.

Hyman, E. J. (1988) "Eros and Freedom: The Critical Psychology of Herbert Marcuse," in A. Feenberg, R. Pippin, and C. Webel (eds.), *Marcuse: Critical Theory and the Promise of Utopia*, London: Bergin & Garvey, 143–69.

Katz, B. (1982) *Herbert Marcuse and the Art of Liberation: An Intellectual Biography*, London: Verso.

Kellner, D. (1984) *Marcuse and the Crisis of Marxism*, London: Macmillan.

Leiter, B. (2017) "Justifying Academic Freedom: Mill and Marcuse Revisited," SSRN, June 3, http://dx.doi.org/10.2139/ssrn.2943774/.

MacIntyre, A. (1970) *Marcuse*, London: Fontana.

Truitt, W. H. (1971) Herbert Marcuse: An Exposition and Polemic, *Journal of Aesthetics and Art Criticism*, Vol. 29, No. 4: 569

Marcuse, H. (1978) "Conversation with Habermas and Others', *Telos*, Vol. 1978, No. 38: 130–31.

Marcuse, H. and Olafson, F. (1977) "Heidegger's Politics: An Interview with Herbert Marcuse," *Graduate Faculty Philosophy Journal*, Vol. 6, No. 1: 28–40, https://doi.org/10.5840/gfpj19776112/.

O'Connor, B. (2014) "Play, Idleness and the Problem of Necessity in Schiller and Marcuse," *British Journal for the History of Philosophy*, Vol. 22, No. 6: 1095–117

O'Connor, B. (2018) "Marcuse on the Problem of Repression," in P. Gordon, E. Hammer, and A. Honneth (eds.), *Routledge Companion to Critical Theory*, London: Routledge, 311–23.

O'Neill, J. (1988) "Marcuse, Husserl and the Crisis of the Sciences," *Philosophy of the Social Sciences*, Vol. 18, No. 3, https://doi.org/10.1177/004839318801800302/.

Postone, M. (2006) "Critique, State and Economy," in F. Rush (ed.), *Cambridge Companion to Critical Theory*, Cambridge: Cambridge University Press, 165–94.

Rush, F. (2006) "Conceptual Foundations of Early Critical Theory," in F. Rush (ed.), *Cambridge Companion to Critical Theory*, Cambridge: Cambridge University Press, 6–39.

Whitebook, J. (2004) "The Marriage of Marx and Freud," in F. Rush (ed.), *Cambridge Companion to Critical Theory*, Cambridge: Cambridge University Press, 74–103.

Whyman, T. (2023) "Two Sorts of Philosophical Therapy: Ordinary Language Philosophy, Social Criticism and the Frankfurt School," *Philosophy and Social Criticism*. Online First. https://doi.org/10.1177/01914537231203525.

Works by others

Adorno, T., Benjamin, W., Bloch, E., Brecht, B., and Lukács, G. (2020) *Aesthetics and Politics*, London: Verso.

Aimar, S. (2019) "Running for Power: The Spectrum Concept of Fascism. Review of J. Stanley's *How Fascism Works*," *Times Literary Supplement*, November: 14–15.

Avineri, S. (1968) *The Social and Political Thought of Karl Marx*, Cambridge: Cambridge University Press.

Basu, R. and Schroeder, M. (2018) "Doxastic Wronging," in B. Kim and M. McGrath (eds), *Pragmatic Encroachment in Epistemology*, New York: Routledge, e-book.

Brandom, R. (1994) *Making It Explicit*, Cambridge, MA: Harvard University Press.

Bürger, P. (1984) *Theory of the Avant-Garde*. Theory and History of Literature, Vol. 4. Trans. M. Shaw. Minneapolis: University of Minnesota.

Carnap, R. (1937) *The Logical Syntax of Language*, London: Kegan Paul.

Cassirer, E. (1910) *Substanzbegriff und Funktionsbegriff: Untersuchungen über die Grundfragen der Erkenntniskritik*, Berlin: Bruno Cassirer.

Cassirer, E. (1923) *Substance and Function, and Einstein's Theory of Relativity*, trans. W. C. Swabey and M. C. Swabey, Chicago: Open Court.

Cohen, G. A. (2000) [1978] *Karl Marx's Theory of History: A Defence*, expanded edn, Princeton: Princeton University Press.

Cohen, G. A. (2009) *Why Not Socialism?*, Princeton: Princeton University Press.

Dews, P. (2018) "Schelling and the Frankfurt School." In *Routledge Companion to the Frankfurt School*, Boca Raton, FL: Routledge, 349–410.

Engels, F. (1890) "Letter to Joseph Block," in *Marx–Engels Reader*, ed. G. Tucker, New York: Norton & Co., 760–765.

Feenberg, A. (2017) *Technosystem: The Social Life of Reason*, Cambridge, MA: Harvard University Press.

Field, H. (2016) [1980] *Science Without Numbers: A Defense of Nominalism*, 2nd edn, Oxford: Oxford University Press.

Fisher, M. (2018) "Acid Communism (Unfinished Introduction)," in D. Ambrose (ed.), *K-Punk: The Collected and Unpublished Writings of Mark Fisher from 2004–2016*, London: Repeater Books, e-book.

Fraser, N. (2016) "Contradictions of Capital and Care," *New Left Review*, No. 100: 99–117, https://newleftreview.org/issues/ii100/articles/nancy-fraser-contradictions-of-capital-and-care/.

Freud, S. (1920) *Beyond the Pleasure Principle*, in *The Standard Edition of the Complete Psychological Works of Sigmund Freud*, Volume XVIII (1920–1922): *Beyond the Pleasure Principle, Group Psychology and Other Works*, London: Hogarth Press, 7–67.

Freud, S. (1923). *The Ego and the Id*, in *The Standard Edition of the Complete Psychological Works of Sigmund Freud*, Volume XIX (1923–1925): *The Ego and the Id and Other Works*, London: Hogarth Press, 1–66.

Fricker, M. (2007) *Epistemic Injustice: Power & the Ethics of Knowing*, Oxford: Oxford University Press.

Friedman, M. (2001) *Dynamics of Reason: The 1999 Kant Lectures at Stanford University,* Chicago: CSLI/University of Chicago Press.

Gerth, H. H. and Mills, C. W. (2009) *From Max Weber: Essays in Sociology,* Abingdon: Routledge.

Geuss. R. (2001) *Public Goods, Private Goods,* Princeton: Princeton University Press.

Geuss, R. (2008) *Philosophy and Real Politics,* Princeton: Princeton University Press.

Habermas, J. (1968) *Antworten auf Herbert Marcuse.* Frankfurt am Main: Suhrkamp.

Heidegger, M. (1962) [1927] *Being and Time,* trans. J. Macquarrie and E. Robinson, Oxford: Basil Blackwell.

Hegel, G. W. F. (1970) *Werke,* ed. E. Moldenauer and K. M. Michel, Frankfurt a. M.: Suhrkamp.

Hegel, G. W. F. (1979) [1807] *Phenomenology of Spirit,* trans. A. V. Miller, Oxford: Oxford University Press.

Hegel, G. W. F. (1991) [1821] *Elements of the Philosophy of Right,* trans. H. B. Nisbet, ed. A. Wood, Cambridge: Cambridge University Press.

Haslanger, S. (2012) *Resisting Reality,* Oxford: Oxford University Press.

Horkheimer, M. (1972) "Traditional and Critical Theory," in *Critical Theory: Selected Essays,* trans. M. J. O'Connell et al., New York: Seabury, 188–244.

Husserl, E. (1970). *The Crisis of European Sciences and Transcendental Phenomenology,* Evanston, IL: Northwestern University Press.

Jay, M. (1973) *The Dialectical Imagination: A History of the Frankfurt School and the Institute of Social Research, 1923–1950,* Boston/Toronto: Little, Brown & Company.

Ladyman, J. (2023) "Structural Realism," *Stanford Encyclopedia of Philosophy,* https://plato.stanford.edu/entries/structural-realism/.

Langton, R. (2009) *Sexual Solipsism: Philosophical Essays on Pornography and Objectification,* Oxford: Oxford University Press.

Larmore, C. (1990) "Political Liberalism," *Political Theory,* Vol. 18, No. 3: 339–60.

Lear. J (2018) "The Difficulty of Reality and a Revolt Against Mourning," *The European Journal of Philosophy,* Vol. 26, No. 4: 1197–1208, https://doi.org/10.1111/ejop.12399/.

Longuenesse, B. (2017) *I, Me, Mine: Back to Kant, and Back Again,* Oxford: Oxford University Press.

Loick, D. (2017) "21 Theses on the Politics of Forms of Life," *Theory and Event,* Vol. 20, No. 3: 788–803.

Manne, K. (2018) *Down Girl: The Logic of Misogyny,* Oxford: Oxford University Press.

Marx, K. (1976) *Capital,* Vol. 1, trans. B. Fowkes, New York: Penguin

Marx, K. and Engels, F. (1978) *Marx–Engels Reader,* ed. G. Tucker, New York: Norton & Co.

McDowell, J. (1994) *Mind and World,* Cambridge, MA: Harvard University Press.

Moyar, D. (2021) *Hegel's Value,* Oxford: Oxford University Press.

Neuhouser, F. (1991), *Fichte's Theory of Subjectivity,* Cambridge: Cambridge University Press.

Neumann, F. (2009) *Behemoth: The Structure and Practice of National Socialism 1933–44*, Chicago: Ivan R. Dee.

Orwell, G. (2013) *1984*, Boston: Houghton, Mifflin & Harcourt.

Peacocke, C. (2019) *The Primacy of Metaphysics*, Oxford: Oxford University Press.

Pelczynski, Z. A. (1984) "Introduction: The Significance of Hegel's Separation of the State and Civil-Society," in Z. A. Pelczynski (ed.), *State and Civil-Society: Essays in Hegel's Political Thought*, Cambridge: Cambridge University Press, 1–14.

Piaget, J. (1950) *Introduction à l'épistemologie génétique*, Paris: Presses Universitaires de France.

Pollock, F. (1978) [1941] "State Capitalism: Its Possibilities and Limitations," in A. Arato and E. Gebhart (eds), *The Essential Frankfurt School Reader*, New York: Urizen Books, 71–95.

Quine, W. V. O. (1961) *From a Logical Point of View: Logico-Philosophical Essays*, New York: Harper & Row.

Rawls, J. (1999) [1971] *A Theory of Justice*, rev. edn, Cambridge, MA: Belknap Harvard University Press.

Rickert, J. (1986) "The Fromm–Marcuse Debate Revisited," *Theory and Society*, Vol. 15, No. 3: 351–400.

Roethlisberger F., and Dickson, W. J (1939) *Management and the Worker*, Cambridge, MA: Harvard University Press.

Russell, B. (1978) [1921], *The Analysis of Mind*, London: George Allen & Unwin.

Russell, B. (2010) *The Philosophy of Logical Atomism*, London: Routledge Classics.

Saul, J., Diaz-Leon, E., and Hesni, S. (2017) "Feminist Philosophy of Language," *Stanford Encyclopedia of Philosophy*, https://plato.stanford.edu/entries/feminism-language/.

Shaw, D. (2020) "Review of J. Stanley's How Fascisms Works," *Marx and Philosophy*, May 13, https://marxandphilosophy.org.uk/reviews/18021_how-fascism-works-the-politics-of-us-and-them-by-jason-stanley-reviewed-by-devin-zane-shaw.

Stanley, J. (2015) *How Propaganda Works*, Princeton: Princeton University Press.

Stanley, J. (2018) *How Fascism Works:The Politics of Us and Them*, New York: Random House.

Thakkar, J. (2018) *Plato as Critical Theorist*, Cambridge, MA: Harvard University Press.

Van Reijen, W. and Bransen, J. (2002) "The Disappearance of Class History in *Dialectic of Enlightenment*: A Commentary on the Textual Variants (1944 and 1947)," in T. Adorno and M. Horkheimer, *Dialectic of Enlightenment*, trans. E. Jephcott, ed. G. Schmid Noerr, Palo Alto, CA: Stanford University Press, 248–53.

Williams, B. (2005) *In the Beginning Was the Deed: Realism and Moralism in Political Argument*, Princeton: Princeton University Press.

Wills, V. (2018) "What Could It Mean to Say that 'Capitalism Causes Racism and Sexism'?" *Philosophical Topics*, Vol. 46, No. 2: 229–246.

Wittgenstein, L. (2001) *Tractatus Logico-Philosophicus*, trans. D. Pears and B. McGuinness, London: Routledge Classics.

Index

Note: Page numbers followed by "n" refer to end notes.

For Product Safety Concerns and Information please contact our EU
representative GPSR@taylorandfrancis.com Taylor & Francis Verlag GmbH,
Kaufingerstraße 24, 80331 München, Germany

Printed and bound by CPI Group (UK) Ltd, Croydon, CR0 4YY
08/06/2025
01896986-0003